TAYLOR SWIFT

Quarto.com

© 2025 Quarto Publishing Group USA Inc.
Text © 2025 Kase Wickman, Joanna Weiss & Moira McAvoy

First Published in 2025 by Motorbooks,
an imprint of The Quarto Group,
100 Cummings Center, Suite 265-D,
Beverly, MA 01915, USA.
T (978) 282-9590 F (978) 283-2742

All rights reserved. No part of this book may be reproduced in any form without written permission of the copyright owners. All images in this book have been reproduced with the knowledge and prior consent of the artists concerned, and no responsibility is accepted by producer, publisher, or printer for any infringement of copyright or otherwise, arising from the contents of this publication. Every effort has been made to ensure that credits accurately comply with information supplied. We apologize for any inaccuracies that may have occurred and will resolve inaccurate or missing information in a subsequent reprinting of the book.

This book has not been prepared, approved, or licensed by Taylor Swift, her management, or her representatives. This is an unofficial publication.

Motorbooks titles are also available at discount for retail, wholesale, promotional, and bulk purchase. For details, contact the Special Sales Manager by email at specialsales@quarto.com or by mail at The Quarto Group, Attn: Special Sales Manager, 100 Cummings Center, Suite 265-D, Beverly, MA 01915, USA.

29 28 27 26 25   1 2 3 4 5

ISBN: 978-0-7603-9749-7

Digital edition published in 2025
eISBN: 978-0-7603-9750-3

Library of Congress Cataloging-in-Publication Data

Names: Wickman, Kase, author. | Weiss, Joanna (Writer) author. | McAvoy, Moira, author.
Title: Taylor Swift : album by album / Kase Wickman, Joanna Weiss, Moira McAvoy.
Description: Beverly, MA : Motorbooks, 2025. | Series: Album by album | Includes index. | Summary: "Taylor Swift: Album by Album follows the megastar from her roots as a country artist to her transition into pop and finally into the cultural phenomenon touring today, covering both her music and her extraordinary life"—Provided by publisher.
Identifiers: LCCN 2025008782 | ISBN 9780760397497 (hardcover) | ISBN 9780760397503 (ebook)
Subjects: LCSH: Swift, Taylor, 1989- | Swift, Taylor, 1989—Criticism and interpretation. | Singers—United States—Biography. | Popular music—History and criticism. | Country music—History and criticism.
Classification: LCC ML420.S968 W53 2025 | DDC 782.421642092 [B]—dc23/eng/20250304
LC record available at https://lccn.loc.gov/2025008782

Design: Cindy Samargia Laun
Cover Photo: Axelle/Bauer-Griffin/FilmMagic/Getty Images

Printed in China

TAYLOR SWIFT

Moira McAvoy | Joanna Weiss | Kase Wickman

CONTENTS

Introduction 6

Taylor Swift — PAGE 8 — 1

FEARLESS — PAGE 20 — 2

1989 — PAGE 58 — 5

reputation — PAGE 72 — 6

evermore — PAGE 108 — 9

Bridge: The Taylor Swift Masters, Explained — Page 120

Midnights — PAGE 146 — 12

Speak Now (Taylor's Version) — PAGE 160 — 13

3 PAGE 32

7 PAGE 84

10 PAGE 128

14 PAGE 168

4 PAGE 46

8 PAGE 96

11 PAGE 136

15 PAGE 176

About the Authors 186   Acknowledgments 188   Index 190   Image Credits 192

INTRODUCTION

Like us, you can probably pinpoint the moment when Taylor Swift inserted herself into your life. Maybe you were a teenager, listening to "Fifteen" over and over, stunned that this stranger was somehow able to tell your life story. Maybe you were a parent, accompanying your kid to the *1989* tour and realizing, on the way out of the stadium, that the songs were now stuck in your head. Maybe you learned about Taylor the businesswoman, toppling industry standards by re-recording her own albums. Maybe you heard "Karma" on the radio by chance and that was that, hooked by the hook.

This book will celebrate Swift's amazing ability to capture our attention, our brain space, and our emotions. It will explore the extraordinary cultural and economic influence that she wields—even among the Dads, Brads, and Chads who claim she's ruining a good ol' game of football (but still allow her to live rent-free in their minds).

Swift has power, and she's built it through masterful use of social media, careful curation of her public image, an innate understanding of what her fans want and need, and the ability to grow with loyal Swifties while continuing to recruit new ones. She's stared down industry titans, defied the doubters, and come out on top. But none of that would matter if she didn't have the music to back it up. So, ultimately, this book is a deep dive into her sprawling catalog of songs. We'll trace her megahits and surprise vault tracks, consider her ability to conquer different genres, dissect the Easter eggs and messages in her lyrics, and marvel at her many, many, bridges and hooks.

Each chapter of this book will cover one of Swift's albums, in chronological order. In the middle, Taylor-style, we've added a "bridge" to illuminate her groundbreaking decision to create new master recordings on her own terms. And once we get to the Taylor's Versions, we'll share the winding conversations the three of us had about what remained and what changed on the re-recorded albums.

Because we're cultural critics, we'll be guided by questions. What's the meaning behind this lyric, this album cover? What reverberations came from a surprise announcement? What was Taylor thinking? How did it matter to her fans? This deep-dive project entailed many hours of listening, meandering trips down internet rabbit holes, long Zoom calls full of memories and ruminations, and a fair amount of sugary snacks. It tapped into our personal experiences: Moira's internet-turned-IRL relationships deep within the Swiftverse, Kase's pop culture immersion, and Joanna's multigenerational collection of Swifties.

It all turned us into fast friends, and that's part of Taylor's legacy, too: As with everything Taylor Swift, the universal lies in the personal, and the personal builds a community. It doesn't matter what road brought you here, or which generation you belong to—you're here with us all the same, and we're all screaming ourselves hoarse to the bridge of "Cruel Summer."

Happy listening, and happy reading,

TAYLOR SWIFT ALBUM BY ALBUM

Dedication

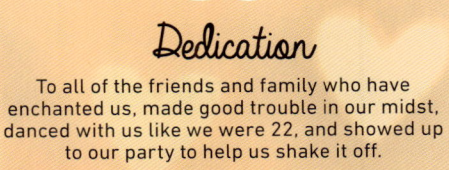

To all of the friends and family who have enchanted us, made good trouble in our midst, danced with us like we were 22, and showed up to our party to help us shake it off.

And to everyone who's sung along to a Taylor Swift song at a concert, in the car, or out in the street in the rain. We're right there with you.

By Moira McAvoy

Track Listing:

Times are from the original release of the first album.

1. Tim McGraw [3:54]
2. Picture to Burn [2:55]
3. Teardrops On My Guitar [3:35]
4. A Place In This World [3:22]
5. Cold as You [4:01]
6. The Outside [3:29]
7. Tied Together With a Smile [4:11]
8. Stay Beautiful [3:58]
9. Should've Said No [4:02]
10. Mary's Song (Oh My My My) [3:35]
11. Our Song [3:24]

Deluxe Edition Bonus Tracks:

12. I'm Only Me When I'm With You [3:35]
13. Invisible [3:23]
14. A Perfectly Good Heart [3:42]
15. Taylor Swift's First Phone Call With Tim McGraw (ft. Tim McGraw) [4:44]

Reissued Edition Bonus Track:

16. Teardrops On My Guitar (Pop Version) [2:58]

Taylor Swift

Recorded at Castles, Quad, Sound Cottage, Sound Emporium (Nashville, Tennessee)

Released October 24, 2006

Produced by Nathan Chapman and Robert Ellis Orrall

Label: Big Machine Records

Notable personnel:

Liz Rose: songwriting

Nathan Chapman: acoustic guitar, banjo, bass, drums, electric guitar, engineer, background vocals, mandolin

Scott Borchetta: executive producer

Robert Ellis Orrall: background vocals

Emily Poe: fiddle, harmonies

Deluxe edition released November 6, 2007

Total units sold: 5,871,000 (as of January 2024)

Notable honors:

4 weeks at number one on the Billboard 200

Taylor Swift spent 24 weeks at number one on the Top Country Albums chart and soon became the longest-charting album of the 2000s on the Billboard 200.

OPPOSITE: Many hallmarks of the Taylor Swift brand were captured in this early photo of the budding megastar; the hair, the confidence, even a touch of color on her lips. Almost 20 years ago, only her closest friends, producers, and fans understood the potential embodied in her music.

Remember the warm, burning smell of making a mixed CD? The sharp scent of a Sharpie's fresh ink drying on the disc while a gloop of nail polish dries on your free hand that is still absolutely ACHING from T9 texting your friend (paid for by the character!)? The insular joy of a joke shot off between BFFs destined to become a battery of AIM away messages and MySpace captions for months to come? The hushed breath and skipped beat as your crush brushes past in the hall? The melodrama of being 14?

Before there was the smartphone panopticon capturing her every move, endless awards to amass, and ceilings to smash through, before there was Taylor Swift™, there was Taylor Swift, an ambitious songwriter and also—simply, crucially—a teenager. Herein lies the magic of Taylor's first album—awash in the overwhelming feelings that come from the best and worst things that have happened in your life being the best and worst things that have happened in your life, and grounded so deeply in these as experienced by a nobody-teen who thinks they're the main character (before they will, less than a decade later, become The Main Character), we have the gift of deeply personal yet infinitely relatable songs about everything from heartbreak to revenge to eating disorders to lifelong friendship.

Pop country, particularly the pop country girlies, had a moment in the early 2000s. Faith Hill, The Chicks, and Martina McBride topped the charts, Reba raked in consistently strong ratings for her sitcom turn, and Carrie Underwood won the fourth season of *American Idol* as a Capital C Country artist. The pop country of the new millennium was also, well, *country*—plenty of songs about love awash in whiskey and cheap beer, many songs about God, and even more songs about revenge.

ABOVE: **Perfect for late-night escapades and early morning drives, Taylor Swift's debut album was a trusty co-pilot for millennials.**

BELOW: **Taylor really did hate that stupid old pickup truck, but she loved hearing her fans' takes on their fave tracks. Swifties loved live versions of "Picture to Burn" so much she decided to release it as a single.**

What the pop country boom was missing was the hordes of adolescents driving pretty much every other major act to stardom. From R&B to nu-metal to pop punk, the hits of the decade were being dictated live on air by the taste-making teens of TRL, but for country? That scene was largely dominated by adults in the machinery of Nashville, singing and writing songs for their peers. Part of the magic of connecting with music is resonating with something not born of your own experience but being inspired to make a melodramatic AIM away message with the lyrics anyway, but it feels like some kind of small miracle when an artist sounds as if they've set your LiveJournal to music. Enter burgeoning songstress and bona fide teen, Taylor Swift.

10   TAYLOR SWIFT ALBUM BY ALBUM

In 2004, Swift played a fateful set at the Blue-bird Cafe (Nashville) that sealed her deal with Big Machine Records. She'd return 14 years later for an intimate set with Craig Wiseman in 2018.

Teenagers, specifically teenage girls, are brats, babies, and bumbling romantics without a lick of sense or emotional regulation. Being taken seriously as an artist is already an uphill battle when you're starting out, but for teenage girls? Where the aspirational career trajectory at the turn of the millennium manifested as skyrocketing fame, being stalked by culture vultures, then being proverbially sold for parts the second the general public even remotely loses interest in you with MAYBE a middle-aged, sexless redemption arc when enough time has passed? Trying to build that sort of career is a war of incantations against an inevitable curse. One way to try to avoid this fate is, of course, to artistically position yourself as not being a teenager.

So many artists write in a zone of inevitable demise. The best pop songs, to me, are tinted with fatalism and jubilation, in spite of the impending doom. Taylor would eventually come to live comfortably in this territory, but Swift's first album (lovingly referred to by fans as "Self-Titled" or "Debut") thrives in the moment in the way only a teenage main character can. We're sneaking out the window, we're whispering on the phone in our bedrooms across town, we're lighting your dumbass ex's house on fire, and we're doing it RIGHT NOW. Even "Mary's Song," a deep cut fan favorite wherein the speaker fantasizes about the long life she and her beau will lead, entrenches the reverie in the now, the wistful longing palpable and immediate.

TAYLOR SWIFT 11

Taylor's lyricism lends itself perfectly to country—narrative by nature, melodramatic, and theatrical, at times approaching a degree of camp, and deeply, painfully earnest—the chemical X of Taylor's success. Not only was she penning hit after hit of relatable teenagerdom, but she was doing so in a way that invites the listener to the slumber party, whispering and giggling and crying and dancing together over a fiddle back track on the proverbial boombox.

This talent radiates all over *Debut*, but is most masterfully obvious in breakout hit—and, in my opinion, the absolutely perfect song—"Our Song." The scene is instantly, viscerally set: I can smell the mix of gasoline and old leather as if I'm in the passenger seat with Taylor. The characters are swiftly (*ahem*) brought to life—the narrator a relatable, giddy love-struck teen, the beloved a charming, coy, and comfortable presence. The story unfolds with narrative tension and obvious stakes, culminating in the joyful declaration and youthful vocalizations at the bridge, and resolving in a perfect circular loop as the narrator breaks the fourth wall, writing the song. All of this is over a melody that will simply never get out of your head, the proverbial napkin holding the song tucked safely in your mind's pocket forever.

In less skillful hands, the confluence of proper nouns throughout the album could alienate fans, but with Taylor, they imbue a sense of personal relatability, where you can slot your own Drews and Corys in as if on cue.

Taylor and Tim McGraw strike up a conversation after she plays the titular "Tim McGraw." The two would share the stage numerous times, and she'd release his first phone call to her in full as a bonus track on the re-release of *Taylor Swift*.

Taylor didn't shy away from the reality of being a teenager—she saw it as power and embraced it. Why write about a universal experience you haven't actually lived? Swift's emphasis on the specifics of her daily life, not to mention the inherent youth of her music, was not only empowering for the artist, but also for her legions of largely adolescent fans. Songs like "Tied Together With a Smile" and "A Place In This World" looked those kids straight in the face and said your schoolyard stories and too-big feelings not only mattered, but were arena-pyro-level interesting.

This was something Taylor felt VERY strongly about, and it proved to be a driving force behind her infamous pursuit of fame. Despite being 14 years old, after RCA declined to extend a record deal in 2004, Taylor felt like she was running out of time. She wanted her debut album to reflect her life as it was right this second, which meant the album needed to come out when she was still connected to its reality. She was, after all, trying to find a place in this world. The music obviously needed to be out before she'd found it!

As self-made as a star could be in commercial country, Taylor embodied the pre-recession possibility of a dying American dream. At 13 years old, she hand-delivered demo CDs to record labels, snagging a development deal from RCA, in addition to a later songwriting deal from Sony/ATV. Her family up and moved to Tennessee so Taylor could be closer to the epicenter of the industry, where she met her first musical co-conspirator, Liz Rose. She performed at any venue she could, from the US Open and opening slots for The Charlie Daniels Band to more modest stages at county fairs and open mics, including the fateful 2004 showcase at The Bluebird Cafe in Nashville where she won over Scott Borchetta. She'd met Borchetta before, playing a few demos in his office, but he—understandably—wanted to see how those songs translated to the stage before signing a 14-year-old as the first artist on his new independent label, Big Machine Records. The rest, of course, is history.

Taylor's grind was absolutely relentless, but it was also intensely approachable. Some of her most enduring hits, like "Our Song," were initially performed at her high school talent shows. Virtually no one reading this is as talented as Taylor Swift, but listening to her teen self talk about her songwriting process, you might just believe you could be.

(continued on page 16)

Fans have been in a frenzy speculating over what unreleased tracks will be included in the Debut Vault since the re-recordings were announced, with many votes going toward songs circulated on Swift's original demo CDs.

ON THE NICE LIST:
THE TAYLOR SWIFT HOLIDAY COLLECTION

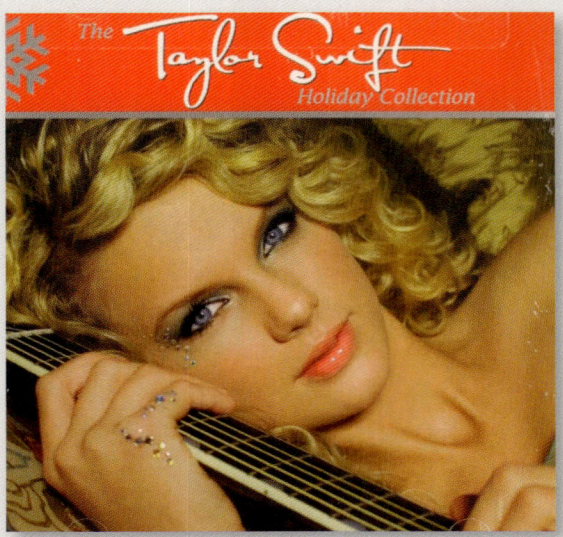

Most artists wait for fame to put out a promotional holiday album. Not Taylor Swift.

LIKE ANY GOOD nascent pop star, Taylor needed a holiday song. In 2019, she would release "Christmas Tree Farm," a catchy, whimsical love letter to her childhood home and the cozy glow of holiday romance, but we're not going to talk about that right now. Instead, we are going to talk about *The Taylor Swift Holiday Collection*, a six-song EP capitalizing on the momentum of 2006's *Taylor Swift*. It has its highs—original track "Christmases When You Were Mine" is a textbook example of endearing Swiftian song, and most of the Christmas standard covers are passable. But hearing an underage Swift belt out her take on "Santa Baby?" It's uncomfortable, and the only other original track, "Christmas Must Be Something More," fails to keep pace with her contemporary country counterpart's religious songs, perhaps the only formally released song from the era where her age shows as naivete instead of sincerity.

The missteps here are just that—missteps made by a teenaged star-in-the-making toeing the line between cut-and-dried country stardom and the sort of career only her talent and ambition could manifest—and her strengths come out swinging at their finest on her next release, sophomore effort and breakthrough smash, *Fearless*.

14 TAYLOR SWIFT ALBUM BY ALBUM

Sisters Danielle and Este Haim joined Swift in a cover of The Chicks' "Goodbye, Earl" more than a decade after her self-titled debut, spanning eras with one foot (boot?) in country and another in Swift's ongoing transformation into a global pop superstar.

SWEETER IN FICTION

WHEN *FOLKLORE* IS released in 2020, Taylor Swift will spend much of her press cycle emphasizing that the album is her first grounded in fiction. Sure, that may be true of the record as a whole, but her songwriting preceding and throughout the debut era is sprinkled with fictitious, other-than-Taylor speakers. Whether it's the album track "Mary's Song" or long-fabled unreleased songs such as "Mandolin" and "Angelina," Swift's work deftly steps into the country tradition of character-driven songwriting. By penning narrative-driven persona anthems—her own teenage-friendly versions of Reba's "Fancy" or The Chick's "Goodbye, Earl"—Taylor continued to cement herself as a country songwriting heavyweight. She'd wink back at this heritage on evermore's "no body, no crime," the HAIM sister-aided homage to "Goodbye, Earl."

TAYLOR SWIFT

(continued from page 13)

Most of my friends' after-school jobs involved working at Tropical Smoothie Cafe or babysitting. Taylor Swift's was songwriting sessions with Liz Rose, 4 p.m. every Tuesday. The pair met at a writer's circle orchestrated by Swift's label and, according to Rose, instantly hit it off, spending hours on end writing through whatever had happened during Taylor's day. A later career criticism of Swift's lyrics is an inability to edit—Rose is on record as saying her primary role was maneuvering the lyrics Taylor herself wrote, an alchemist melding lyrics and melody into country magic.

Liz Rose is a legend in the Taylor Swift mythology, a co-writer on many of her early career's most successful songs, including *Debut*'s lead single "Tim McGraw." According to Taylor, the melody for the song struck her during math class, when her mind started wandering to her inevitable breakup with her soon-to-be-graduating boyfriend. Processing this with Rose and discussing the little details that make you love and miss a person—like a favorite song—was lightning in a bottle. The song, which would go on to earn double platinum, was done in under 20 minutes.

Taylor earned her "Voice of Her Generation" crown before she became a household name thanks to her personal lyrics and intimate storytelling.

16   TAYLOR SWIFT ALBUM BY ALBUM

"Picture to Burn" video co-star and real-life best friend, Abigail Anderson, accompanies Taylor to one of many red carpets throughout their friendship.

"Tim McGraw" was not only an aching slice-of-life love ballad, but a declaration of presence, entrenching Swift in the language of country writ large. By intertwining her personal narrative and artistic debut with the established titans and tropes of the country world, "Tim McGraw" gives Swift a sense of ownership over the genre, helping center her as the heir to country stardom.

Taylor didn't need to stake a claim to her rising star, her songwriting was doing it for her. The only song motivated by anger on the album (according to Swift), standout revenge anthem "Picture to Burn" comes out swinging with a string quartet and never once stops landing punches, leaving the listener breathless, invigorated, and ready to burn some shit down. "Should've Said No," a track definitely also motivated by anger, opens with a sinister chord progression evoking noon in an old Western, when the sun is high and a duel is about to begin. Tension builds throughout the verses, with Swift firing the proverbial shot at the chorus, building one of the first in a career defined by powerful bridges.

Sure, she was at the top of her class for bubbly love songs and gleeful revenge anthems, but Taylor didn't shy away from heavier topics, like the suffocating reality of living with an eating disorder in "Tied Together With a Smile," or the desperate disappointment driving "Cold As You," her first-ever track 5.

Track 5 is the emotional heart of any Taylor album. Over time, Taylor would confirm that whatever song was placed in that slot was the most vulnerable, emotional, or heavy song on the album, and you can see how "Cold As You" unwittingly started the tradition. "Cold As You" is an inconceivably bleak song from a 14-year-old, riddled with the sort of resignation and frustration that often simmers inside a person for decades before being cogently articulated. Here, acknowledging and pining after her own agency in this crumbling relationship, Swift is not being melodramatic—she is astoundingly mature.

Taylor Swift the brand would come to be defined by relatability, diluted over time with an inevitable manufactured and distant aura. But on her first few albums? That reputation was earned. She'd wait for hours on end to meet every fan at free meet and greets. Her vlogs and MySpace pages were accessible, intimate, and unfiltered, just like your high school best friend's might be if they were about to become a breakout country star. Part of this is thanks to Taylor's friendship with HER high school best friend, Abigail, who cameos in her over-the-top teen dream

TAYLOR SWIFT 17

LEFT: **From the earliest days of her career, Swift stunned on stage.**

BELOW: **Long before the inescapable friendship bracelet craze, Taylor was busy making friends with fans like Alyssa (pictured).**

Taylor adds a personal touch to her meet-and-greet mementos.

music videos and constant mentions on her MySpace. Taylor has a real, living best friend? And THEY have silly revenge fantasies and inside jokes? Maybe you could be her best friend, too.

And man, did Taylor want you to be her friend. She was intensely active on MySpace, once telling *CMT Insider* that she "really tries to give back to people and you know you can't give back to everybody, but I try as hard as I possibly can. I'm always putting up blogs, and anytime anything happens, I'm just, 'Hey, you guys, look what happened today!'" She'd keep this rapport up for nearly another 15 years, interacting with fans on Tumblr, Twitter, and Instagram, often instantly remembering fans years after first meeting them.

Thanks to Taylor's omnipresence, the Swiftie community blossomed naturally online. Beyond interacting with Taylor herself, a robust library of shared demos and leaked songs made the rounds among the most dedicated fans. Trading tracks rewarded fans with both relationships and rarities, and having certain MP3s was seen as a badge of honor, a sort of ordination of proximity to Taylor and her process. Hundreds of these songs were known to be in wide circulation and a handful have gone on to be Vault Tracks on the Taylor's Version projects, including "You All Over Me" and "We Were Happy."

Like so many of my peers, many of my earliest Taylor memories exist in two places: my family's desktop computer and my family's minivan. *Taylor Swift* lends itself to long drives alone, long drives with friends, long drives with your beloved. Bombastic and dynamic and brimming with potential, it's the perfect soundtrack for a drive before the horizon, when everything and everyone feels possible in the way it only can when you're 17. I'd blast "Picture to Burn" on my pink iPod mini, and would take my earbuds out when "Our Song" came on in rotation on my father's country channels of choice. In a season of life when agency seems so distant and possibility so urgent, Taylor proverbially met me with open arms, showing me—and her legions of fans—we could all have a place in this world.

TAYLOR SWIFT

By Joanna Weiss

FEARLESS

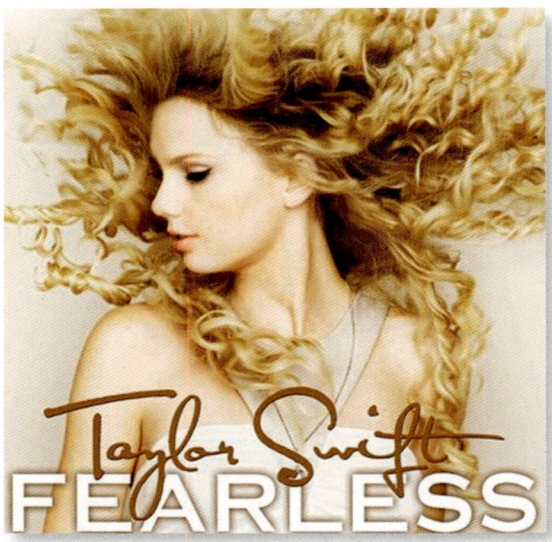

Track Listing:

1. Fearless [4:01]
2. Fifteen [4:54]
3. Love Story [3:55]
4. Hey Stephen [4:15]
5. White Horse [3:54]
6. You Belong With Me [3:51]
7. Breathe (feat. Colbie Caillat) (4:23]
8. Tell Me Why (3:20]
9. You're Not Sorry (4:21]
10. The Way I Loved You (4:03]
11. Forever & Always (3:45]
12. The Best Day (4:05]
13. Change (4:40]

Recorded at Blackbird (Nashville), Fool on the Hill (Nashville), Quad (Nashville), Sound Cottage Sound Emporium Starstruck (Nashville), Sound Kitchen (Franklin)

Released November 11, 2008

Produced by Taylor Swift & Nathan Chapman

Label: Big Machine Records

Notable personnel:

Nathan Chapman: producer, acoustic guitar, bass guitar, electric guitar, keyboard, Hammond organ, mandolin, mixing, percussion, piano, programming, steel guitar, vocal harmony

Sammie Allan: backing vocals

Colbie Caillat: finger snapping, guest vocals

Eric Darken: percussion, vibraphone

Kenny Greenberg: electric guitar

Dan Dugmore: steel guitar

Rob Hajacos: fiddle

Bryan Sutton: acoustic guitar, mandolin

LeeAnn Ramey: cover art, graphic design

Sandi Spika: hair stylist, make-up artist, wardrobe stylist

Deluxe edition released October 26, 2009

Total units sold: 7,285,000 (as of January 2024)

Weeks at Number 1 on the Billboard 200: 11

OPPOSITE: **Ready to sing the title track on the Fearless Tour, Taylor Swift was a rising star who was about to become a worldwide phenomenon.**

The Taylor Swift on the cover of *Fearless* looks to all the world like a fairy-tale princess, searching for happily ever after. She's innocent and hopeful, fashioned like a doll, her hair splayed out in carefully curated windswept ringlets, eyes closed as if she's dreaming. In the videos, she gazes out from medieval castle parapets or plays the parallel role of a freshman in distress, contemplating the deep, dark woods of high school and the princes who might be inside.

What happens to those fantasies—and whether they're worth wishing for—is the conflict at the heart of Swift's second album. The songs toggle between innocence and hard-earned wisdom, prom dresses and grungy high-tops, believing in fairy tales and acknowledging they don't exist. The title track is the sugar rush at the start of a relationship; "You're Not Sorry" is the song you scream into your pillow after a breakup. In "You Belong With Me" the underdog gets the guy of her dreams; in "White Horse," the dream falls apart spectacularly. In "Hey Stephen," the boy across the hallway is a prince; in "Tell Me Why," the prince turns out to be a jerk. It's all of the joys and stresses of teenage romance, rolled into a country-pop confection.

Fearless, released in November 2008, is unequivocally a country album, produced in Nashville at a time when Nashville was Swift's center and aspiration. The trappings are abundant: the fiddle leading off "Tell Me Why," the mandolin filling the spaces on "Breathe," the Hammond B-3 organ beneath the chorus of "Hey Stephen." Swift's airy vocals have a decided twang; it's almost like she's practiced a Southern pronunciation of "mind" and "drive" and "times." Still, there's plenty of pop peeking through the crevices, a sign of what was to come, from the banging drumbeat at the start of "Tell Me Why" to the sly finger snaps at the close of "Hey Stephen." And some reviewers seemed a bit confounded about where this 18-year-old upstart, poised for crossover success, fit in to the larger music industry landscape. *Entertainment Weekly* marveled that Swift wasn't "some manufactured vixen-Lolita" like the pop starlets of the early aughts. *American Noise* called *Fearless* "a bipolar album that dips its feet into both pools." *Slant* griped that Swift was hardly a lights-out singer (she "wouldn't make it out of the first round of *American Idol* auditions"), but conceded that the album was destined to be a juggernaut anyway.

OPPOSITE: **Dressed for medieval times, Taylor performs "Love Story" at the 42nd CMA Awards in November 2008.**

Even the not-quite haters had to acknowledge the real source of *Fearless*'s power—Swift's heart-on-her-sleeve lyrics and her preternaturally skilled songwriting. She wrote eight songs on the album and co-wrote the rest, which means that unlike the passive girl on the cover, not to mention most of her pop star peers, she was fully invested in telling her own stories. (A few reviewers sniffed that some of her lyrics verged on cliché but conceded that the tweens and teens would love them anyway. There's a fine line, in pop music, between cliché and universal truth.)

Technically, the songs aren't sophisticated, but they're skilled: a string of indelible hooks lodged in simple chord progressions. Emotionally, they're pathos bombs. Each one is a self-contained story, a window into a problem, a strongly held wish, or an identifiable moment when the dream begins or ends. The lyrics to "Tell Me Why" tumbled out in real time, Swift once recalled, when co-writer Liz Rose invited her to vent about a boy: "If you could say everything you were thinking right now, what

FEARLESS   23

would you start with?" It's not the only song that feels like being on the receiving end of a breathless rant or a quiet confession. And that's where the real alchemy comes in.

There was, let's admit, something counterfactual about the image Swift presented at the time *Fearless* came out. Country girl? She'd grown up in Pennsylvania, the daughter of a stockbroker. Wide-eyed naif? She'd willed a music career into existence before she was even a teenager. But she managed to pour enough authenticity into *Fearless* to neutralize any doubts. Partly that comes from the unmistakably teenage mood: the petulance in her voice as she gripes about broken promises in "Forever & Always," the twisted self-awareness of the girl who's drawn to bad boys in "The Way I Loved You," the sweetness on "The Best Day," as she thanks her mother for rescuing her from the mean kids. And partly, it comes from her raw emotions, no matter how adolescently low the stakes seem. Juliet was just 13 in Shakespeare's play; you can be young and still *feel*.

Hence, "Fifteen," the ballad of high school longing that tapped directly into the brains of American teenage girls. It's full of specifics, some of them verifiable: Taylor *did* spend two years in a place called Hendersonville High School, where, in English class on the first day, she *did* meet a redhead named Abigail who would become her lifelong friend. But the generic images could ring equally true. Plenty of girls have walked through school hallways pining for romance, wondering where they fit in, barely aware of a world beyond the personal mini-tragedies they felt so fully. ("I CRIED WHILE RECORDING THIS," was Taylor's secret message in the liner notes.) Even the country lyrics about small-town life make sense in context here, because what is high school if not a sometimes-cruel small town?

It's a trick Taylor would pull off again and again, in *Fearless* and the albums that followed: The specificity makes fans feel like they know her, and the generality makes people feel like she knows *them*. On one of Swift's later tours, I saw groups of teenage girls who had probably been in elementary school when *Fearless* came out, singing "Fifteen" as if they were reading pages from their own diaries. Taylor also spoke to them in the conspiratorial language of high school camaraderie, as she did on her debut album: hidden comments in the liner notes, delivered via code; detective work assignments on social media; a track 5 that does its level best to eviscerate you. (Here, it's "White Horse," which enlists the cello for maximum mournfulness.)

The difference between those two albums, and what launched *Fearless* into the stratosphere, was that, here, she also had a verifiable megahit. "Love Story" is the ultimate Romeo-and-Juliet saga, if you overlook the fact that the original play was a tragedy. Even now, it might be the ultimate Taylor Swift song, a place where the whole package comes together: country roots and pop sensibilities, a universal emotion, and the music to match.

It starts quietly, like a country ballad: a mandolin arpeggio, a modified version of "once upon a time," an invitation to a storybook romance filled with gardens and

(continued on page 29)

OPPOSITE: **Taylor Swift won the CMT Country Music Award for Female Video of the Year for "Love Story"—one of many statuettes she'd take home for *Fearless* in 2009.**

FEARLESS

It was supposed to be a fairy-tale night at the VMAs. Swift arrived in a gilded, Cinderella-like carriage, but the night turned into a pumpkin more quickly than Taylor expected.

THE PRINCESS AND THE TROLL

TAYLOR SWIFT ROLLED up to Radio City Music Hall, the site of the 2009 MTV Video Music Awards, in a horse-drawn carriage fashioned after Cinderella's. She wore a silver off-the-shoulder floor-length gown, sparkles all around, and she was ready for another fairy-tale moment in her so-far charmed career when the announcers called her name: She had won Best Female Video for "You Belong With Me." Onstage, she launched into an aw-shucks speech: "I sing country music, so thank you so much for giving me a chance to win a VMA award."

And then Kanye West appeared.

Where had he been lurking? From a TV viewer's vantage point, he seemed to conjure himself from thin air, appearing in front of Swift with his big-star swagger. Grabbing the mic from Swift's hand, he unleashed his infamous line, "Imma let you finish," then declared that "Beyoncé had one of the best videos of all time."

26   TAYLOR SWIFT ALBUM BY ALBUM

"Imma let you finish…" That moment—and that quote—would be seared into pop culture history.

Beyoncé, shocked as anyone by Kanye's eruption, handed the stage to Taylor Swift after winning the award for Video of the Year.

Audience members shifted uncomfortably. Beyoncé herself, caught by the cameras, gasped in disbelief. And then, in what might have been the cruelest move of all, West handed the mic back to Taylor, as if she could just pick up where she left off.

Taylor Swift, compulsive diarist and social media natural, a person who, since her preteen days, had written songs at the speed of her thoughts, was suddenly speechless. She stood still for a moment, like a statue. Then she turned and left the stage.

She would later say that, in the chaos of the moment, she mistook what was happening inside the hall. She heard boos and thought the crowd was booing her, the interloper who had displeased a musical genius. After all, she was just 19, a country artist with big hopes; he was 32 and already larger than life. ("Were you a fan?" one reporter asked her after the event. "Yeah," Swift replied, almost sheepishly. "He's Kanye West.")

In fact, the room had been on Taylor's side. Pink went up to Kanye and chewed him out. Beyoncé cried backstage in her father's arms. Mechanisms were put in place to make speedy amends: When Beyoncé won the award for Album of the Year, she invited Swift back onstage, where she gave the short speech she'd intended.

The backlash continued long after the event; Barack Obama, then US president, would call Kanye a "jackass." Still, in the days and weeks afterward, Swift evaded questions about the controversy. She told reporters she didn't want to cause trouble or make the moment a bigger deal than it already was.

But she would get her retribution, in due time—delivered the way she knew best.

RIGHT: **When she performed at the start of the VMAs, Taylor had no idea that she'd be getting an early lesson in megastardom.**

FEARLESS 27

ABOVE LEFT: **Fans have speculated that "Forever & Always" was about Joe Jonas, who broke up with Swift by phone in 2008 after a summer romance. It's part of a string of "Was it him?" breakup references she'll never officially share.**

ABOVE RIGHT: **The code in the liner notes for "Hey Stephen" spelled out "Love and Theft"—the opening act for her 2008 tour. It was confirmation she had written the song for the band's handsome co-vocalist, Stephen Barker Liles.**

OPPOSITE: **On the Fearless Tour, Taylor sang "You Belong With Me" dressed as girl in the bleachers in the marching band—the one who eventually gets the guy.**

(continued from page 24)

ballgowns and secret trysts. The story unfolds, the drums weigh in, the strings build intensity. The bridge arrives when the romance seems doomed; the instruments fall quiet along with Taylor's voice. And then suddenly—yes!—a plot twist, a key change, and soaring strings as the story reaches its fairy-tale ending. If you don't feel compelled to whirl around the room when that modulation hits, you should hire a detective to conduct a multistate search for your soul.

This is the best of what *Fearless* had to offer, and fans showed their appreciation. The album spent 11 weeks at the top of the Billboard 200, the longest number-one run for a country female album. "Love Story" was the first country song to hit number one on *Billboard*'s Pop Airplay chart. "White Horse" won the Grammy for Best Song and Best Female Country Vocal Performance. *Fearless* won for Best Country Album and Album of the Year. The video for "You Belong With Me"—in which Taylor played both a mousy girl in glasses and her raven-haired cheerleader rival—won Best Female Video at the MTV Video Music Awards, leading to a pop culture moment that would change the trajectory of more than one career (see sidebar, page 26).

All in all, it wasn't a happy ending so much as a fierce beginning. If *Taylor Swift* lit the spark that would become Taylor Swift, Inc., *Fearless* turned the flame into a wildfire. *Fearless* set the stage for her future mythology, unleashing images that would come up again and again: beckoning stairwells and favorite dresses and lonely Tuesday nights and kissing in the rain. *Fearless* launched the mysterious breakup songs that

FEARLESS   29

sent fans hunting for real-life clues. (Was "Forever & Always" about Joe Jonas? Taylor will never tell.) *Fearless* snuck in the meta commentary that would characterize so much of her future work: that laugh in "Hey Stephen" when Swift acknowledges she's different from other girls because she has the power to write a song. *Fearless* gave Swift her first stadium-sellout headlining tour, turned her from upstart to phenomenon.

Did the girl with the ringlets on the album cover, dressed and primped by Nashville handlers, know what was coming next? Did she expect the highs and lows that happen when your fairy tale comes true? Already, as Taylor sang in the album's final song, her life had changed. She spent only two years at Hendersonville High before her growing career intervened. Within years of the *Fearless* release, she'd be buying mansions for her parents and herself, and she'd be able to escape small towns in a private jet. Older Taylor would still write songs from the teenage perspective, at least from time to time, but her personal drama would shift to the privileges and pressures of celebrity and the vipers in a cutthroat music industry (with some bad boys to love and lose along the way). But the original *Fearless* is preserved in amber, a moment when her life was as down to earth as it was ever going to be. And those stories endure, because everyone wants to relive the fairy tale.

Whenever you happen to encounter these songs, whether you're a teenager or a former teenager or someone who hasn't been a teenager yet, you'll find a way to understand. Which brings us to a September day, far away from Nashville, some 15 years after *Fearless* was first released. In a postage-stamp park in a town outside Boston, as dusk began to bring a hint of chill into the air, a local band was playing a cover of "Love Story." A little girl who couldn't have been older than four, with long, curly hair that looked like Taylor's tresses on the *Fearless* cover, had pushed herself to the front of the crowd, in the grassy space in front of the band. As the song played, she did an interpretive dance—acting out the words with literal gestures, falling to her knees and rising again, spinning in circles as the couple in the song embarks on its happy ending.

This was love as she understood it, Taylor's Version. And as she writes her own story, it's safe to assume that *Fearless* will be part of the background score.

Some child stars have notoriously terrible relationships with their families. Not Taylor Swift. "The Best Day" is a tribute to her close relationship with her family, especially her mother, Andrea, who would be a mainstay on her tours as a teenager.

30 TAYLOR SWIFT ALBUM BY ALBUM

In the liner notes for "Fifteen," Taylor's coded message read, "I cried while recording this." It was a message embedded in the lyrics in capital letters—something she did for her first five albums. Here, she performs "Fifteen" at the Stagecoach Music Festival in 2008 in California.

FEARLESS

3

By Kase Wickman

Track Listing:

1. Mine [3:50]
2. Sparks Fly [4:20]
3. Back To December [4:53]
4. Speak Now [4:00]
5. Dear John [6:43]
6. Mean [3:57]
7. The Story Of Us [4:25]
8. Never Grow Up [4:50]
9. Enchanted [5:52]
10. Better Than Revenge [3:37]
11. Innocent [5:02]
12. Haunted [4:02]
13. Last Kiss [6:07]
14. Long Live [5:17]

Deluxe Edition Bonus Tracks:

15. Ours [3:57]
16. If This Was A Movie [3:54]
17. Superman [4:35]
18. Back To December (Acoustic) [4:52]
19. Haunted (Acoustic) [3:37]
20. Mine (Pop Mix) [3:50]

Speak Now

Recorded at Aimeeland (Nashville), Blackbird (Nashville), Pain in the Art (Nashville), Starstruck (Nashville), Capitol (Los Angeles), Stonehurst (Bowling Green)

Released October 25, 2010

Produced by Nathan Chapman and Taylor Swift

Label: Big Machine Records

Notable personnel:

Martin Johnson: co-writer "If This Was A Movie," Deluxe edition only

Deluxe edition released October 25, 2010

Selected awards:

Grammy Awards: Best Country Song ("Mean")

Grammy Awards: Best Country Solo Performance ("Mean")

American Music Awards: Favorite Album (Country) 2011

Billboard Music Awards: Top Country Album 2011

Notable honors:

6 weeks at number one on Billboard 200

Six-time Platinum certified by RIAA

2010 Guinness World Record: Fastest-selling album in the United States by a female country artist

Tour: Speak Now World Tour, February 2011–March 2012; 110 shows, 18 countries

OPPOSITE: **Swift flashes a now-familiar heart during the beginning of the Speak Now tour in Omaha, Nebraska.**

On October 25, 2010, with five Grammy Awards under her belt for her first two country-accented records, a twang inserted into her native Pennsylvania cadence, Taylor Swift released *Speak Now*, her third studio album. For anyone who clutches their pearls in shock at the reinventions, re-reinventions, and re-re-*re*inventions Swift would pull off later in her discography, pivoting between genres smoother and faster than a disco ball's spin, one listen to *Speak Now*, in retrospect, feels like warning enough of what was to come in her then-young career.

A few months shy of her 21st birthday, Swift released the 14-track album, its cover art featuring the singer twirling in an ethereal deep-purple dress in front of a white background, a scattered cloud of little-girl fairy dust added with the help of post-production photo editing to surround the album's title and Swift's name in her recognizable loopy script. The album art is legible to fans who had begged their moms to take them to Borders bookstore or the FYE down at the mall to buy her first two releases: same curly-haired blonde girl gazing out from behind the jewel case with an inscrutable expression, same signature scrawl, that posed soft-focus romance. But the contents of *Speak Now* reveal a Swift with one foot in what she'd been—the autobiographical songstress strumming along to accompany herself on songs about the boys she wants and the ones who broke her heart—and the other stepping into thin air, imagining the mature artist and adult she was already plotting how to become.

John Mayer and Taylor Swift perform together at the Z100 Jingle Ball in New York City in December 2009. Their short-lived relationship is the stuff of legend—and song.

And there's no way this isn't intentional: Swift is nothing if not the obsessive curator of her own museum and mythology. *Speak Now* is the only album of her now-vast discography on which she has the sole songwriting credits—for Every. Single. Track.

And she has a lot to say! Cute little ditties these aren't: Of the 14 tracks on the standard edition of the album, only three—opener "Mine" at 3:50, the scathing "Mean" missing the mark by just three seconds, and the album's shortest song, "Better Than Revenge," at a still-hefty 3:37—have a runtime shorter than four minutes. At the risk of being yet another person comparing Swift to The Beatles, the go-to yardstick of super-duper-popular music of an earlier era, consider that their early musical efforts typically clocked in between two and three minutes. And she was just getting started: The famed 10-minute version of "All Too Well" wouldn't be released for years yet, but the clues were already there on *Speak Now*, with Swift proving she could—and absolutely would—hold her fans captivated for longer than it takes to rinse out last night's coffee grounds and get a fresh pot brewing.

That Swift wrote all of this album's songs solo wasn't an act of ego or rejection of earlier collaborators such as Liz Rose, her Nashville mentor and frequent co-writer. In a webcast for fans on July 20, 2010, ahead of the album's release, Swift explained herself.

"It didn't really happen on purpose, it just sort of happened," she said, the result of long nights alone while touring *Fearless*, her first time taking an album on the road. "Like, I'd get my best ideas at three a.m. in Arkansas, and I didn't have a co-writer around and I would just finish it."

The odd hours and solitude that led to Swift's Herculean solo writing credit, that disorientation that comes with feeling unmoored in both time and physical location, always on the move and beholden to the weirdest schedule ever, almost certainly also contribute to the album's inward gaze—Swift turning over the stones of her innermost memories and feelings and examining them in great detail in the same space as dreaming of what her future might hold.

In "Never Grow Up," she flinches at a memory of her younger self asking her mom to drop her off around the corner, then looks ahead with the shock of realizing that "everything I have is someday gonna be gone." On a lighter note, title track "Speak Now" sees Swift imagining busting up a wedding, lurking behind curtains like some kind of emotionally covetous gremlin, tossing off comments about the "snotty little family all dressed in pastels" and snarking about the bride and her "gown shaped like a pastry." (Worth pointing out that nearly a decade and a half later on Swift's supersized The Eras Tour, where she puzzlingly only performed one song, "Enchanted," to represent the *Speak Now* era, she cycled through at least nine different gowns throughout the tour, all notably pastry-esque. Forget the pot calling the kettle black, Swift, in this song, is the personification of the petit four calling the cupcake frosted.) The event itself is purely imagined (*something* tells me we would have heard about this at some point if it wasn't), but the emotion that comes with watching secretly from the sidelines, playing at being tough and critical while

(continued on page 38)

ENCHANTED WITH "ENCHANTED"

ON AN ALBUM full of fan-favorite tracks and six Platinum-certified singles, it's somewhat surprising that an album cut has emerged over the years as the sonic distillation of *Speak Now*: The nearly six-minute-long "Enchanted." On Swift's 2023–2024 The Eras Tour, "Enchanted" was the only song from the album that made the show's permanent setlist. Swift floated out onto the stage in a variety of bedazzled fairy princess looks. The song was reportedly written in reaction to meeting Adam Young, the lead singer of Owl City, and liking the cut of his jib enough to daydream about whether they might have a future together; Swift even hid A-D-A-M in the liner notes to make its subject even more obvious.

A few months later, Young wrote on his Tumblr about buying *Speak Now* at midnight on release day and having his socks knocked off by the track, not knowing ahead of time that Swift had written it. "Needless to say, I was lost for words and utterly smitten. I couldn't stop smiling," he wrote, before a brief note addressed to Taylor herself. Oh, and it's important to note: This was on Valentine's Day 2011. The note reads, in part, "Everything about you is beautiful. You're an immensely charming girl with a wonderful heart and more grace and elegance than I know how to describe. You are a true princess from a dreamy fairy tale; a modern Cinderella." He posted a cover of himself singing "Enchanted" and swapping in Swift's name, saying, "I was enchanted to meet you, too."

Swift reportedly never responded to the post.

Beyond the pop culture lore it inspired, "Enchanted" has always been the undercover heart of *Speak Now*, and was nearly the title track. In a 2010 interview with Reuters, Scott Borchetta, CEO of Swift's then-label Big Machine Records, revealed the title that almost was and why it changed. "We were at lunch, and she had played me a bunch of the new songs," he said. "I looked at her and I'm like, 'Taylor, this record isn't about fairy tales and high school anymore. That's not where you're at. I don't think the record should be called Enchanted.'" Swift stood up from the table and disappeared briefly, he said. When she came back, she had the new title, *Speak Now*.

As Swift wrote in a journal entry dated April 13, 2010, "Scott freaked out. He loved it. We have a title, ladies and gentlemen!" In the album's liner notes she elaborates that, of course, the words were inspired by the infamous line in traditional wedding vows, but that in the context of the album, they had a still more personal meaning yet: "These songs are made up of words I didn't say when the moment was right in front of me," she wrote. "These songs are open letters. Each is written with a specific person in mind, telling them what I meant to tell them in person. To the beautiful boy whose heart I broke in December. To my first love who I never thought would be my first heartbreak. To my band. To a mean man I used to be afraid of. To someone who made my world very dark for a while. To a girl who stole something of mine. To someone I forgive for what he said in front of the whole world."

And, hey, if "Enchanted" didn't get the title track treatment, having not one but two fragrances named after it isn't the worst consolation prize, is it? Swift's Wonderstruck, a "fruity floral," was released in 2011, and the "exotic vanilla" Wonderstruck Enchanted followed in 2012. If you can't sing it, as they say, smell it.

On his Tumblr blog, Adam Young revealed he was blown away by Taylor's "Enchanted," though Swift never responded to the post. At least, that's what was reported.

Barefoot and in a hairstyle and dress nodding to what she'd worn when Kanye West told her he was gonna let her finish (he did not, actually), Swift returned to the VMAs a year later, in 2010, to debut "Innocent," a song inspired by the incident.

(continued from page 35)
really feeling left out and sad, fantasizing about springing into action and blowing up everyone else's fun to grab the thing you really want, is very real.

Speak Now is Swift at her late-adolescent finest. She articulates that early 20s empowerment and bewilderment so well in these songs, the giddiness at having your own place and rules that are your own, not your parents', a feeling that can morph in a blink to the "now what?" panic of realizing that, without that scaffolding of dos and don'ts, you're not just free to fill your own time, you're also *responsible* for filling it. In album opener "Mine," Swift imagines lying on a couch with her boyfriend, feet tangled together indoor-pants level of intimacy, reminiscing about their beginnings and past fights. She has a drawer at "your place," his part-time waiter gig is behind him. It's cozy and domestic. You can imagine that Ikea furniture is probably involved, as were the attendant domestic squabbles while assembling it. It's relatable, the whole thing.

In reality, Swift *had* recently gotten her first place of her own, but almost certainly without even a splinter of DIY furniture. In 2009, she purchased a 3,240-square-foot condo in Nashville for $1.99 million. Later that year, she bought the apartment right below it, too. She masterminded the interior design, according to a 2013 *Vulture* profile, down to the heart-shaped kitchen backsplash, a human-size birdcage, and, Judy Rosen wrote, "a topiary rabbit, as tall as an NBA shooting guard, wearing a marching-band hat." It's *slightly less* relatable, the whole thing.

Taylor's gift on *Speak Now* is alchemizing universal feelings (the crush-at-first-sight giddiness and obsession of "Enchanted" and that imagined fighting and making up and years of history with a childhood sweetheart in "Mine") with her own specific lived experiences (having her heart bruised in a fling with John Mayer for "Dear John," and bruising Taylor Lautner's via the mistreatment of cut flowers in "Back To December") and borrowed sonic signifiers layered on top of her own piano and acoustic guitar–based sound to move her work forward (the insult to injury of using the Mayer-signature steel guitars to great effect on "Dear John," the way "Better Than Revenge" could well be recorded by Paramore, whose lead singer Hayley Williams she not coincidentally spent New Year's Eve 2009 with, banjo tracks and twang turned to 11 for "Mean" to make it clear she sees those critiques of whether she's "country enough," and the wailing, intense, Evanescence-coded orchestrations of "Haunted"). The same way Swift herself was navigating the shift from teenager to adult right alongside the transition from rising songwriter to Grammy-winning superstar, her music slyly edged closer to the pop sound she would more openly embrace on her next album, *Red*, and throw itself fully into on *1989*, nary a banjo or affected twang to be found.

Speaking of twang, let's address the "Mean" elephant in the room. By the time *Speak Now* rolled around, Swift's fame had already grown into the type where mention of her name was just as likely to inspire squeals of adoration as too-cool eyerolls and scoffing denunciations. She'd been lambasted for being too boy crazy; she'd already been interrupted onstage by Kanye West at the MTV Video Music Awards with a rant

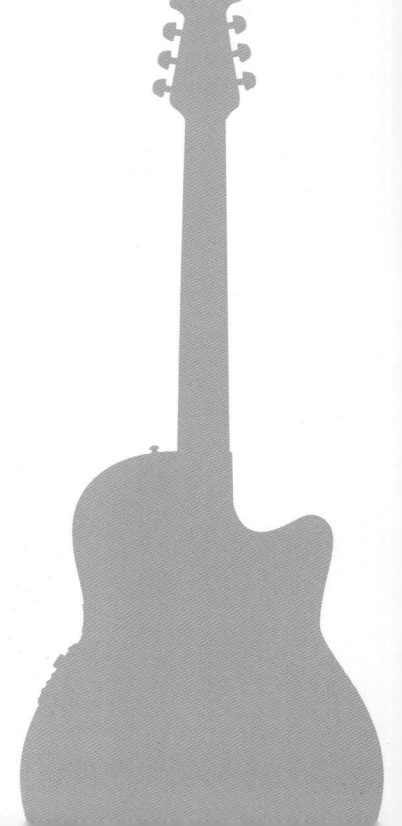

RIGHT ON TARGET

SPEAK NOW MARKED the true beginning of a business relationship that has outlasted so many personal ones: the blessed union between Taylor Swift and retail giant Target. While Swift dipped a toe into the balmy bull's-eye waters with the "Platinum Edition" reissue of *Fearless*, a re-release of the sophomore album roughly one year after its original drop featuring six new songs that had one cover variation exclusive to Target, it wasn't a true exclusive.

That changed with *Speak Now*, when Swift had gained enough popularity and power to garner a Target-exclusive Deluxe edition of the album, released on the same day as the standard edition. The difference, beyond a cover with Swift's purple dress instead edited to red (perhaps a hint at the next album Swift was already mulling?), was the addition of three bonus tracks ("Ours," "If This Was A Movie," and "Superman"), two acoustic versions ("Back To December" and "Haunted"), and a pop remix of "Mine." Separate sales numbers for the two versions of the album were not released, but the experiment must have been successful enough: For all of Swift's subsequent releases, there have been Target-exclusive tie-ins, and in 2024, the chain was the exclusive retailer for Swift's The Eras Tour Book and the long-awaited vinyl and CD versions of The Anthology double-album edition of *The Tortured Poets Department*, the full tracklist of which had previously been available only in digital form.

Between the recolored dress and her trademark crimson lipstick, Swift's Target-exclusive version of *Speak Now* delighted fans and was impossible to miss on retail endcaps.

about how lesser than she was; and been picked apart in every way imaginable regarding her wardrobe, hair, singing, songwriting, all of it. It seemed to be open season on everything about her, always. She didn't say anything—until she did.

Speak Now is notably the first album on which Swift publicly apologizes for anything, sharing her regrets about how she ghosted a relationship on "Back To December." It's also the album that plays host to her most vicious how-dare-you tracks, "Better Than Revenge" and "Mean." The latter song appears to be in response to a blog post by critic Bob Lefsetz in which he eviscerates her performance at the 2010 Grammys with Stevie Nicks, the same night she nabbed her first Album of the Year Grammy, for *Fearless*. He said it was "awful," "dreadful," questioned why she was "sharing a stage with a legend," said she should have employed autotune to "save her career" and that she's "too young and dumb to understand the mistake she made."

SPEAK NOW 39

TAYLOR SWIFT ALBUM BY ALBUM

ABOVE: **Performing with longtime pal Selena Gomez in New York City on the Speak Now World Tour. Fun fact: When Gomez got engaged in 2024, Swift congratulated her friend in an Instagram comment and volunteered herself for flower girl duty.**

OPPOSITE: **For "Mean," Swift went back to her roots for a full banjo-twang country sound.**

"In one fell swoop, Taylor Swift consigned herself to the dustbin of teen phenoms," Lefsetz wrote. Elsewhere in the rant: "It's hard to be a singer if you can't sing."

And Taylor, as Michael Jordan might say, took that personally.

The uncalled-for comments not only garnered Lefsetz a few personal telephone calls from Swift, which he also wrote about on his blog, further claiming he had been the first person in history to suggest to Swift that she listen to Joni Mitchell's "Blue," but a musical ode in the shape of "Mean."

The song's music video is a movie-trope romp, featuring Swift both in a singing role outside the narrative and as a vaudevillian damsel in distress, tied up on the railroad tracks by twirly-mustached villains, collaged with a sharply dressed boy getting elbowed by the jocks as he reads a magazine simply called *Fashion*, a girl who slips pennies earned from her demeaning fast-food mascot gig into a piggy bank marked "college," and a very young Joey King in a frilly white dress, no room for her at the lunch table with the other girls, picking at her cafeteria tray in a bathroom stall. By the end of the song, Swift has thrown off her bindings and strutted off the tracks as her captors drunkenly snooze on barstools, the *Fashion* reader is being applauded at his runway show, the redhead has traded up to a power suit and a degree from college (the college is called "College," naturally) hangs on her office

SPEAK NOW

wall, and the little girl claps, inspired, from the audience where she has watched singer Swift transform from a hayseed to the sparkliest star over the course of the song. The choices are at once incredibly earnest in their stereotypes as well as winking in Swift's self-recognition of the public perception that she plays the victim for her own benefit.

The song itself is interesting, lyrically. Michelle Obama hadn't yet dropped her "when they go low, we go high" tidbit, but even if she had, Swift certainly wouldn't have been listening. In response to a bully's critique, her lyrics jump to name-calling and some bullying of her own. "A liar and pathetic and alone in life and mean," she calls her tormenter. She imagines him "alone in life" and drunkenly bitching into the wind at a sports bar where nobody wants to hear what he has to say, but he's saying it anyway. Ouch. The whole thing flies in the face of the conflict resolution curriculum my public school presented in seventh grade, but then one subtle change in verb tense unlocks the entire song for me: "I just wanna feel ok again," Swift sings.

Apart from that line, the entire song makes definitive statements, Swift prophesying her future "living in a big old city," "big enough so you can't hit me." She knows for a fact, grammatically, that this unnamed man is always going to be mean, just as much as she knows that he'll still be able to get to her with that bitchery: "You will knock me off my feet again." It's just that one line where she expresses a wish, one she's not sure will come true. This transforms the song from fighting fire with immature fire to a little-kid tantrum, the yelp and tears that come with the sadness and disappointment of being told you spelled the word wrong in your essay and have been marked down, or that there's just not time for you to take another turn on the rollercoaster before we go. It's the outward manifestation of a big, hard-to-process feeling. That line, too, is her little-kid truth. Taylor wishes this didn't get to her, she wants to be secure enough on her own to not be bothered by it, but it does and she isn't. Again, Swift manages to express an adolescent emotional truth, the calling card of this album, to which fans can relate, even if it arose from a situation they will never face.

"Innocent," her response to Kanye West's infamous VMAs "Imma let you finish," a photograph of which she reportedly hung in a gilt frame in that same first Nashville pad, has had plenty of ink spilled in its honor. Despite West claiming that Swift had played the victim in the situation (in which she was, undoubtedly, the victim), she actually didn't offer a substantial response until she debuted "Innocent" at the 2010 Video Music Awards, ahead of *Speak Now*'s release. With the backing of a full orchestra and wide, earnest Bambi eyes, Swift did the most infuriating thing possible: She forgave him.

Swift pauses with fans during the Speak Now World Tour.

Because there's no winning when you're Taylor Swift, the song was called condescending by some in its proclamation that "who you are is not what you did" to a man who's "32, but still growing up now." But, really, can we remember that Swift was 19? She didn't have a lot of authority in the "growing up" space, but she also shouldn't have been put into a situation where she'd need to. It's also worth pointing out that Mayer, another older man who got on Swift's bad side and was reprimanded in song, was also 32. Lefsetz, the apparent "Mean" inspiration, was in his late 50s when he hit publish on his post. It's damned if you do (imply any conflict with men your own age, resulting in that boy-crazy characterization), damned if you don't (respond to older men punching down on a teenager and be accused of playing the victim).

The album ends on a note of triumph with the soaring "Long Live," a tribute to Swift's band and the spotlight they've shared. After her first big stadium tour, the singer had forged something special with her band, who would go on to also play on her albums, not just on stage, the ones who had been there for the times you just had to have been there to get.

"This song for me is like looking at a photo album of all the award shows, and all the stadium shows, and all the hands in the air in the crowd," Swift wrote of the song on her website. "It's sort of the first love song that I've written to my team." Again, she pulls in relatable imagery—the naming of the prom king and queen, the fantasy novel knights slaying dragons—of situations she's never experienced but are more legible to her listeners than her actual inspiration of looking out at seas of adoring fans, all screaming for her. Even as she appreciates the experiences she's had and the memories she made, in typical Swift fashion, she's looking forward at her eventual legacy, begging her compatriots to someday tell their children about her, and all the wonderful things they did together.

When Swift sings that it's "the end of a decade, but the start of an age," there was no way to tell what would come her way in the next decade-plus, or even exactly how much she was closing out her own fairy princess, country ingenue chapter. This was the last time we'd see Swift donning a tulle cloud of a dress in which to spin on an album cover, no more Swift as the storybook Juliet. She was growing up, and so was her music. Soon, everything would be *Red*. 🦋

ABOVE: **During the Speak Now World Tour, Swift would write different lyrics on her arms every night. Here, she borrows one of Selena Gomez's lyrics.**

NEXT PAGE: **Swift onstage in her home state of Pennsylvania (in Philadelphia) during the Speak Now World Tour.**

SPEAK NOW 43

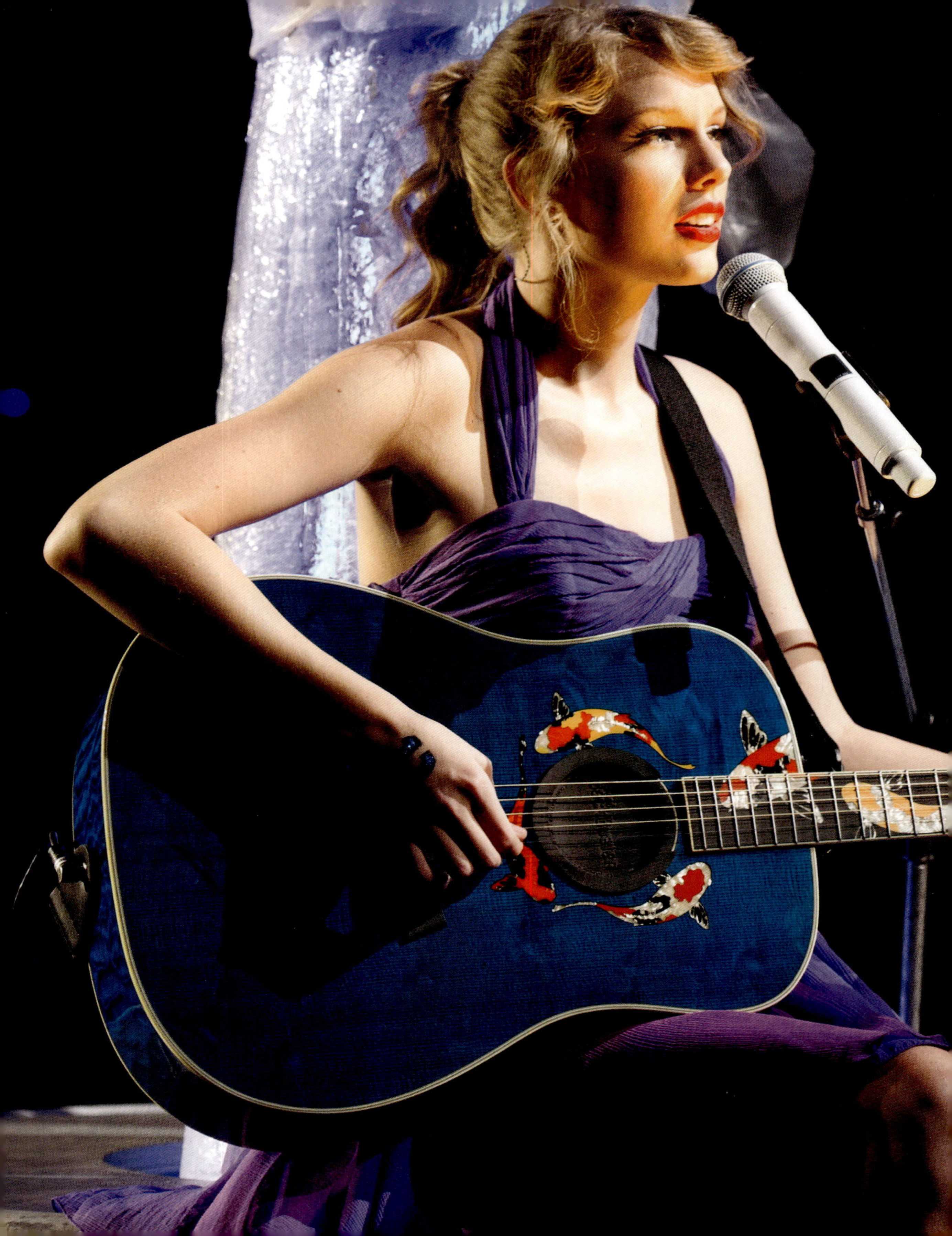

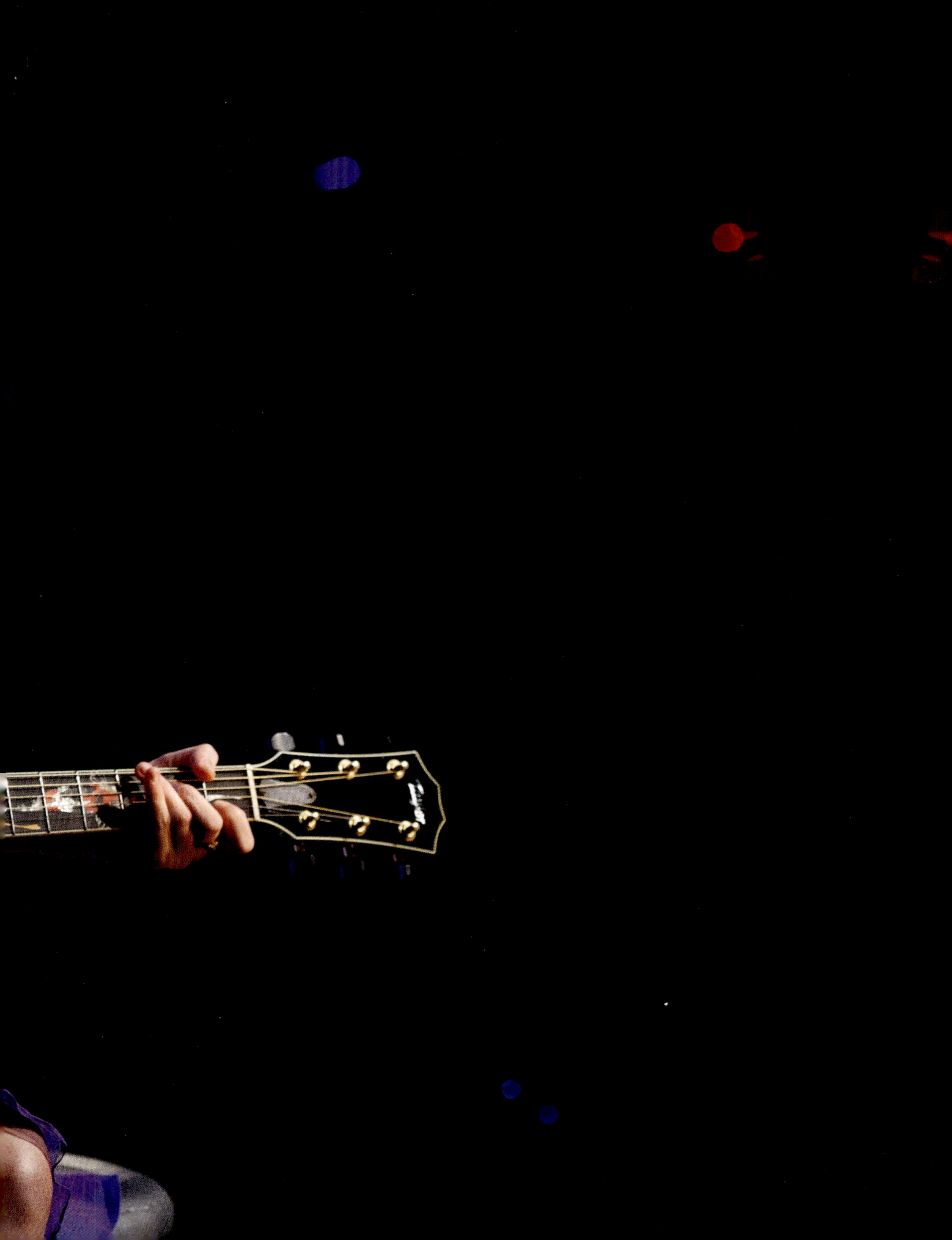

By Kase Wickman

RED

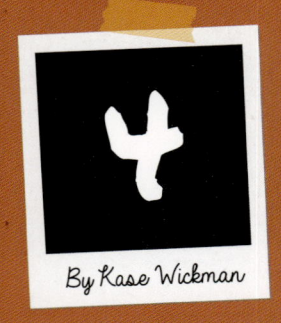

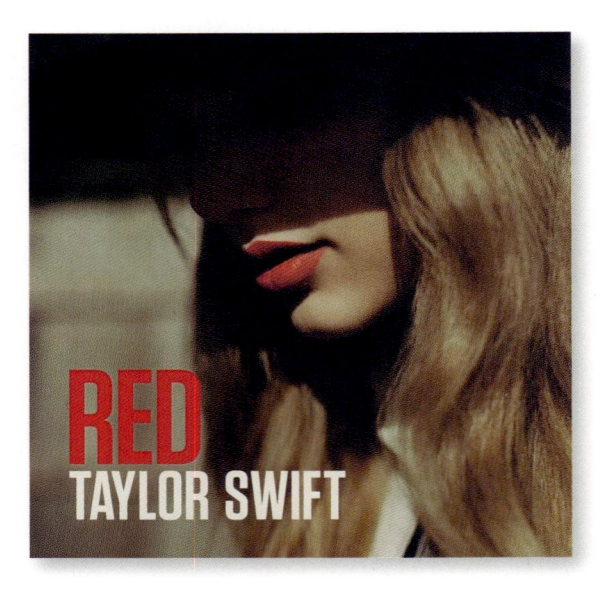

Track Listing:
1. State Of Grace [4:55]
2. Red [3:43]
3. Treacherous [4:02]
4. I Knew You Were Trouble [3:39]
5. All Too Well [5:29]
6. 22 [3:52]
7. I Almost Do [4:04]
8. We Are Never Ever Getting Back Together [3:13]
9. Stay Stay Stay [3:25]
10. The Last Time (ft. Gary Lightbody) [4:59]
11. Holy Ground [3:22]
12. Sad Beautiful Tragic [4:44]
13. The Lucky One [4:00]
14. Everything Has Changed (ft. Ed Sheeran) [4:05]
15. Starlight [3:40]
16. Begin Again [3:57]

Deluxe Edition Bonus Tracks:
17. The Moment I Knew [4:46]
18. Come Back...Be Here [3:43]
19. Girl At Home [3:40]
20. Treacherous (Original Demo Recording) [4:00]
21. Red (Original Demo Recording) [3:47]
22. State Of Grace (Acoustic) [5:23]

46

Recorded at Blackbird (Nashville), Pain in the Art (Nashville), Ballroom West (New York), Instrument Landing (Minneapolis), MXM (Stockholm), Conway Recording (Los Angeles), Village (Los Angeles), The Garage (Topanga Canyon), Ruby Red (Atlanta)

Released October 22, 2012

Produced by Taylor Swift, Nathan Chapman, Jeff Bhasker, Dann Huff, Jacknife Lee, Max Martin, Shellback, Butch Walker, Dan Wilson

Label: Big Machine Records

Notable personnel:

Ed Sheeran: vocals

Jacknife Lee: bass guitar, guitar, keyboard

Gary Lightbody: vocals

Max Martin: keyboards

Owen Pallett: conducting, orchestration

Shellback: bass guitar, guitar, acoustic guitar, electric guitar, keyboards

Butch Walker: drums, guitar, keyboards, percussion, background vocals

Dan Wilson: bass guitar, electric guitar, piano, background vocals

Deluxe edition released October 22, 2012

Selected awards:

American Music Awards: Favorite Country Album 2013

Billboard Music Awards: Top Album 2013

Billboard Music Awards: Top Country Album 2013

MTV Video Music Awards: Best Female Video ("I Knew You Were Trouble")

Notable honors:

7 (nonconsecutive) weeks at number one on Billboard 200

Seven-times Platinum certified by RIAA

Second-highest selling album of 2012

16 weeks at number one on *Billboard*'s Top Country Albums chart; year-end number-one album of 2012 and 2013

Tour: Red Tour, March 2013–June 2014, 86 shows, 12 countries

OPPOSITE: **Though she's admitted to being disappointed by the lack of awards recognition for *Red*, there's no doubt the album was a commercial success.**

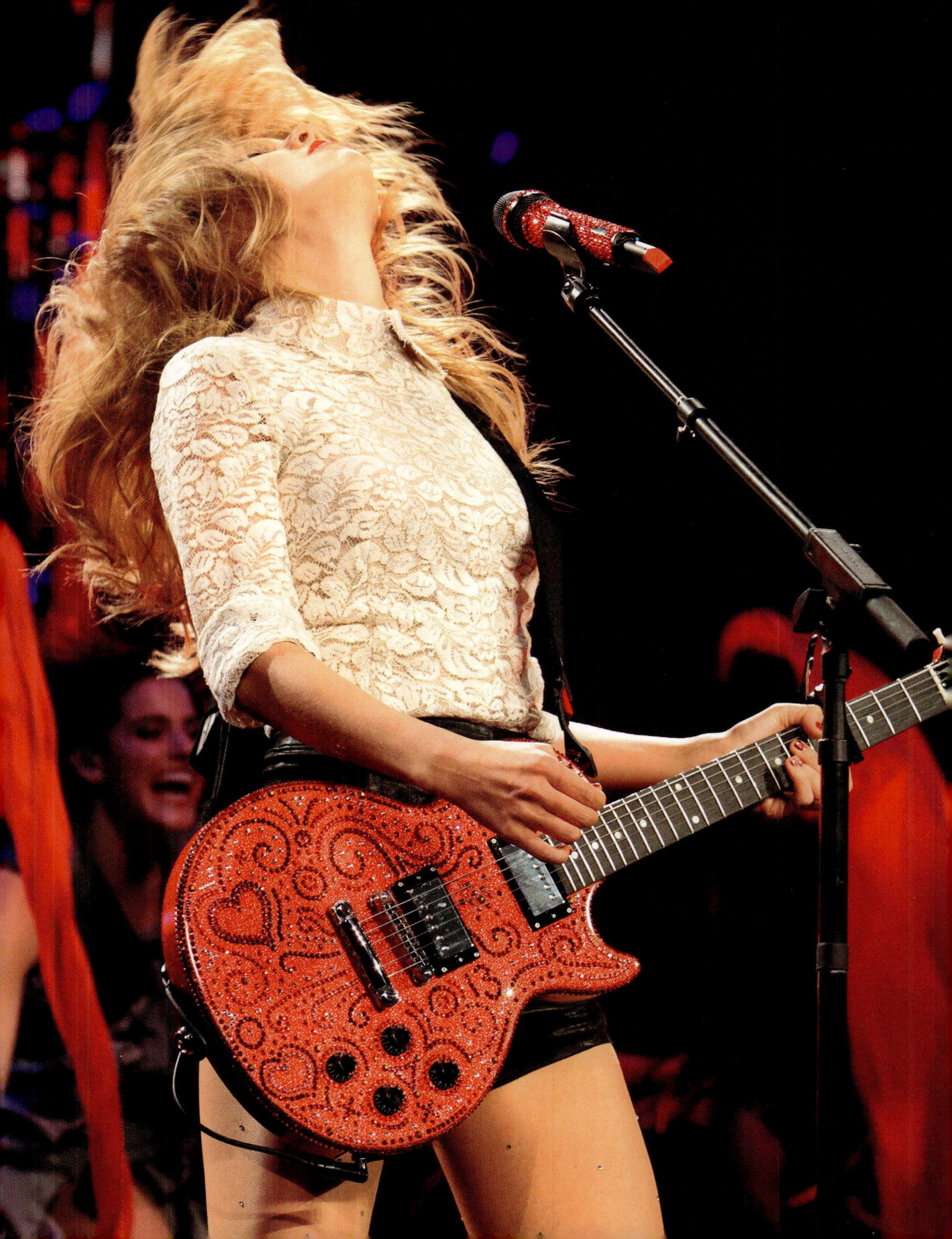

From the first note of *Red*'s opening track, Taylor Swift tells her listeners that we're somewhere new, somewhere we've never been before with her. We're in a "State Of Grace," and we're stepping in sync with Swift into an undeniably dance-y, pop-inflected sound. Remember the girl who, on Swift's self-titled debut album, looked back on a past romance and hoped the boy would think of her when he heard a Tim McGraw song? Well, she grew up. In "State Of Grace," Swift's narrator is doing the same kind of rumination, but this time she's on the move, and she's not melancholy. Weaving her way expertly through the masses on a sidewalk, she reflects on a relationship that took her by surprise, wrecked her, and left her to rebuild. "This love is brave and wild," she sings of a romance that nonetheless inspired her to build a gallery of "mosaic broken hearts." It's another breakup song, but the Swift of "State Of Grace" would put her arm around her younger "Tim McGraw" self and give her a "honey, live and learn, life goes on" pep talk, sans affected twang.

Swift gave us clues to her next musical evolution on *Speak Now*, but on *Red*, she gets some new producers, the most notable and impactful for this sound being hitmaker Max Martin and Shellback, and leans all the way in to her new status as a pop superstar, the persona she'd been trying on for a few years but was too shy to leave the house in. And you know what? It looks great on her.

OPPOSITE: **On the *Red* Tour, Swift performs at the BRIT Awards at the o2 Arena in February 2013 in London a few months after the album's release.**

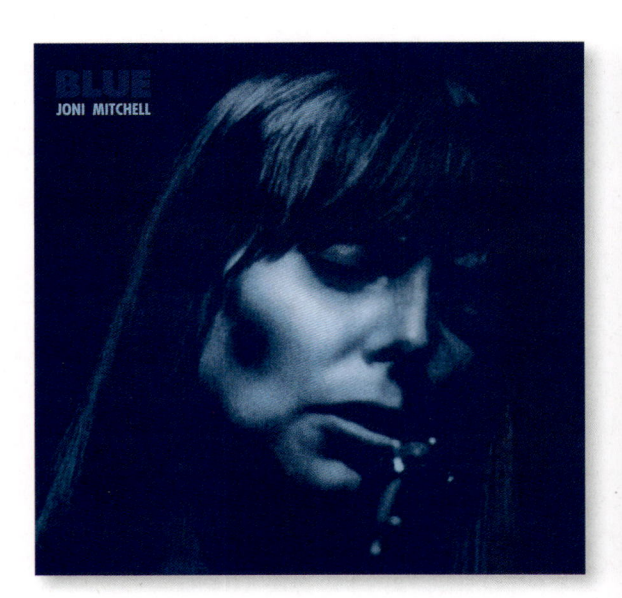

Swift's original *Red* album art was a clear homage to Joni Mitchell's *Blue*. On *Taylor's Version*, the album art was less of a direct reference.

Jake Gyllenhaal wearing what fans have pinpointed as The Scarf, borrowed from Swift, in November 2010. As history tells it, after Swift and Gyllenhaal spent Thanksgiving 2010 in Brooklyn with his sister, the singer forgot her scarf. A piece of misplaced knitwear became a legend.

TAYLOR SWIFT ALBUM BY ALBUM

RED 49

After the entirely self-written, confessional *Speak Now*, on *Red* Swift leaves adolescence, turns 21, meets some new friends, hits the bar, and continues on the never-ending experiment of being an adult person in the world. In a 2020 interview with *Rolling Stone* in honor of *Red* being included on the publication's list of the 500 greatest albums, Swift called the project her only true "breakup album." Breakup songs, sure, she's done those. But a whole album of them? Just *Red*.

"I look back on this as my true breakup album, every other album has flickers of different things," she said. "But this was an album that I wrote specifically about pure, absolute, to the core, heartbreak."

Fresh off the album's release, a then 22-year-old Swift had more to say in a 2012 interview with *Billboard*.

"It's all the different ways that you have to say good-bye to someone," she said. "When you're experiencing the ups and downs of a relationship, especially when you're 22 years old, they all strike you different ways. Every different kind of missing someone, every kind of loss—it all sounds different to me. When you are missing someone, time seems to move slower and when I'm falling in love with someone, time seems to be moving faster. So I think, because time seems to move so slow when I'm sad, that's why I spend so much time writing songs about it. It seems like I have more hours in the day."

"Like, ever." For her Red Tour, Swift wore hotpants, circus costumes, and, of course, red lipstick, by then her signature.

TAYLOR SWIFT ALBUM BY ALBUM

On the reputation Stadium tour, Swift said of "All Too Well" that, "I feel like this song has two lives to it in my brain . . . there's the life of this song, where this song was born out of catharsis and venting and trying to get over something and trying to understand it and process it. And then there's the life where it went out into the world and you turned this song into something completely different for me . . . a collage of memories of watching you scream the words to this song, "And that is how you have changed the song 'All Too Well' for me."

On *Red*, Swift isn't just reflecting on past romantic relationships, Harry Styles and Jake Gyllenhaal and the "All Too Well" misplaced red scarf that shall forever live in infamy, but there's a sense of saying good-bye to the old her, too, a dramatic musical reintroduction. That beat drop in "I Knew You Were Trouble," a shock in the context of Swift's earlier work? It's the sonic equivalent of grabbing the scissors post-breakup and going, "I mean, how hard could it even be to cut my own bangs?" (Swift did also begin her long follicular love affair with bangs around this period.) *Red*, in my mind, is the delineation in Swift's body of work where she's officially done with "the early stuff" and on to a new chapter in what, it was clear by then, would be a long career.

Further evidence of this turning point: *Red*, Swift's fourth album, is the last one for which she was nominated in country categories at the Grammys, garnering nods but no wins at the 2014 ceremony for the Best Country Album, Best Country Song, and Best Country Duo Performance. In 2018, she was nominated for her writing credit on "Better Man" as performed by Little Big Town, handed over to the group after she cut it from *Red*'s original tracklist—which Swift later recorded herself and released as a Vault Track on *Red* (*Taylor's Version*). Another Vault Track, "I Bet You Think About Me," got a nod in 2023 for Best Country Song after the *Taylor's Version* release, a resurfaced relic she wrote way back when. No entirely new Swift material written post-*Red* has been honored by the Grammys in a country category, which feels telling. The album also delivered Swift's very first Billboard Hot 100 number-one track, with "We Are Never Ever Getting Back Together," further cementing her pop crossover status.

RED

Swift co-produced half of the album's original tracks with her go-to guy, Nathan Chapman, whom she'd been working with since the beginning, but three songs—"I Knew You Were Trouble," "22," and "We Are Never Ever Getting Back Together"— were crafted by Martin and Shellback, the Swedish hitmakers whose past collaborators include Britney Spears, the Backstreet Boys, NSYNC, Pink, Katy Perry, Ariana Grande, and so many more boldface, decidedly not-country-music acts. Martin and Shellback's names together virtually gleam Platinum, such is their track record. So when the first single from *Red*, "We Are Never Ever Getting Back Together" emerged with those screamable hooks and those names in the producing and songwriting credits? As Swift herself would proclaim later on the album in a duet with Ed Sheeran, it was a clear sign everything had changed.

She had a rapport with the two, and even, according to her, included a hot mic moment of her in-studio bitching about her love life to them in that first single. As she told *Billboard* in 2012, a friend of some ex came by while she was recording with the two and "he made some comment about how he heard how I was gonna get back together with my ex. And after he left I was talking to Max and Shellback and was like, 'We are never ever getting back together!' And after that happened I just grabbed my guitar." The song "just kind of happened," she said, and the rest is a dubstep beat-drop match made in heaven, an angelic chorus of liberated single ladies skipping around the club gleefully shaking off those no-good guys and making grand "never-ever" proclamations.

In with the new, but not out with the old. A Swift signature is reaching into the past for inspiration, and *Red* is no different. Not just her past personal experiences, though there's plenty of those to be found here (it's a breakup album, after all), but her musical forebears. Whether critic Bob Lefsetz, the apparent subject of *Speak Now*'s "Mean," really was the first to suggest she listen to Joni Mitchell, as he claimed, *Red* makes it more than clear that her love affair with the singer's work was in full swing. The album title is an obvious homage to 1971's *Blue*, as is the cover art, Swift's downward-tilted face taking up most of the frame on *Red*'s cover, eyes in shadow, and her most important instrument, weapon, and tool, her mouth, on full display. On Mitchell's *Blue* art, Mitchell's somewhat-obscured face, tinted blue, too, is the main event, eyes hidden not by shadow but by being closed. Both albums, too, feature the single-word title in large font with the singer's name in block letters underneath. Farewell to Swift's loopy little-girl cursive of record art past; *Red* declares right off the bat it's different.

In a 2011 diary entry later released with the *Lover* album, Swift wrote while touring *Speak Now*, "I've been thinking about getting old and irrelevancy and how all my heroes ended up alone. I wrote a song on

Swift's relationship with Gyllenhaal left a lasting, not entirely positive, impression on her fans, as this homemade t-shirt shows.

TAYLOR SWIFT ALBUM BY ALBUM

the plane ride from Sydney to Perth on the Appalachian dulcimer I bought the day of my flight. I bought it because Joni played it on most of the record. I taught myself to play 'A Case of You.'" In the title track "Blue," Mitchell might as well be outlining Swift's approach to songwriting in the simple lyrics: "There is a song for you/Ink on a pin/Underneath the skin/An empty space to fill in." Swift is a master of works that are very personal and specific to her experiences but which allow the listener to project their own stories and let the light seep in to those purposeful cracks Swift leaves for them. It's Swift's song and story, yes, but she also always knows and leaves space for it to inevitably become unique to each listener.

(continued on page 57)

For those curious what an *Appalacian zither* is, it's the spearpoint-shaped instrument resting on Joni Mitchell's lap; that Swift could adopt one of her hero's instruments and instantly write a song with it speaks volumes about her early commitment to her music, her heroes, and herself.

RED 53

"ALL TOO WELL:" THE 10-YEAR VERSION

TO PARAPHRASE THE poet Pablo Neruda, love is so short, the lore of "All Too Well" is so long.

Occupying the infamous track 5 slot on *Red*, a space Swift typically tends to hold for her most devastating songs, "All Too Well" is one of the most infamous tracks in Swift's songbook, the never-returned red scarf that launched a thousand ships, not to mention some 1,490 minutes—roughly 24.8 hours, more than an *entire day*—of performance altogether throughout Swift's The Eras Tour, which she typically introduced by asking the crowd if they "had about ten minutes to spare." The song was never a single, but it's undoubtedly legendary among fans.

"All Too Well" was the first song Swift wrote for *Red*, the first shreds of the song about going upstate, losing some knitwear, and having her heart broken by some boy who didn't deserve to have his hands on it in the first place, emerging as Swift and her band noodled around during a rehearsal for the Speak Now World Tour. "My band joined in and I went on a rant," Swift recalled of that fateful freestyle session, which a wise sound guy reportedly recorded for posterity. She knew she had something good, something real, but also something that was, as she recalled on *Good Morning America*, "probably like a ten-minute song, which you can't put on an album." (Cue the omniscient narrator's "Or can you?") "I had to filter it down to, like, a story that could work in the form of a song. I called my friend and coworker Liz Rose and I said, 'Come over, we've gotta filter this down.' It took me a really long time to get it to its final form."

Rose hadn't worked with Swift since *Fearless*, and told *Rolling Stone* that it was a surprise to get a call from her asking what she was doing that day and if she could write. It was also a great excuse to get out of what she was doing: packing up her Nashville house for a move to Dallas. She delegated the packing to the moving guys and headed over to Swift's, where she found that "she had a story and she wanted to say something specific. She had a lot of information. I just let her go. She already had a melody and she started singing some words, and I started writing things down, saying, 'Okay, let's use this, let's use that.' She mentioned a plaid shirt, and I wrote that down in a corner, and when we got to the end, I said, 'Let's put the plaid shirt in there.' That turned into one of the best lines." She called it "the most emotional, in-depth song we've ever written. She's such a force. You remember the songs you write with Taylor, because the emotion that goes into them is so palpable." In another interview, she recalled Swift having "about twenty-four minutes" of material, then whittling it down to 10 minutes, then finally the 5:29 of the album cut.

But when Swift talks, fans listen, so the apparent existence of a supersize 10-minute version of the song did not go ignored. They asked her about it. All the time. In one instance of Taylurking, a pastime of Swift's in which she'll pop into fans' Instagram comments or whatnot to blow minds and cement that parasocial relationship, she began interacting with fans in the comments of a livestream and was asked, yet again, where the 10-minute version of "All Too Well" might be. "IT'S SOMEWHERE IN A DRAWER I DON'T KNOW I DON'T KNOW," she responded. The original song was such a fan favorite that though it wasn't a radio single and didn't get a music video, Swift chose to perform it at the 2014 Grammys, later explaining that "the fans wanted to hear it a lot."

And, again, what Swift's fans want, Swift's fans often get. And they got the 10-minute version of the song when Swift released the re-recorded album *Red (Taylor's Version)* in November 2021, in addition to a revamped version of the original song in the same track 5 slot, the big boi slipped in as a Vault Track. It has so many parenthetical subtitles that it's like a multispecialty doctor trailing their degrees behind them on a CV: The full title of the expanded track is "All Too Well (10 Minute Version) (Taylor's Version) (From The Vault)," or "ATWTMVTVFTV" if you're nasty. Fans even got that long-promised f-bomb in the song's expanded lyrics (if you're wondering, there are photos of a woman holding a "fuck the patriarchy" sign at a 1989 protest, evidence that the phrase has been around for a long time).

TAYLOR SWIFT ALBUM BY ALBUM

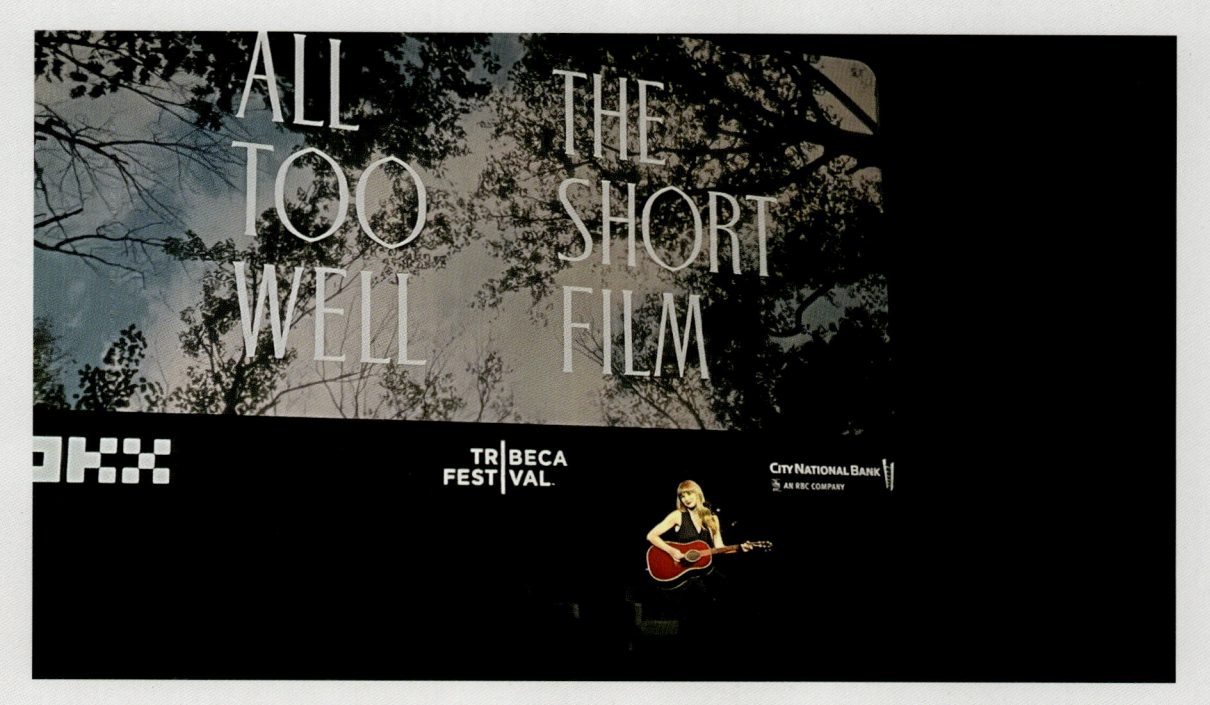

Swift's deft songwriting often plays with time and memory, refracting and distorting what she thought she knew as a narrator in the song *and*, it is often speculated, as a real, living artist. "All Too Well" is less a song and more a literary essay.

"I'm promoting so many albums, went on so many tours, tried to move past the *Red* album. Every time I would talk to you—every time I'm doing a livestream, every time there's a Q&A, every time there's a meet and greet, there's, 'When are you going to release the ten-minute version of 'All Too Well'?" she said in 2022. "You guys just wouldn't let it go."

Rehashing the song's origin story in an appearance on *The Tonight Show Starring Jimmy Fallon*, Swift laughed, "Ten minutes is absurd, that's an absurd length of time for a song to be. Who thinks that they can put out a ten-minute song? I mean, obviously, me."

Not just that, but a short film to visualize that 10-minute song. Swift directed *All Too Well: The Short Film*, starring Sadie Sink and Dylan O'Brien as the story's doomed lovers. The film opened with the same Neruda line that Swift included in the album booklet for *Red*, a pull from the poet's "Tonight I Can Write (The Saddest Lines)," splashed across the screen: "Love is so short, forgetting is so long." She once said of the line that "it's a violent thing to read something that poignant."

The short film got special screenings at the Tribeca Film Festival and the Toronto International Film Festival. At Tribeca, branded tissues were distributed for audiences to have at the ready. They needed them.

Introducing the short film at Tribeca, Swift described the themes of the song and album as "girlhood calcifying into this bruised adulthood." In early performances of the song, Swift would often be visibly teary, the subject matter still obviously painful. As the years went by, that changed, and she began to smile while singing it, time and distance evidently transforming the experience. The 10-minute version of the song hit number one on the Hot 100, and stayed there long enough to break the all-time record, previously held by Don McLean's "American Pie."

"A record label didn't pick this as a single," Swift said at Tribeca in 2022. "It was my favorite. It was about something very personal to me. It was very hard to perform it live. Now for me, honestly, this song is one hundred percent about us and for you."

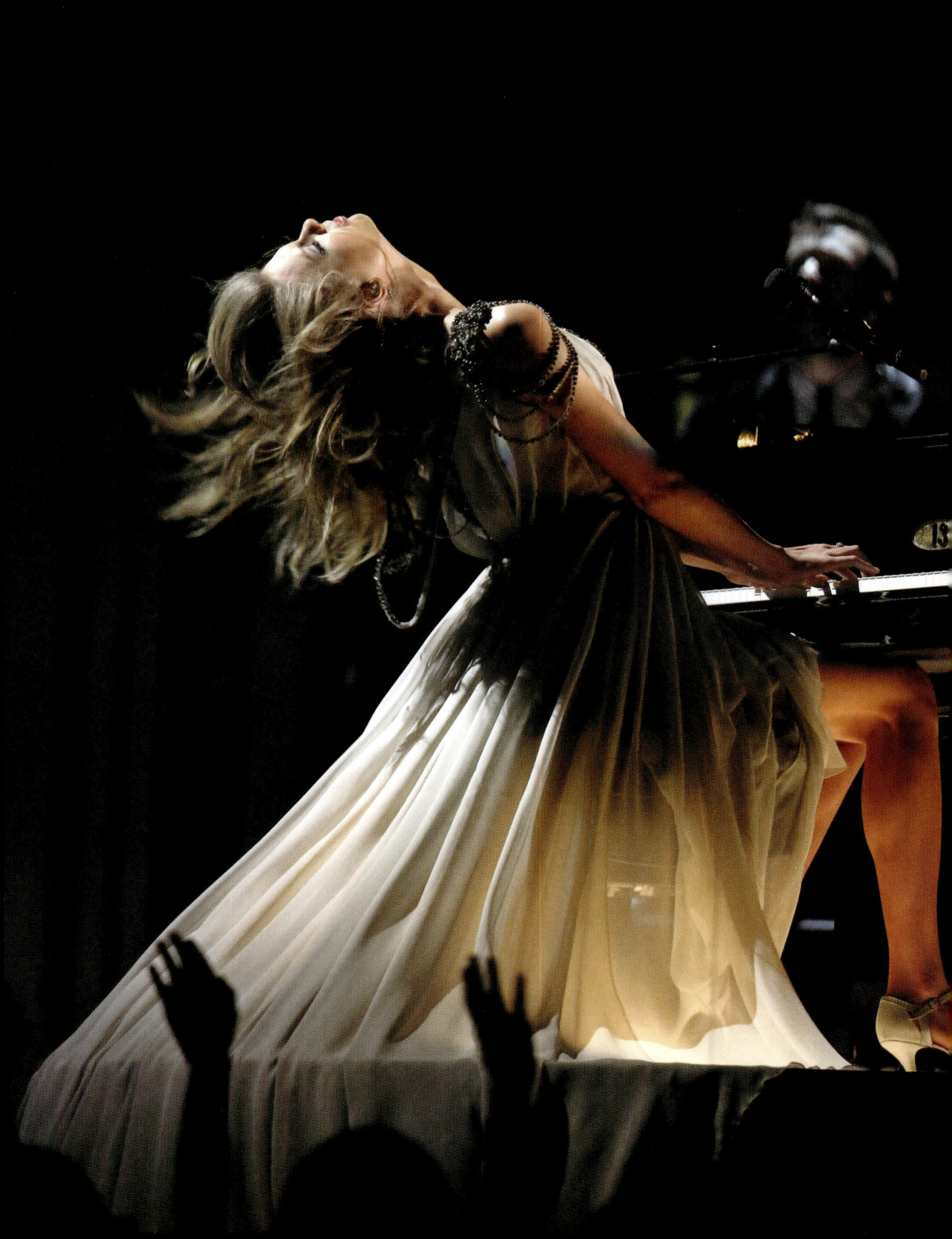
13

(continued from page 53)

That's her thing, providing the universal by way of the specific, while always striving for evolution. As she told *Billboard* in 2012 before the release of *Red*, as "We Are Never Ever Getting Back Together" held fast to the peaks of the Hot 100, her goal with the fourth album was "to be different from what I've been, and somehow end up where I'm going. You want to provide your fans with something exciting, but you don't want them to be listening to the album going, 'I don't recognize her.' So it's somewhere in the middle. You have to find a balance."

Swift, who in the album's lyrics recalls her ex blowing her off for listening to "indie records much cooler than mine" and who hesitates before reaching for high heels because her beau prefers her small, signaled her own future indie-ish and folk-flecked sounds on the record, even as she also introduced the bombastic Martin/Shellback pop moments. On "The Last Time," she duets with Gary Lightbody of Snow Patrol, and co-wrote the track with Lightbody and his bandmate Jacknife Lee. This is well after Snow Patrol's "Chasing Cars" blew up thanks to a 2006 episode of *Grey's Anatomy*, which Swift loved enough to name one of her beloved cats, Meredith Grey, after, so it could be seen as a little self-indulgent, but musically, it's a new direction for her. Singer-songwriter Butch Walker, a real "guy with a guitar"–type guy, produced her Ed Sheeran duet, "Everything Has Changed," and Jeff Bhasker worked on "Holy Ground" and "The Lucky One" based on the strength of his work with fun., and his part in turning the indie band's "We Are Young" into a smash. Could Bhasker have been her inroad to Jack Antonoff, a member of fun. and future hall of fame Swift collaborator? The bread crumbs, as they always seem to be with Swift, are all there.

On *Red*, Swift is a woman in transition in so many ways, wondering and grasping at who she'll be on the other side of all of this: She's emerging from adolescence into adulthood, from ingenue to music mainstay, from wannabe country artist to mainstream icon, and so much more. Romantically, she seems to be nursing a perpetual broken heart and doing her best to make sure the scar tissue heals into something she'll be able to handle. She spends the first five tracks of *Red* talking about her exes before blasting into "22" and deciding not to give them any more of her time or emotions, and then, oops, she's right back into it with "I Almost Do." Who hasn't been there, obsessing and planning, trying to make the most of a bum deal and a broken heart?

And, true to Swift's habit, she'll reinvent herself once again, more fully, on the next album, *1989*, with the groundwork she's laid on *Red*. As the last track on the standard edition announces, it's time, once more, to "Begin Again."

OPPOSITE:
Swift performs "All Too Well" at the 2014 Grammys.

RED 57

5

By Moira McAvoy

1989

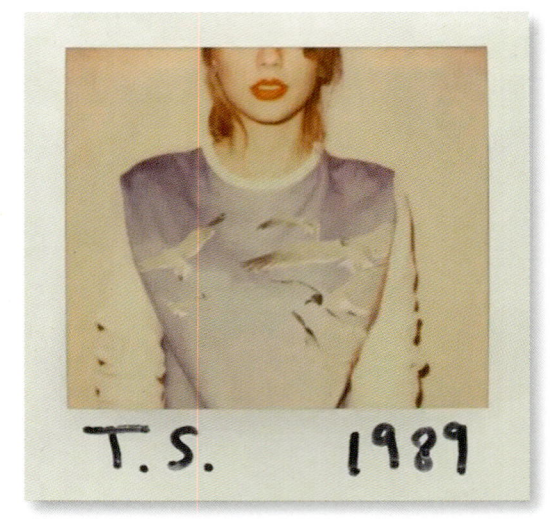

Track Listing:

1. Welcome To New York [3:32]
2. Blank Space [3:51]
3. Style [3:51]
4. Out Of The Woods [3:55]
5. All You Had To Do Was Stay [3:13]
6. Shake It Off [3:39]
7. I Wish You Would [3:27]
8. Bad Blood [3:31]
9. Wildest Dreams [3:40]
10. How You Get The Girl [4:07]
11. This Love [4:10]
12. I Know Places [3:15]
13. Clean [4:31]

Deluxe Edition Bonus Tracks:

14. Wonderland [4:05]
15. You Are In Love [4:17]
16. New Romantics [3:50]

Recorded at Conway Recording (Los Angeles), Jungle City (New York City), Lamby's House (Brooklyn), MXM (Stockholm), Pain in the Art (Nashville), Elevator Nobody (Göteborg), The Hideaway (London)

Released October 27, 2014

Produced by Max Martin, Taylor Swift, Jack Antonoff, Ryan Tedder, Noel Zancanella, Ali Payami, Nathan Chapman, Imogen Heap, Mattman & Robin

Label: Big Machine Records

Notable personnel:

Max Martin: writer, programming, executive producer, keyboard, piano, claps, shouts, background vocals

Shellback: writer, programming, acoustic guitar, electric guitar, bass, keyboard, percussion, shouts, stomps, additional guitars, knees, noise, claps, drums, background vocals

Imogen Heap: writer, recording programming, vibraphone, drums, mbira, percussion, keyboards, background vocals

Jack Antonoff: writer, acoustic guitar, electric guitar, keyboards, bass, drums, background vocals

Ryan Tedder: recording, writer, additional programming, piano, Juno, acoustic guitar, electric guitar, drum programming, additional synth, background vocals

Ali Payami: writer, producer, programming, keyboards

Noel Zancanella: additional programming, drum programming, synthesizer, bass, additional synth

Nathan Chapman: recording, electric guitar, bass, keyboards, drums

Mattman & Robin: programming, drums, guitar, bass, keyboard, percussion

Laura Sisk: recording

Deluxe edition released October 27, 2014

Total units sold: 12,300,000 (as of August 2023)

Selected awards:

American Music Awards: Favorite Pop/Rock Album 2015

The Japan Gold Disc Awards: Album of the Year (Western) 2015

iHeartRadio Music Awards: Album of the Year 2016

Grammy Awards: Album of the Year and Best Pop Vocal Album 2016

Notable honors:

11 weeks at number one on the Billboard 200

500 weeks (as of July 2024) on the Billboard 200

Tour: 1989 World Tour, May-December 2015, 85 shows, 11 countries

Taylor stuns on the 1989 World Tour in Shanghai, China.

After the dust from *Red*'s album and tour cycle settled, Swift's career trajectory was a "choose your own adventure" of professional possibilities, though hindsight—and the commercial success of *Red*'s pure pop singles—makes her next move seem not only obvious, but inevitable. She was not just going to be a pop star. She was going to be The Pop Star.

Red's simultaneous strength and weakness lie in its genre-spanning tracklist, with Swift walking an oftentimes tenuous artistic tightrope. Taylor would go on record to say that *Red*'s scattershot stylistic and narrative choices were intended to mirror the messiness of heartbreak as an emotional process: You're up, you're down, you're country, you're pop, you're 2000s soft rock with the guy from Snow Patrol. When it works, it works (see: the one-two tracklist punch of career highs and fan favorites "All Too Well" and "22"), but some detractors argue the listener can feel overwhelmed by the maximalism of it all. All other success, accolades, and sales aside, *Red* lost the Album of the Year Grammy to focused tour de force *Random Access Memories* by Daft Punk, and Swift took it hard. Her next move needed to be perfect, and it needed to look effortless.

If *Red* was an experiment with excess, *1989* is an exercise in restraint. Long an artist whose bread and butter had been the theatrical and emotional, Taylor pivoted on an artistic about-face: The songs themselves and album as a whole would be sleek, succinct, and cohesive. The title, homage to the year Taylor was born, operates as a declaration of resurrection—short, direct, and grounded inherently in Taylor herself.

1989 is about a lot of things—self-love and self-awareness, and the sort of earth-shattering self-discovery that comes only from being in your 20s and being in New York City, so much so that the opening track is dedicated to setting the scene squarely in Manhattan. The album is not just adjacent to New York. It IS New York. And now? So is Taylor. Good-bye, Hendersonville! Good-bye, Christmas Tree Farm (for now). Hello, Tribeca!

And who can blame Taylor, really? I mean, who among us has not, seemingly overnight, found ourselves, cut our hair, moved to a new city, and subsequently made it our entire personality? New York was a fresh artistic start in a fresh era of her life—it really HAD been waiting for her.

"Welcome To New York" relies on syncopated beats throughout the verses, breaking momentarily into sweeping vocals and joy at the chorus, perfectly setting the tone for the album. At its core, *1989* is electrified and jubilant self-determination. It is also calculated and precise, a response to allegations of a career of Too Much and Too Many: too many feelings, too many songs, too many boyfriends. Even within this era of reinvention, Taylor remains on brand: The intentionally short album still clocks in with 13 tracks, her favorite and famously lucky number.

We're not out of the woods—we're luckily just getting started with Jack Antonoff's collaborations with Taylor in the *1989* era.

That's the thing about reinvention—you can run off to a new city, cut off all your hair, and proclaim yourself the beguiling It Girl about town, but, at the end of the day, you're still left with yourself. *1989*'s power lies in the fact that in reincarnation Taylor wasn't actually running away from something else, but racing faster toward possibilities still untapped within herself. From the outset, "Welcome To New York" seems to say that a new city does not a new person make, but it can make you a truer version of yourself, a thesis that, below the bobbed hair and flock of models, Taylor continued to take to heart.

Iridescent at the 57th Grammy Awards, Taylor introduced Sam Smith and Mary J. Blige.

The bridge between an old and new self spans the personnel list on the album: Max Martin and Shellback signaled Taylor's turn to chart-topping pure pop with chart toppers like "Blank Space" and "Shake It Off." New—now ubiquitous—collaborator Jack Antonoff ushered in a fresh ever-so-slightly experimental flavor to tracks like "Out Of The Woods," and yet the traces of the Old Taylor remained with Nathan Chapman's work on classic Swiftian ballad "This Love."

This makes sense as Taylor put her heart into *1989*—literally. "Wildest Dreams," a sensuous, slinking highlight, is set to a recording of Swift's actual heartbeat. On one hand, this could drive home the interpretation of the album as a fully fresh rebirth of Swift as an artist, one who is Mature and Adult and is entirely removed from her past iterations as country ingenue, her new roots permeating the music itself.

The other argument—and the one I like more—is Taylor is signaling that despite the trappings of a brand new Taylor, the heart of what has made her herself remains thrumming as the centerpiece of her art. This heart is no longer vulnerably exposed on her sleeve or projected onto elaborate, theatrical narrative songs; it is a foundation for her reinvigorated sense of self.

SO LONG, TRIBECA

HOME IS WHAT we make it, and *1989* is our first true glimpse at where Taylor has built hers. New York is not just a setting, it is its own character in *1989*'s arc (and much of Swift's albums to follow). New York is Taylor's new beginning, yes, but also a harbor of safety, a secluded and intimate love affair, a deeply personal refuge and anchor to her sense of care and security. This is a fascinating contrast to the role London will come to play in her work—a place first of visible possibility and excess, then still hypothetical escapist privacy, then finally a dreary depressive dungeon, dank and desolate. On *Lover*, we see Taylor holding on to both at the same time—cheerily pining after her London Boy all the while passionately worshipping her beloved as the West Village of New York. Both locales are dreams and visions, dissolving as the relationships to both the beloved and herself begin to collapse over the course of the albums to follow.

The album promo cycle, too, saw Taylor still indulging in most of what had, publicly and personally, so endeared her to her fans. The press junket was never-ending, each interview punctuated by Swift's signature passion for her work and self-deprecating humor. She became extremely active on Tumblr, further befriending fans and selecting several for Swiftmas, wherein Swift delivered gifts to fans over the holidays (sometimes by hand). This relationship with fans took an even more intense form than previously in her career with the inception of Secret Sessions, wherein Swift literally invited fans into her actual home to chat, eat cookies, and hear *1989* before its public release. And for the fans who weren't lucky (or online) enough to be invited? They could still feel closer to Swift thanks to the official inclusion of voice memos detailing the composition process of "Blank Space," "I Know Places," and "I Wish You Would" on the album.

This was, perhaps, the most heavily exposed era of Taylor's life until the 2020s. Paparazzi were following her home, to her friends' homes, to the gym. Investigations into her daily interactions were on the cover of every major tabloid and minor blog.

Swift's deepening and widening connection with fans went hand-in-hand with the wall she had been constructing between herself and the non-Swiftie general public. The album invited plenty of speculation, of course. "Blank Space" lampoons the idea itself all the while begging the listener to, as Swift would say later, paternity test the tracks, but its careful construction sends a message that would solidify in the next stages of Swift's career: This is the story I am telling you; this is the story I want you to hear. This is the Taylor Swift I want you, the public, to know.

1989

I'VE GOT A BLANK CHECK, BABY

PICKED CLEAN BY critics and fans alike, Taylor's strategy seemed to embrace the notion of Taylor as a product, and that product? She knew it was valuable. When she didn't think she was getting what she's worth, she pulled her entire catalog off Spotify's streaming platform before *1989*'s release, calling their bluff and selling more than 10 million copies without any streaming numbers in the interim.

Few artists could pull their own records from streaming services and expect them to survive. Swift did not see this as a problem as her influence and confidence grew as a musician, performer, and brand unto herself.

Taylor accepts the iHeartRadio Music Awards Best Lyrics Award for "Blank Space," a nod to her enduring talent in her pivot to pop.

She was surveilled at concerts by fans with grainy cell phones. The fact that her attempt at setting boundaries and controlling her perception failed—all on an album about self-determination and reclamation—would haunt Swift for a decade. "I Know Places," a song explicitly about desperately searching for any place of privacy with a beloved free from the feeding frenzy of the press, being included on the album implies Taylor knew this was a doomed pursuit from the start, and wants to have a little fun with it.

Taylor indulges her critic's perception of her own romantic and emotional indulgence on satirical romp "Blank Space." The music video (one of my personal favorites) leans into the excessive, filmed at a Oheka Castle in Long Island, Swift taking a golf club to an AC Cobra, slashing priceless portraits to shreds, and stabbing delicate cakes with a steak knife in her lingerie.

The song is addressed to an unnamed beloved (their name will be slotted into, and eventually erased from, the titular blank space), enticing them with a luxurious but inevitably doomed tryst. This direct address being aimed at an unnamed lover is the obvious, canonical point. However, the song also shines as a wink toward fans and the invitation to this new and improved Taylor Swift experience. It will still include the haters, the naysayers, and the heartbreak, but you'll have a hell of a good time on the way to the top.

In a Grammy campaign interview with Radio.com, Taylor elucidated that "Shake It Off" was not simply conceived as a banger about stunting on the haters and achieving serenity through joy, but also specifically as a song to be played at weddings. In classic Swift fashion, she frames this sweetly as inspiring a reception's shyest attendees to blossom into the party, and yet it pings on a notable concept on *1989*: Every song has its purpose. "Clean" is the ultimate recovery companion, and has captioned many of my own posts about sobriety and eating disorder recovery. At the end of the day, the classic Taylor success story runs its course: Her earnestness and business prowess collude, and "Shake It Off" is inescapable at any millennial wedding over a decade later.

The high seemed worth the pain, as Taylor once again wins the Grammy Award for Album of The Year for *1989*.

66   TAYLOR SWIFT ALBUM BY ALBUM

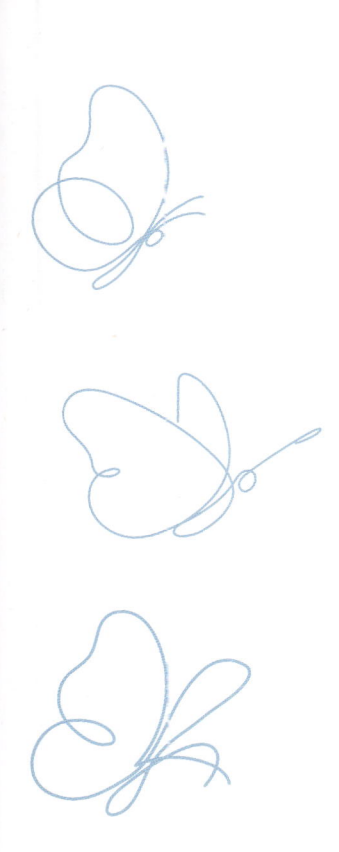

Lorde appeared when the 1989 Tour stopped in Washington, DC, a concert I (Moira) was thrilled to attend.

The haters really were gonna hate hate hate when "Shake It Off" hit the charts. Fans and critics alike highlighted the relatively simplistic chorus as evidence that Taylor had lost her spark as a songwriter, which misses the mark on how she'd honed her generational talent for creating an inescapable earworm. It's on the same album as "Clean"—the sharp lyrics come up on other tracks to show this is a choice, not a mistake.

1989

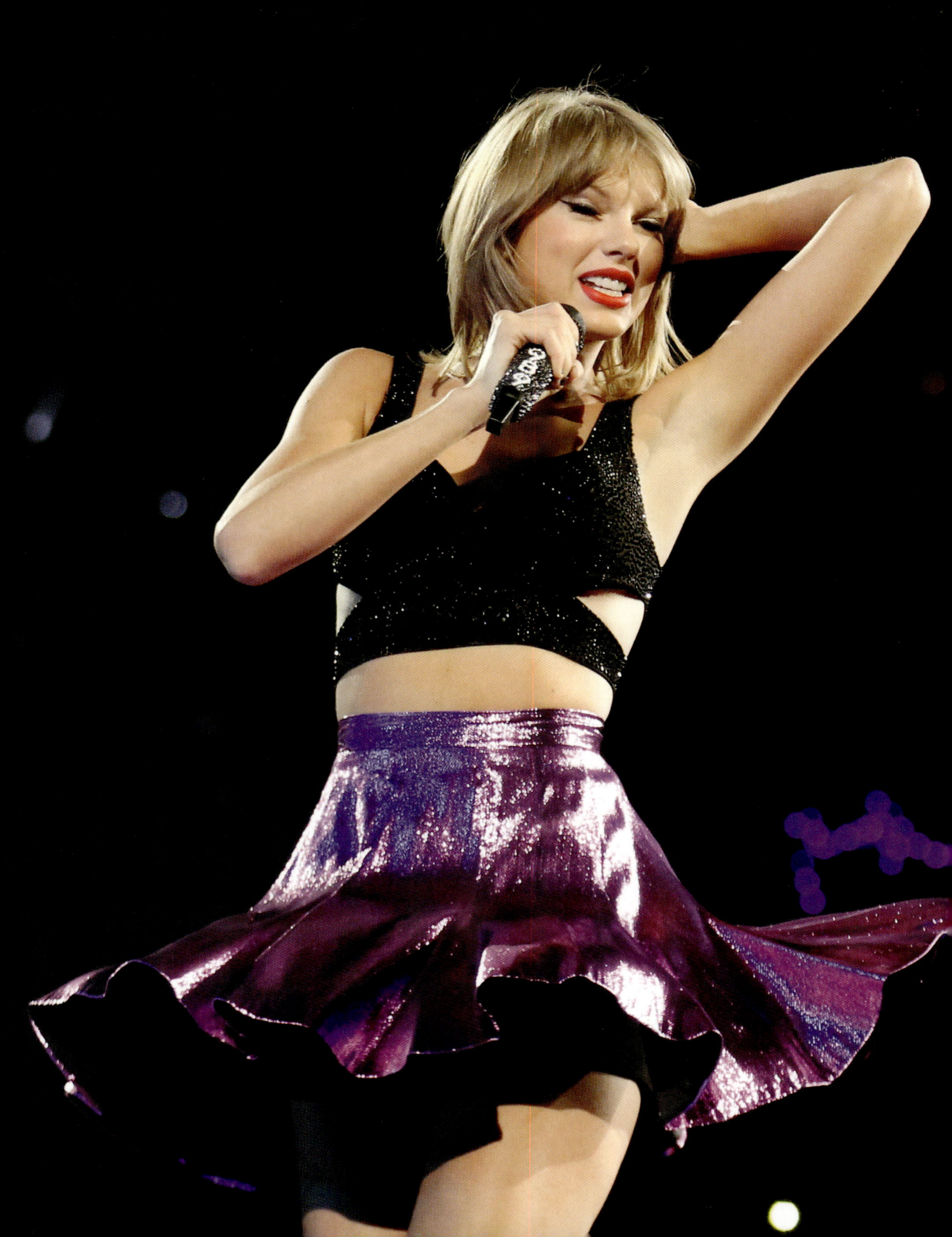

Taylor's vault to pop stuck the landing. "Style," Vox Media's so-declared Perfect Pop Song, struts to the forefront as an artistic thesis for the album. "Style" opens with alluring, thrumming guitars punctuated by Taylor's confident vocals setting the scene with a pointed "midnight," opens the passenger door, and we're along for the ride. Lyrically, Swift jumps back and forth between "he" and "you" to reference the other in the song. The genderless aspect of this empowers the listener to imagine themself as a fashion plate who never goes out of style.

It's a genius move to incorporate the somewhat dated '50s pop culture references into a record made entirely of '80s and '90s musical motifs. By interweaving enduring icons into her declaration of timelessness, she preemptively places herself in the same legacy of monoculture. The images themselves—James Dean and blue jeans—hint toward the "Miss Americana" moniker half a decade in advance, the first chess piece moved toward reclaiming the crown from detractors of Taylor as embodiment of white American femininity.

Swift would make another move against this with the Kendrick Lamar feature on the "Bad Blood" remix, a track with a video entirely revolving around the nebulous line between public and private life. The first song of Taylor's to explicitly identify its subject—in this case, Katy Perry—"Bad Blood" finds Taylor really angry, practically rapping over an unchanging drumbeat and flanked by a pantheon of famous friends and muses alike. It's simultaneously an homage to community and anger, and to never letting anything go.

Despite all jokes to the contrary, Taylor Swift does know how to let things go—it is arguably the foundation of her most moving songs, including Imogen Heap–helmed stunner "Clean." On "Clean," a classically Swiftian ballad awash in twinkling synths, Taylor wrestles with an intoxicating love long lost, but lingering, then suffocating. She acknowledges that sometimes you need to let the worst thing be the worst thing, sink beneath it, then punch yourself back up and out, cleansed and freed in the open sea, where you can find yourself again and anew.

I'm writing this from the era of genre fluidity. Everything is a dramedy, and the gamification of the algorithm reward broad appeal. That was not the case back in 2014 when a new Taylor was being born into the world. Reincarnation is impossible without death, and the country world lamented the loss of Old Taylor. The County Music Association Awards, the premier event of the year for the genre, even dedicated a whole bit to Brad Paisley and Carrie Underwood diagnosing the "national epidemic" of Post-Partum Taylor Swift Disorder. In quintessential Opry-worthy harmony, they asked who would fill her singular (and very tall) shoes.

OPPOSITE: **Swift performs "I Know Places" during the 1989 World Tour in Los Angeles.**

On the one hand, this shows the strong bias toward genre adherence of the era that Taylor was working against. On the other, it shows that Taylor herself was irreplaceable in her niche. Her move toward pop cemented that although she wasn't country, she also wasn't pop—she was, as always, Taylor. 🦋

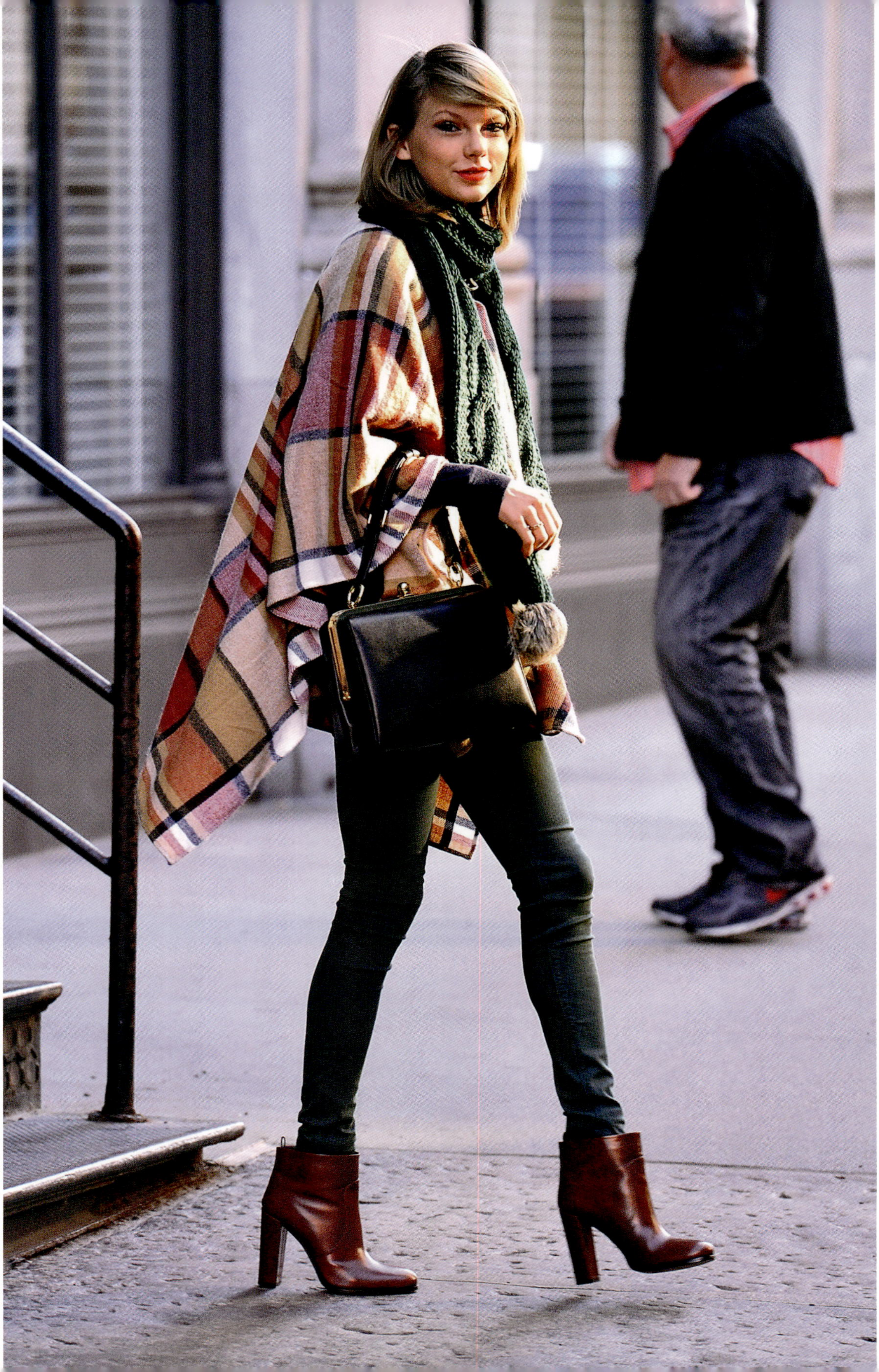

RIGHT: **Swift holds center stage on the 1989 World Tour in Shanghai in November 2015.**

BELOW: **Another tour, another show, another clutch of accolades at the 2015 Billboard Music Awards at the MGM Grand Garden Arena in Las Vegas.**

OPPOSITE: **Swift treats the Manhattan streets as a runway, claiming her seat at the NYC fashion table.**

reputation

By Moira McAvoy

Track Listing:

1. . . . Ready For It? [3:28]
2. End Game (ft. Ed Sheeran and Future) [4:04]
3. I Did Something Bad [3:58]
4. Don't Blame Me [3:56]
5. Delicate [3:52]
6. Look What You Made Me Do [3:31]
7. So It Goes . . . [3:47]
8. Gorgeous [3:29]
9. Getaway Car [3:53]
10. King Of My Heart [3:34]
11. Dancing With Our Hands Tied [3:31]
12. Dress [3:50]
13. This Is Why We Can't Have Nice Things [3:27]
14. Call It What You Want [3:23]
15. New Year's Day [3:53]

Recorded at Conway Recording (Los Angeles), MXM (Los Angeles/Stockholm), Rough Customer (Brooklyn), Seismic Activities (Portland), Tree Sound (Atlanta)

Released November 10, 2017

Produced by Taylor Swift, Max Martin, Shellback, Jack Antonoff, Ali Payami, Oscar Görres, Oscar Holter

Label: Big Machine Records

Notable personnel:

Max Martin: keyboards, programming, recording, piano, backing vocals

Shellback: keyboards, programming, drums, bass, guitars

Ali Payami: keyboards, programming

Jack Antonoff: programming, instruments, backing vocals, piano, bass, guitar, synths

Ed Sheeran: featured artist

Future: featured artist

James Reynolds: baby voice intro

Oscar Görres: keyboards, programming, piano

Oscar Holter: keyboards, programming

Laura Sisk: engineer

Mert and Marcus: photography

Total units sold: 7,000,000 (as of February 2024)

Selected awards:

American Music Awards: Favorite Pop/Rock Album 2018

Billboard Music Award: Top-Selling Album 2018

Notable honors:

4 weeks at number 1 on the Billboard 200

300 weeks (as of June 2024) on the Billboard 200

Best-selling album on Billboard (in the United States) 2017

Tour: Reputation Stadium Tour, May-November 2015, 53 shows, 7 countries

OPPOSITE: **People do throw rocks at things that shine, like a radiant Taylor at the 2018 AMAs, where she won four awards including Artist of the Year and Favorite Album - Pop/Rock for** *reputation*.

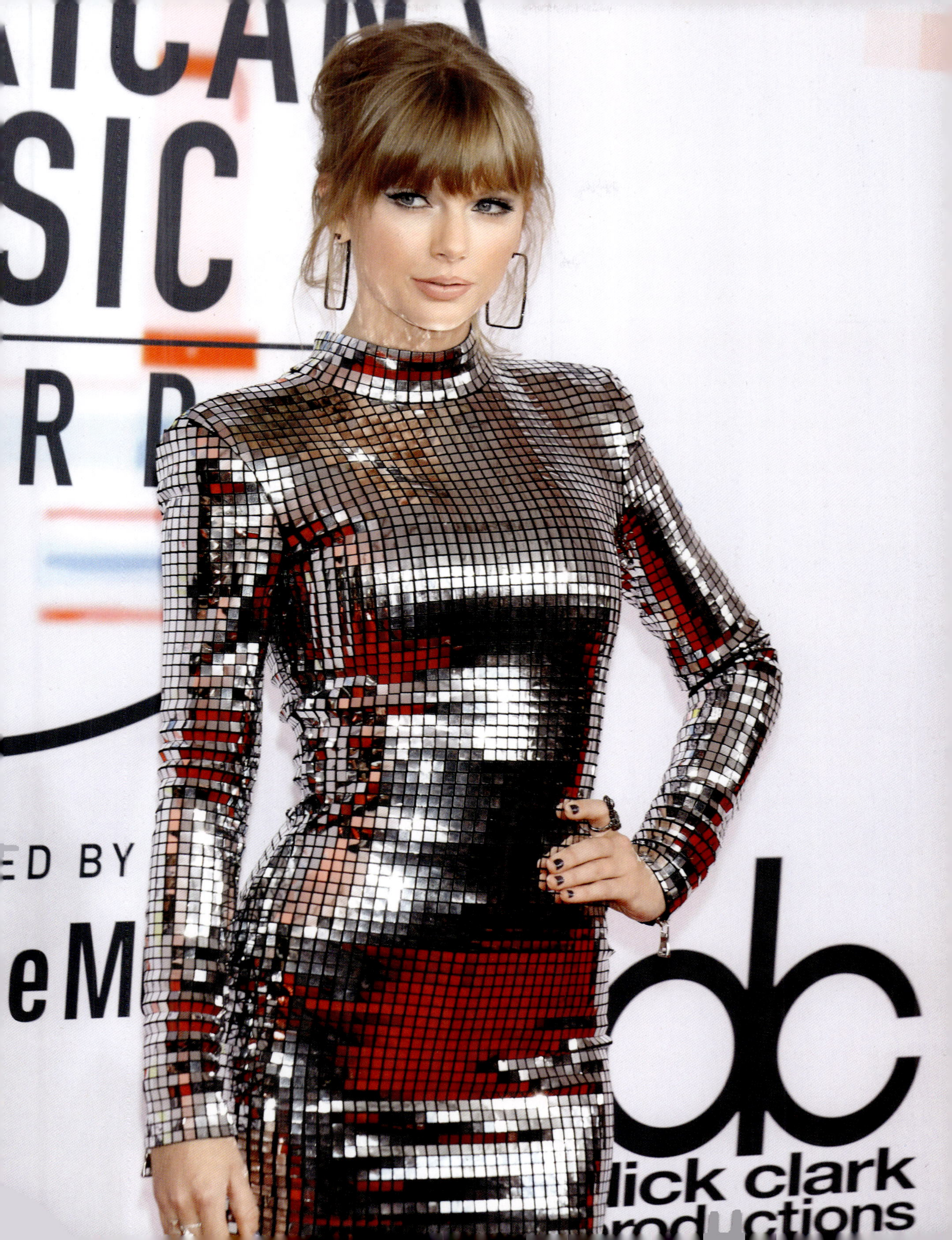

Where do you go after you've been raptured to the apex of pop superstardom? You fall, long and hard. In the wake of *1989*'s ubiquitous success, the Kanye West and Kim Kardashian "Snakegate" scandal, and an escalating barrage of criticism over everything from alleged racism to alleged romances, 2016 threw Taylor Swift headlong into her own version of hell, a proto-Eden panopticon where salvation lies tantalizingly out of reach. There are a few paths down here: You can fashion yourself into an Eve, awaiting the potential pardon of your own cultural awareness and conformity, or, recognizing you've found yourself here BECAUSE of knowing the realities of the world above all too well, you can embrace your fate and become the snake. Taylor, of course, chose the latter.

This is the dramatic, dangerous story Taylor wants us to hear on 2017's *reputation*—a woman scorned, cursed, and canceled welcoming darkness and reclaiming the narrative over EDM beats from Shellback and guest features from Future. Lead single "Look What You Made Me Do," premiering at the VMA's—a callback to the original Kanye West "Imma let you finish" incident in 2009—was dropped as a sort of warning shot for her return after two years out of the studio and spotlight. Here is Taylor Swift—oh, she's dead?!—raising herself from the dead. Here is Taylor Swift siloed away in a gilded birdcage. Here is Taylor Swift crashing a car, amassing an army, blowing up a bank, and *it's all our fault*.

This is the story Taylor wants us to hear on *reputation*. This, of course, is not the story Taylor is actually telling on *reputation*. Beneath the spikes and scorn, rebuttals and revenge, there lies the hushed corners of a world built just for the artist and her lover. Amidst endless overexposure and over-observation, the album's layered narratives appear to be Swift's attempt at privacy in plain sight, the singular gleeful joy of a long glance shared across a crowded room.

It's fitting, then, that the *reputation* promotion cycle was defined by silence. On August 18, 2017, every single one of Swift's social media channels was wiped clean—all posts and profile pictures deleted, every account unfollowed, her official website a blank, black page. She would eschew her previous strategy of endlessly relatable appearances on an endlessly vast press junket in favor of inviting select fans personally into her home(s) to hear the album before its release. In lieu of statements where her words could be twisted, redacted, or remixed, she published poems. Her message was clear: The art—and only the art, not even herself—would define this chapter of her life.

To a degree, it worked. The internet went into a frenzy. In less masterful hands, an eviscerated online presence and vacuum of press could have stretched the canvas onto which the naysayers and superfans alike projected their vision of her. This phenomenon still continued, as it always will with fame, but, ever the mastermind, Swift's gambit paid off. The static cultivated a dueling sense of intrigue and humanity. In the wake of an era swirling around refutations of anything Swift said or did (or allegedly said or did), erasure proved to be her most potent weapon.

TAYLOR SWIFT ALBUM BY ALBUM

The *reputation* tour marked a stark contrast from what fans were used to, all menace and snakes, stilettos and sneers. Here Swift performs at Miami Gardens, Florida, in August 2018.

reputation's prologue, stylized as a newspaper editorial, tells us from the outset that the album is not what it seems, and, perhaps, that we as listeners are not entirely invited to know what its true nature is. This sense of secrecy is heightened by the fact that this booklet was Swift's first to not include a case-sensitive skeleton key secret message to fans. It is her only album without any bonus tracks, the album in and of itself a complete statement.

reputation signaled a shift in the way in which Taylor's personal life intertwines with her work. A first in the meta-autobiographical trend that would come to define the back half of her catalog, *reputation* winks, somewhat sardonically, at Taylor's lyrical history of sprinkling personal—and public—narrative Easter eggs into otherwise nonspecific lyrics: the tilted stage from Kanye West's Saint Pablo Tour, the

(continued on page 78)

REPUTATION

"LOOK WHAT YOU MADE ME DO:" THE TRACK 6 SPECTACLE

LET'S GO BACK to the track 5 mythos for a minute, and, more interestingly, the bait-and-switch of track 6. In the grand Swiftian canon, track 5 is portrayed, in large part, by Taylor (and in larger majority by Swifties) to be the most emotionally significant and capital T true track on an album. Underdiscussed is the function of the following track, track 6, usually a poppy anthem meant to distract from the vulnerable emotional centerpiece and re-center the listener in the glittering spectacle of a Taylor Swift album.

Take, for example, "White Horse" into "You Belong With Me," tracks 5 and 6 on *Fearless*. "White Horse" finds Taylor's fevered fairy tale falling to pieces around her as she admits her faults in the first moment of accountability in her career. It is slow, devastating, raw. The somber violin fades, and in swell the joyous chords opening "You Belong With Me," the buoyant high school crush megahit. No more of THAT vulnerability! We're back in the realm of sly digs, silly costumes, and the abundant possibility of teen romance!

For *reputation*'s track 5, we have "Delicate," an insecure and searching, understated song set to a video in which Taylor dances across New York, invisible to all but her beloved. Taylor questions her artistry and persona and this context elevates the nearly cartoonish revenge anthem, track 6, "Look What You Made Me Do" to a state of true camp, one in which Taylor is mocking our perception of her anger, and underscores the intimacy thrumming in *reputation*'s chest. The anger is clearly something that's been processed and is being rehashed, a pantomime of rage. The title itself nods to this—just LOOK at how we needed to be distracted after peeking too close. The romance and intimacy, however, cloaked beneath layers of detachment and revenge and, at times, overproduction, is palpable. This is an album about the outside world, written for Taylor and her nameless beloved.

Taylor maintains this dynamic throughout her discography, using *folklore*'s track 6, "mirrorball" to smash the fourth wall and spell the whole thing out for us, paving the way for additional meta riffs on the concept, such as "But Daddy, I Love Him!"

OPPOSITE: **"Look What You Made Me Do" marked an almost violent shift from her traditional track 5 games and references; in it, she channels Susan Sontag's definition of camp: "Camp sees everything in quotation marks,"** Sontag wrote, "not a woman, but a 'woman.' "

TAYLOR SWIFT ALBUM BY ALBUM

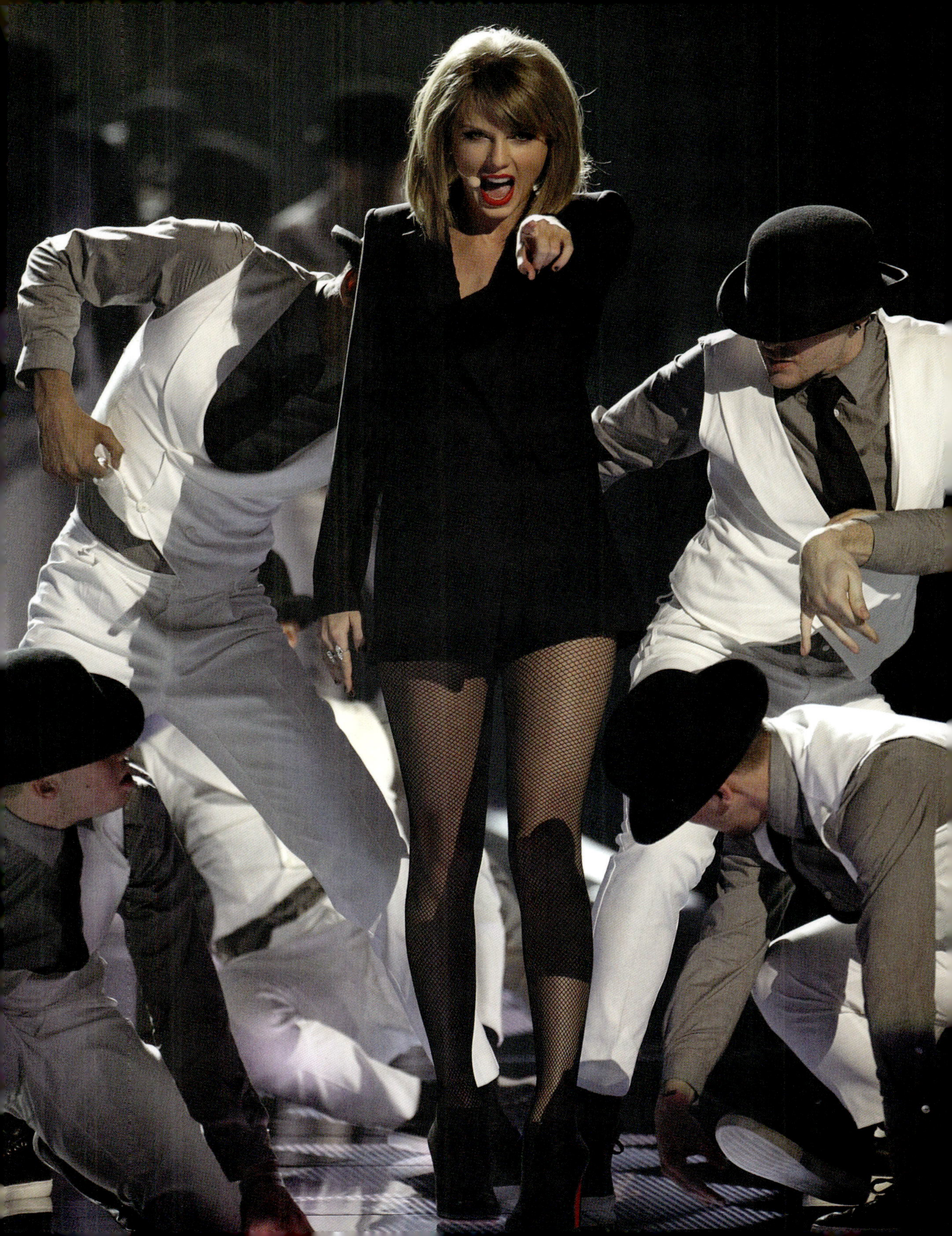

(continued from page 75)
Greenwich Village enclave to which Taylor retreated in 2016, daisies plucked from her 2014 trip to Big Sur, a full opening verse conjuring the Gatsbyesque parties once a regular fixture of her Rhode Island mansion, in a bid to challenge the public who supposedly know her so well, to suss out truth from fiction, emotion from performance, a Shakespearean bait-and-switch.

Taylor sets this stage in album opener "...Ready For It?". Opening with a blaring synth riff, Taylor clearing her throat, and a barrage of hitherto unheard Swiftian rap, *reputation* makes it clear from the start that it does not want us to be comfortable. We are in the underworld, after all, and we are about to meet its cast of characters—Swift, a criminal on the lam; her beloved, first a tantalizing myth, then a phantom accomplice; an unnamed traitor and their legions; and "they," us, the public, judge and audience peeking behind the wings. Swift sings, simultaneously haughtily and wearily, that she knows how this will all pan out, and implies that we do not, cannot. The rules are simply not the same here in the twilight pseudo reality of *reputation*.

The subsequent three tracks lean in to turning mores and morality on their head, with Taylor defiantly declaring over and over that she, America's Decade-Long

Taylor commits to her hardened, powerful persona throughout the *reputation* stadium tour.

TAYLOR SWIFT ALBUM BY ALBUM

Sweetheart, is actually Bad, very Bad, and, in fact, she wants to get worse if it will bring her closer to her muse. Despite the overarching discourse seemingly at the center of the album, that Swift's reputation is forever tarnished due to being a Machiavellian puppet master and perpetual victim, Taylor makes it clear that the true threat to her reputation is not her alleged nature as a liar or traitor but her relationship to her lover, the accomplice to her crimes. On fourth track pop ballad "Don't Blame Me," Taylor evokes original sin at the mere thought of touching her muse, implying the ensuing backlash is what actually damned her into *reputation*'s underworld, and she's seemingly all the more eager to indulge.

Here, however, Swift's bravado begins to waver into vulnerability. *reputation*'s track 5, the emotional thesis of any Taylor album, is "Delicate," the first sign of vulnerability and anxiety on the record. A syncopated backbeat evokes Swift's cyclical intrusive thoughts: IS it cool to put all of that out into the world? IS it chill to be seen and understood so well? Taylor seems skeptical at the idea that someone could, indeed, want all of her and her career as she is, even after all she has sacrificed at the altar of their love.

These are big, fragile questions, and Taylor does not give herself time to answer before launching into *reputation*'s linchpin, inarguable tour de force "Look What You Made Me Do."

Out of context, "Look What You Made Me Do" is not Swift's best pop effort, to say the least. But as a narrative device and thesis statement? It is brilliant. Is it intentionally bad as a piece of satire on both musical and personal criticisms plaguing Swift? Is it an overly earnest, classically Swiftian moment of melodrama? Where does the performance of rage end and the actual emotional core of the album ease in?

"Look What You Made Me Do" closes as Taylor rises to the pinnacle of fame built upon her murdered past selves and embraces the treachery she believes we believe lives in her. She's a snake, she's the thief, she's the problem, and it's brought her back to life.

With the listener distracted by her bombastic descent into evil, Swift is free to return to seclusion with her lover in the sensual "So It Goes..." a song so intimate it feels almost voyeuristic to experience after the album's aggressive first act. It begs the lover to lean in, the listener to look away.

Bookended between the ellipses of "...Ready For It" and "So It Goes..." lies the story from the public's lens—the treacherous, insatiable snake lashing out at anyone and everyone in her path. The story ends with intimacy weaponized against the public, and rightfully so. How dare we entitle ourselves to Swift's private longings and hidden trysts after throwing her to the wolves? So it goes, indeed.

Freed of the constraint of the general public's script, we are now peeking behind the curtain, retracing our steps through the album's first narrative as Taylor and her beloved slink through secluded corners of New York's dive bars.

REPUTATION

LEFT: **In addition to the memory of a lifetime, the lucky Rep Room fans also received a signed lithograph and a personalized photo op with Taylor.**

OPPOSITE: **The reputation Stadium Tour found Taylor reveling in her hardships, like partying under gigantic luminescent snakes at Levi's Stadium in Santa Clara.**

Here on out, we're in a delightful, drunken, dizzy tryst. "Gorgeous" giggles and winks like your fourth glass of champagne on New Year's Eve. "King of My Heart" shines with self-determination, and "Dress" continues Swift's bid to be seen as an artist capable of sensuality. We leave the Max Martin and Shellback tracks largely behind and emerge into the buoyant efforts of Jack Antonoff, such as cult favorite track "Getaway Car."

"Getaway Car" empowers Taylor to reclaim her role as robber while revealing that her accomplice was merely a vehicle for obscuring her true love, her actual partner in crime, all at the public's loss, acts as thesis for act two. She is not only reclaiming the narrative—she is stealing back what was always hers.

80   TAYLOR SWIFT ALBUM BY ALBUM

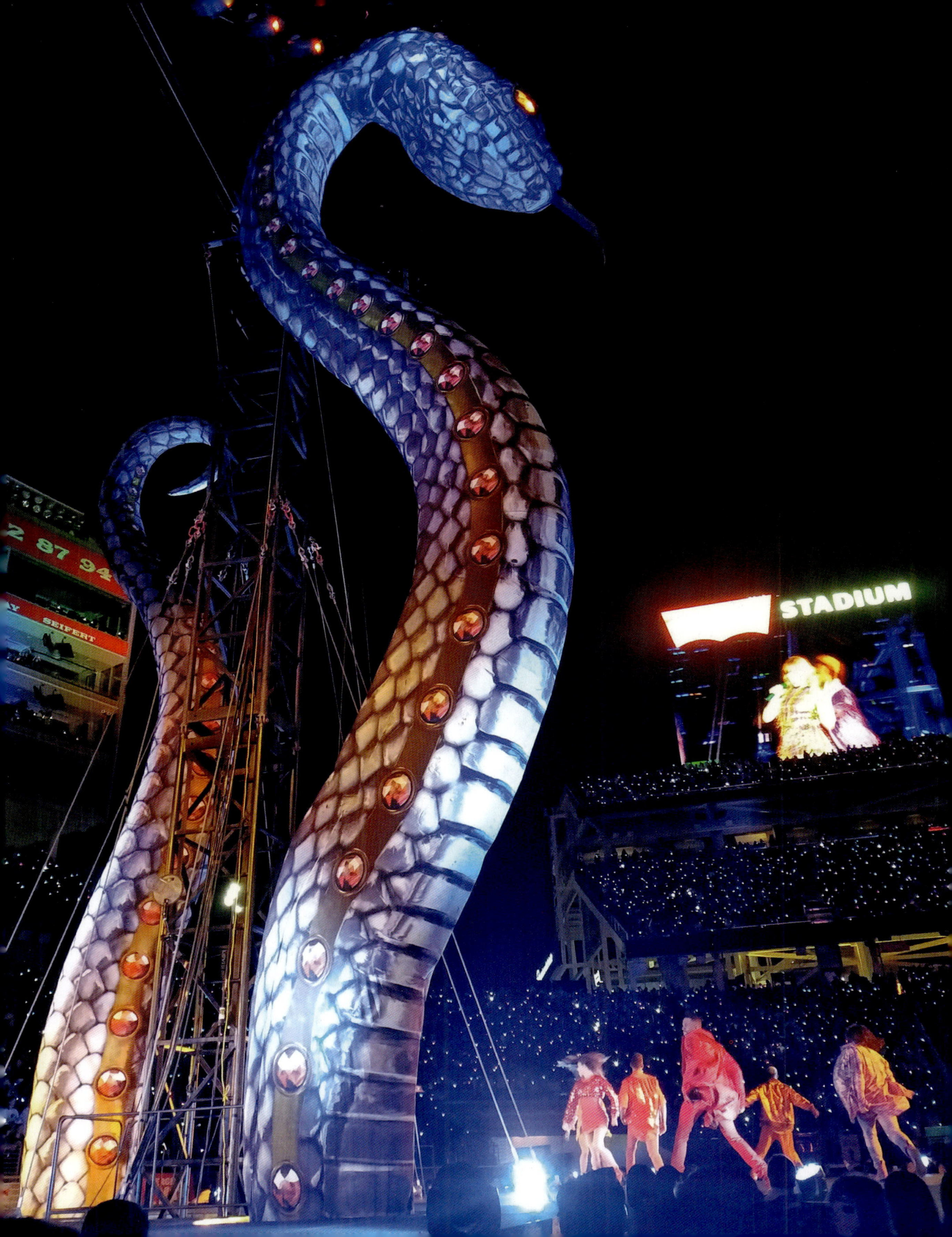
STADIUM
2 87 94
SEIFERT

The album closes with the intimate, bare ballad "New Year's Day." The track beautifies the small, unseen moments that come to define a relationship—secret gestures on a car ride home, the unspoken rhythm of two bodies moving together amongst the clamor and scrape of last year's trash. The addressee, at the beginning, is seemingly Taylor's beloved. The bombast of the album has fallen away and they're left here, alone and quiet, amongst the last glittering and empty mementos of last night's spectacle. The acoustic piano tracking does not exclude the surrounding sound pollution, evoking a sense of a cozy corner amidst the bustle of a party, inviting the listener to lean in closer.

The bridge seems to drive this home—a repeated plea to stay familiar—before opening the song up to the general you, a volta turn and nod to the fans who have so loyally stuck by her through what is seemingly the most trying era of her life. Indeed, the live rendition of the song on the *reputation* stadium tour–mashed up with "Long Live"–was a cherished high point of the era, seen as less of a thank you and more of a communion.

Swift's ability to make her fans feel not only heard but also *seen* continued to reap rewards as she embraced herself on *reputation*. Fireworks ignite the night at the Rose Bowl, reminiscent of her legendary Fourth of July parties.

If you know you'll never be out of the headlines, as a younger *Red*-era Swift began to realize, you might as well make your own, as Taylor would do with the *reputation* prologue.

Herein lies the Swiftian genius. No matter who she is or is not dating or avenging, Taylor can make you believe that you, the fan, are the ultimate collaborator and accomplice in her story. Every night she replied to fans on Tumblr, summoned them to the rep room (the post-show free meet and greet), and embraced their communal traditions like the "1, 2, 3, let's go bitch!" chant during "Delicate." In a stadium filled with tens of thousands of fans, Swift still had the unparalleled ability to make every single one feel as if the show was just for them, the album now theirs to hold.

Perhaps the old Taylor never died at all. 🦋

7

By Joanna Weiss

Lover

Track Listing:

1. I Forgot That You Existed [2:50]
2. Cruel Summer [2:58]
3. Lover [3:41]
4. The Man [3:10]
5. The Archer [3:31]
6. I Think He Knows [2:53]
7. Miss Americana & The Heartbreak Prince [3:54]
8. Paper Rings [3:42]
9. Cornelia Street [4:47]
10. Death By A Thousand Cuts [3:18]
11. London Boy [3:10]
12. Soon You'll Get Better (ft. The Chicks) [3:21]
13. False God [3:20]
14. You Need To Calm Down [2:51]
15. Afterglow [3:43]
16. ME! (ft. Brendon Urie of Panic! At the Disco) [3:13]
17. It's Nice To Have A Friend [2:30]
18. Daylight [4:53]

Deluxe Edition Bonus Tracks:

19. I Forgot That You Existed (Piano/Vocal) [3:30]
20. Lover (Piano/Vocal) [5:39]

Recorded at Conway Recording (Los Angeles), Electric Lady (New York City), Golden Age West (Auckland), Golden Age (Los Angeles), Electric Feel (Los Angeles), Metropolis (London)

Released August 23, 2019

Produced by Taylor Swift, Jack Antonoff, Joel Little, Louis Bell, Frank Dukes

Label: Republic Records

Notable personnel:

Jack Antonoff: keyboards, piano, drums, acoustic guitar, electric guitar, percussion, bass, vocoder, synthesizer, Wurlitzer organ, background vocals

Louis Bell: keyboards

Frank Dukes: guitar

Joel Little: keyboards, drum programming, synthesizer, guitar

Laura Sisk: background vocals

Annie Clark: guitar

Joe Harrison: guitar

Serafin Aguilar: trumpet

David Urquidi: saxophone

Steve Hughes: trombone

Michael Riddleberger: drums

Sean Hutchinson: drums

Mikey Freedom Hart: keyboards, background vocals

Evan Smith: keyboards, saxophone

Emily Strayer: banjo

Martie Maguire: fiddle

The Chicks: featured artist, vocals

Brandon Bost: background vocals

Cassidy Ladden: background vocals

Ken Lewis: background vocals

Matthew Tavares: guitar

Brendon Urie: featured artist, vocals

Deluxe edition released February 14, 2020

Selected awards:

MTV Video Music Awards: Video of the Year ("You Need To Calm Down")

MTV Video Music Awards: Video for Good ("You Need To Calm Down")

MTV Video Music Awards: Best Visual Effects ("ME!")

MTV Video Music Awards: Best Direction ("The Man")

iHeartRadio Music Awards: Pop Album of the Year 2020

Notable honors:

1 week at number one on the Billboard 200

Taylor accepts the award for Favorite Album: Pop/Rock for *Lover* at the 2019 American Music Awards.

Lover begins with a declaration. After years of fighting demons—an obnoxious rapper, a cutthroat producer, a fickle fandom—Taylor Swift has discovered the awesome power of letting go. *reputation* was an album-length hiss at the haters, full of growling vocals and aggressive synths. The opening track to *Lover* swaps that seething for finger snaps, giggles, and petulant spoken word. It's called "I Forgot That You Existed."

There's a lightness that comes from abandoning a grudge, and for months leading up to the *Lover* release, Taylor has been bathing in that light. She's teased her fans with images of butterflies and released "ME!"—a piffle of a single that proclaims self-love to a marching band beat. In pastel-colored videos, she's been prancing in hair curlers, dancing in an oversized yellow suit, singing in a dress that dissolves into rainbow-colored goo.

But the fun and games are a kind of tease, too. Because *Lover* goes beyond the technicolor fizz to share a deeper message about accepting yourself and relating to someone else. The love songs are sensual but grounded, celebrating intimate habits and comfortable routines. The breakup songs are self-aware: stories of imposing your will at the start of a relationship and taking responsibility at the end. Overall, this is an album about adulting.

What does it mean to be an adult, when you're a few months shy of 30 and you've been a megastar for nearly half your life? By the time *Lover* came out, Swift had been through every high and low of the pop music industry, from the rush of early recognition to the dark side of success. She had lost control of her master

BELOW LEFT: **Taylor poses in front of a mural in Brooklyn introducing** *Lover* **in August 2019.**

BELOW RIGHT: **Taylor's** *Lover* **outfit, on display at the Museum of Arts and Design in New York at the** *Taylor Swift: Storyteller* **exhibit.**

TAYLOR SWIFT ALBUM BY ALBUM

recordings, experienced scorching internet hatred, discovered that not everything she touched would turn to gold. (Earlier that year, she filmed *Cats*.)

And she had learned that the force that most threatened to unravel her was the very fame she'd dreamed of as a child. In the Netflix documentary *Miss Americana*, filmed as she was making *Lover*, Swift talked about how much she'd bound her self-worth to award-show voters, stadium crowds, and internet fans. In diary entries she included with physical copies of the album, she marveled at the cheering fans but fretted about the pressure she felt to give them what they wanted (see sidebar on page 90).

So yes, she's delivered a confident synth-pop confection of an album, billed as a celebration of love. The tracks—produced and co-written, variously, by Jack Antonoff, Joel Little, and Lewis Bell and Adam King Feeney—are layered with sound and loaded with pop flourishes, from blips of percussion to the occasional trumpet.

Still, there's a faint throughline of darkness in nearly every song, a realization that even the highs come with a shot of compromise and a twinge of regret. The biggest hit single, "Cruel Summer"—co-written by Antonoff and Annie Clark of St. Vincent—is a bass-heavy banger about longing and accountability that may or may not have its roots in a real-life summer fling. Its chorus rolls out like a sigh and its bridge feels like a shout to the heavens, punctuated by an uncharacteristically ugly Taylor shriek.

And if there's one track that serves as *Lover*'s thesis, it's the sly "Miss Americana & The Heartbreak Prince," which uses the high school metaphor that has served Swift so well to explore her disillusionment with fame. Carried by melancholy low notes, punctuated by a haunting hook on the high end of the keyboard, it imagines Swift as a prom queen, seeking a future with her fandom. It ends with a grim chant backed up by a chorus of voices, as if her cheerleading squad has morphed into a sinister force.

No wonder Taylor sings about wanting to run away from it all. But there's no indication she'd actually want to quit. And if you're not going to back away from fame, the grown-up thing to do is leverage its power for your own ends.

Taylor found this newfound strength by way of some unwanted battles. After failed negotiations with her previous label, Big Machine Records, her back catalog was sold to a hated industry rival, compelling her to lash out online (see page 120). The groping hands of a Colorado deejay had inadvertently turned her into a feminist icon.

The indignities gave Swift a new perspective on the business and a new awareness of her place in it. Around the time of the *Lover* release, she told *Vogue* that she hadn't recognized sexism in the music industry at the start of her career, because "men in the industry saw me as a kid. I was a lanky, scrawny, overexcited young girl who reminded them more of their little niece or their daughter than a successful woman in business or a colleague." The passage of time changed all of that: "The second I became a woman, in people's perception, was when I started seeing it."

(continued on page 92)

88 TAYLOR SWIFT ALBUM BY ALBUM

Swift held court in a dazzling display at the 2019 Billboard Music Awards.

LOVER 89

DEAR DIARY

NO ONE COULD possibly be surprised that Taylor Swift started a diary. Someone with a penchant for musical confessions has to write the first drafts somewhere. Someone teeming with ideas needs a blank page to serve as an uncritical sounding board. And someone in middle school needs a place to spill her frustrations.

And so, sometime circa 2008, a 13-year-old Taylor Swift opened the pages of a journal, scribbled, "Property of Taylor Swift," and added a parenthetical beside her signature:

(That could be worth money someday!! Just kidding hehe)

Was she really kidding, though? Already, Swift had sights on a music career, and the drive to keep pushing until she got it. Even then, she might have imagined that these entries would serve a different purpose someday—as windows into her thinking, insight into her lyrics, artifacts in the mythology she was building about herself. That's what they turned out to be. And with the release of *Lover*, Swift decided to share them—well, a carefully selected sample of entries she had written over the past 18 years.

She doled them out in four special physical editions of the album, each page photographed and marked with her date and age at the time. The result is an out-of-sequence hodgepodge of emotions and ideas: school-day memories, exuberant reports of writing new songs, early drafts of lyrics to "All Too Well." And many, many scribbled lines that trace her evolving relationship with fame and success.

- At 13, on the first day of eighth grade: "I think my teacher's gonna give me a spotlight solo in chorus!"
- At 16, on a tour stop in Las Vegas: "all these fans wanted their picture with me and were calling out my name and stuff and I loved it."
- At 20, after a Grand Ole Opry show: "Criticism of my performance has been the biggest source of pain in my life. I sometimes feel like my college degree is in acting like I'm OK when I'm not."
- At 23, in her Rhode Island mansion: "This mostly perfect life can feel a lot like being a tiger in a wildlife enclosure. It's pretty in there, but you can't get out."
- At 26, at the heart of a bitter internet-driven fight with Kim Kardashian and Kanye West: "This summer is the apocalypse."

These are, in many cases, the kinds of dark thoughts you only dare to tell yourself in private. The fact that Swift decided to share them with the world says something about her sense of trust, her relationship with her fans, her expectations for the future.

What would Swifties do, now that they'd been invited to peek at her intimate story?

That's part of the chapter that comes next.

TAYLOR SWIFT ALBUM BY ALBUM

Used to being in the limelight, Swift emerged at the 2012 Jingle Ball with an agenda, fulfilling a journal entry from her younger 13-year-old self; not just a "spotlight solo in the chorus," as she wrote, but into a much larger spotlight to the world.

LOVER 91

(continued from page 87)

Now, the damsel in distress was ready to fight back. The making of *Lover* coincided with Swift's growing desire to use her stadium-size megaphone to advocate for women and LGBTQ rights. *Miss Americana* captures her arguing with her father and her management team over whether she should endorse a Democrat in Tennessee's US Senate race. Taylor wants to speak, and speak *now*, but the men in the room don't want to risk alienating fans or, worse, devaluing the brand.

Taylor would win that fight, though her candidate would lose the race. She'd also allow politics to seep into a few *Lover* tracks. Sometimes the messaging is subtle: She enlists The Chicks—blackballed by country music in 2003 for criticizing President George W. Bush—to accompany her on the intimate "Soon You'll Get Better." Sometimes, her political statements are almost embarrassingly on the nose: The upbeat romp "The Man" airs her grievances by way of *Barbie*-movie-grade Feminist 101.

And sometimes, she overshoots. The video for "You Need To Calm Down" namechecks nearly every LGBTQ A- and B-lister in the land, and ends with a link to a Change.org petition for the antidiscrimination Equality Act. But the queer community wasn't uniformly impressed. Some complained that she looked like another pop star jumping on a bandwagon and turning pride into a commodity.

They had a point: Even if her allyship was heartfelt, it could seem a little awkward, like Taylor showing her work. Her strength as a songwriter, after all, isn't in making broad social statements or waving banners for giant causes. It's in navigating complex, intimate relationships.

That's why the most authentic part of the "You Need To Calm Down" video, after every Easter egg and reference to internet battles and LGBTQ rights, is the wholly apolitical final shot, when Taylor and her onetime-rival Katy Perry—dressed, respectively, as a cheeseburger and a carton of fries—stare at each other shyly, then embrace like long-lost besties. This is the language Taylor Swift speaks most fluently: the language of love.

It's a good thing, then, that *Lover* is overstuffed with songs about relationships. At this point in her life, she's in the middle of what seems to be a good one: her long-term union with British actor Joe Alwyn, her muse and occasional collaborator (he would co-write songs on subsequent albums, under the pseudonym William Bowery). Swift has been intent on keeping the details of this one quiet—the *Miss Americana* documentary acknowledges his existence but never shows his face—but she can't help but shout from the rooftops about the happy state of her life.

So we get songs filled with the signature details that make a Taylor Swift love song feel like a history document: shopping trips and dips in the pool and intimate car rides. "London Boy" is a groovy celebration of a cross-ocean romance. "Paper Rings" is all lighthearted energy; at one point, you can make out a happy Taylor sigh.

On The Eras Tour: "Lover" boots at a show in Paris, France, on May 9, 2024.

92 TAYLOR SWIFT ALBUM BY ALBUM

Taylor arrives at the 2019 American Music Awards, where she won six awards—including Artist of the Decade.

We get cheeky songs about the start of a relationship: "I Think He Knows," about the euphoria when a woman in pursuit realizes the attraction is mutual, and "It's Nice To Have a Friend," which tracks the slow build of a love affair from childhood to intimate adulthood.

And we get "Lover," the title track, which might be the most romantic song Swift has ever written, precisely because it isn't about the storybook clichés she used as a dreamy teenager. Here, no one kisses in the rain or declares his love on a parapet; instead, Swift celebrates mundane routines and inside jokes and quiet understanding. It's a slow dance—a waltz—with a bridge that offers an alternate wedding vow. Is Taylor allowing herself to believe she's in this one for good?

Or is she afraid that "Lover" is an unattainable dream? Taken out of order, a handful of other songs on the album trace the arc of a long-term union, from exuberant beginnings on to darker times, when imperfections surface and doubts settle into the cracks.

Some of them feel almost literally like prayers. "False God," a sensual song about conflict and resolution, explores the kind of faith you need to make a relationship last through rough patches. "Death By A Thousand Cuts" starts with a kind of madrigal chant and picks at the challenge of letting go after the end. "Cornelia Street" explores the fear of losing a relationship so rich it blends into the landscape. "Afterglow" simmers with self-blame when it might be too late.

And then there's track 5, where Swift has traditionally voiced the plaintive wail of an innocent heroine wronged by a man. In "The Archer," she looks inward, instead. The spare production, backed by the quiet heartbeat pulse of a kick drum, evokes the feeling of being alone in a room with your dark thoughts. This isn't a song about realizing the fairy-tale prince isn't all he's cracked up to be. It's a song about acknowledging that the myths you've told about yourself might not be true.

LOVER

LOVE OF HER LIFE

WHO'S GOING TO love Taylor Swift? It's a subject she returns to repeatedly, in songs about relationships begun and ended, hopes that end in heartbreak. But in her life, there is one story of consistent, undeniable, unconditional love: the kind she shares with her mom.

Andrea Finlay Swift, mother of two, marketing professional, daughter of an opera singer, has been by Taylor's side at every step in her career. She accompanied 13-year-old Taylor to meetings with record executives, set up her early website and MySpace page, chaperoned her Fearless Tour. She's been her plus-one at award shows and presented her Milestone Award at the Academy of Country Music Awards in 2015. She carries guitars on international trips and watches tour performances from backstage.

And she was and remains Swift's pillar of emotional support. The long car rides they'd take together to rinse off the middle-school drama—one of which made it into the *Fearless* song "Best Day"—were the template for Taylor's true love language, seeking meaning from the tiniest moments and intimate details. The courtroom embrace they shared when Swift won her case against a Colorado deejay was a reminder that, as she navigated a cutthroat world, Swift always had a safe harbor.

So it's hard to overstate Taylor's devastation and fear as she confronted her mother's multiple bouts of cancer—or the emotional gut punch of *Lover*'s 12th track, "Soon You'll Get Better." A chronicle of hospital rooms and difficult treatments and desperate hope, elevated by The Chicks' backing vocals and mournful fiddle, it's full of sound, but pitched like a whisper. This drama has to have a happy ending. There's no other way Swift could bear to write it.

Swift has said her family agreed to include the song in *Lover*, but she can't bring herself to sing it onstage. And maybe that's as it should be. Swift's fandom clearly shares her hopes for recovery and good health. But even when you've invited the entire world into your life—making your mother nearly as famous as you—there are still messages that stay between people who share a special kind of love.

Taylor's mom presented her with the Milestone Award for Youngest ACE Entertainer of the Year at the Academy of Country Music Awards in 2015.

Not a roadie—but carrying a guitar on tour in Narita, Japan, in 2014.

In short, it's about accountability—something Swift was grappling with when *Lover* was in progress, as she figured out how to make sense of her setbacks and take responsibility for her failings. She was well past the point of getting everything she wanted from the music industry: The *Miss Americana* documentary captures her when she learns she got only one Grammy nomination for *reputation*. (It's for pop vocal album, and she'll eventually lose it to Ariana Grande.) But what happens next is telling. Swift allows herself a nanosecond of disappointment before formulating a new plan. She's just going to have to make an album that's better.

Lover was that attempt, and it might well have taken over the world if a mysterious virus hadn't begun to snake through the population a few months after the album's release. The pandemic got in the way of Swift's plans for a worldwide "Lover Fest" tour. The lockdown sent her down other creative paths.

But the next phase of her business life was still on track. *Lover* dropped right after Swift lost control of her master recordings. Before long, she was hatching plans to reclaim her financial stake in her own work by recording new versions of her old albums.

It was a boss move, straight out of the feminist fantasy world of "The Man," and quite possibly the most grown-up thing she'd ever done. This is what you learn in 15 hard-fought music industry years, facing off with producers and staring down the haters and coming out the other side. To win over the long haul, wallowing in anger doesn't help, and vowing to get even doesn't matter. What you really need to do is get to work. 🦋

LOVER   95

folklore

8

By Kase Wickman

Track Listing:

1. the 1 [3:30]
2. cardigan [3:59]
3. the last great american dynasty [3:51]
4. exile (ft. Bon Iver) [4:45]
5. my tears ricochet [4:15]
6. mirrorball [3:28]
7. seven [3:28]
8. august [4:21]
9. this is me trying [3:15]
10. illicit affairs [3:10]
11. invisible string [4:12]
12. mad woman [3:57]
13. epiphany [4:49]
14. betty [4:54]
15. peace [3:54]
16. hoax [3:40]

Deluxe Edition Bonus Track:

17. the lakes [3:31]

Recorded at Conway Recording (Los Angeles), Kitty Committee (Los Angeles), Electric Lady (New York City), Long Pond (Hudson Valley), Rough Customer (Brooklyn)

Released: July 24, 2020

Produced by Aaron Dessner, Jack Antonoff, Taylor Swift, Joe Alwyn

Label: Republic Records

Notable personnel:

William Bowery: (aka Joe Alwyn) co-writer and production

Aaron Dessner: orchestrations, cowriter, various instruments

Bryce Dessner: orchestrations

Jack Antonoff: vocals, cowriter, percussion and various instruments, background vocals

Justin Vernon of Bon Iver: vocals, co-writer on "Exile"

Deluxe edition released July 24, 2020

Selected awards:

Grammy Awards: Album of the Year 2021

iHeartRadio Music Awards: Best Pop Album 2021

Notable honors:

8 weeks at number one on Billboard 200

Two-time Platinum certified by RIAA

Spotify's biggest first day for a 2020 album, more than 80.6 million global streams on the platform

Guinness World Record for most opening-day streams for an album by a female artist

International Federation of the Phonographic Industry named it the year's best-selling album by a woman, and Swift the best-selling solo act of 2020

Swift, with her key *folklore* collaborators at the Grammy Awards, where they took home Album of the Year. *L to R*: Aaron Dessner, Swift, and Jack Antonoff.

Believe it or not, there was a time when there wasn't a bespoke cable knit cardigan color-coded to correspond with each of Taylor Swift's albums. Shocking, but true. We have, of course, *folklore* and its second track, "cardigan," to thank for that now-ubiquitous and endlessly iterated merch, along with so many other things. *folklore* marked a turning point in Swift's career, even beyond its melancholy, stripped-down vibe, the saddest pianos and loneliest acoustic guitars you've ever heard. No, *folklore* also signals when Taylor Alison Swift became an entire planet unto herself, dictating her own laws of gravity and writing her own mythology.

On July 23, 2020, Swift broke the internet when she broke the news via Instagram: "Most of the things I had planned this summer didn't end up happening, but there is something I hadn't planned on that DID happen. And that thing is my 8th studio album, *folklore*. Surprise," she began a caption next to the black-and-white photo that would serve as the first cover art for the album, Swift in a long plaid coat standing in the woods, gazing up at the trees. She's in the middle of the frame, but also the middle distance, hardly the focus of the photo. Her usually impressively tall 5-foot 10-inch (1.77 m) frame is dwarfed by these old, gargantuan wonders of the world, and Swift, her coat hanging open and unbuttoned, all the more room for the deepest emotions to come spilling unchecked out of her belly as they do on this album, seems to signal she's aware of just how inconsequential she is in the grand scheme of the world's history. Breakups, makeups, whatever bad blood with Katy Perry—with the horror of the global COVID-19 pandemic hanging over us all, who cares about little old Taylor? Widespread isolation in an attempt to stop the spread of coronavirus began mid-March 2020, with many thinking it would be, whatever, two weeks until we knocked this thing out. By late July, with no end in sight to masking and 6 feet (1.8 m) of distance minimum from all but your most trusted

A peak pandemic look for a peak pandemic album: Swift donned a mask to match her gown at the 2021 Grammy Awards.

TAYLOR SWIFT ALBUM BY ALBUM

loved ones and the impossibilities of daily life—remote work, childcare, maintaining sanity, you name it—the bright summer sun almost felt like a mockery in the face of all that profound darkness.

"Tonight at midnight I'll be releasing my entire brand new album of songs I've poured all of my whims, dreams, fears, and musings into," she went on to write in that announcement caption, giving Swifties worldwide, themselves isolating at home, just 16 hours to lose their minds before the album dropped on digital. She called out key collaborators, among them co-writer and co-producer Aaron Dessner of The National, Jack Antonoff, dubbed "basically musical family at this point," and the mysterious William Bowery, credited with co-writing two songs. (This turned out to be a pseudonym for Swift's long-term boyfriend at the time, actor Joe Alwyn, who got a Grammy out of their relationship.)

The surprise album drop was a first for Swift, a thrilling twist that signaled that, 14 years after releasing her debut album, the singer had some new tricks up her sleeve. Namely, she could knock listeners' socks off at any given moment. Easter eggs are one thing, but an entire album, recorded over Zoom during a time when most people weren't able to hug their grandparents or go grocery shopping outside of strictly designated hours? That's another level entirely. Is Taylor Swift a witch, or?

"Before this year I probably would've overthought when to release this music at the 'perfect' time, but the times we're living in keep reminding me that nothing is guaranteed," she wrote in the Instagram announcement. "My gut is telling me that if you make something you love, you should just put it out into the world. That's the side of uncertainty I can get on board with. Love you guys so much."

Uncertainty? It's something Swifties are now more than familiar with, as a rule.

Weeks into COVID-19 quarantine, Swift had already started work on *folklore*. "Not a lot going on at the moment," she told her followers on Instagram. Here, she streams a few songs during the One World Together at Home concert in April 2020.

FOLKLORE 99

WHAT'S IN A CODENAME?

IF THERE'S ONE thing Swift loves, it's an Easter egg, but if you take her at her word, *woodvale* is not one of them. Eagle-eyed fans noticed the word "woodvale" in faint white italics on the album art of *folklore* and lost their minds. Was it yet another secret album? Was it a clue?

It was not a mastermind move. It was an oopsie.

As Swift explained on *Jimmy Kimmel Live!* in December 2020, "I tend to be kind of annoyingly secret agent-y" when it comes to work. "Woodvale" was a code name for folklore, and was used on mockups of album art, as even Swift's closest collaborators weren't in on the album's true title until just before release. It had the same number of characters, and Swift wanted to see how it would look over Beth Garrabrant's photos. She just...missed deleting it. "Sometimes I take it too far and I make a mistake," she said of that secret agent schtick. Swifts: They're just like us.

Less than a year after *Lover*'s August 23, 2019, release date, *folklore* followed and couldn't be more of a pivot from *Lover*'s superproduced tracklist of bops, from the head-on-shoulder slow dance of the title track to the scream-along "Cruel Summer" and the giddy, handclappy "Paper Rings." Swift had expected to be touring that album with the April-to-August Lover Fest, a series of stops at festivals beginning with something of a warm-up gig headlining a free concert series in Atlanta on April 5. Then, the tour proper would begin, meandering throughout Europe for a series of dates beginning June 20, then two shows in Brazil before wrapping up with two Lover Fest West shows in Los Angeles and the final two Lover Fest East concerts just outside Boston, the last one originally set for August 1.

The terrible perfection of the timing of an airborne illness taking over the world almost exactly when thousands of fans had planned to scream and cry and dance together, sweat-slicked under the summer sun, is almost poetic, you have to admit.

On March 12, that first Atlanta concert's cancellation was announced, along with the NCAA's March Madness Tournament, which it was set to coincide with. Then, on April 17, Swift postponed the rest of her planned shows until 2021, writing, "I'm so sad I won't be able to see you guys in concert this year, but I know this is the right decision. Please, please stay healthy and safe. I'll see you on stage as soon as I can but right now what's important is committing to this quarantine, for the sake of all of us."

On February 26, 2021, having released not only *folklore* but its sister album *evermore*, too, she gave up the ghost entirely and canceled the tour.

In that middle time, before she said that the pandemic meant "nobody knows what the touring landscape will look like in the near future," Swift was in the same boat as the rest of us: home alone and losing her mind for the foreseeable future.

How quickly life changes! In January 2020, Swift was celebrated in Park City, Utah, at the premiere of "Taylor Swift: Miss Americana," the same week folklore **debuted at No. 1 on the Billboard 200, her seventh No. 1 title on the chart.**

A lot of people made sourdough bread or got bangs. Swift made what many consider to be her career-best album. Six on one hand, a half-dozen on the other, you know?

"When lockdown happened, I just found myself completely listless and purposeless—and that was in the first three days of it," she said in the Long Pond Sessions documentary, a November surprise that made many "what I'm thankful for" lists, in which she performed the album in its entirety with Dessner and Antonoff for the first time, discussing the project with them in interludes where absolute goblets of white wine serve as another participant in the flannel-swaddled conversations. (Pinterest, eat your heart out, this album could easily come with a jar of fireflies and a cozy throw blanket.)

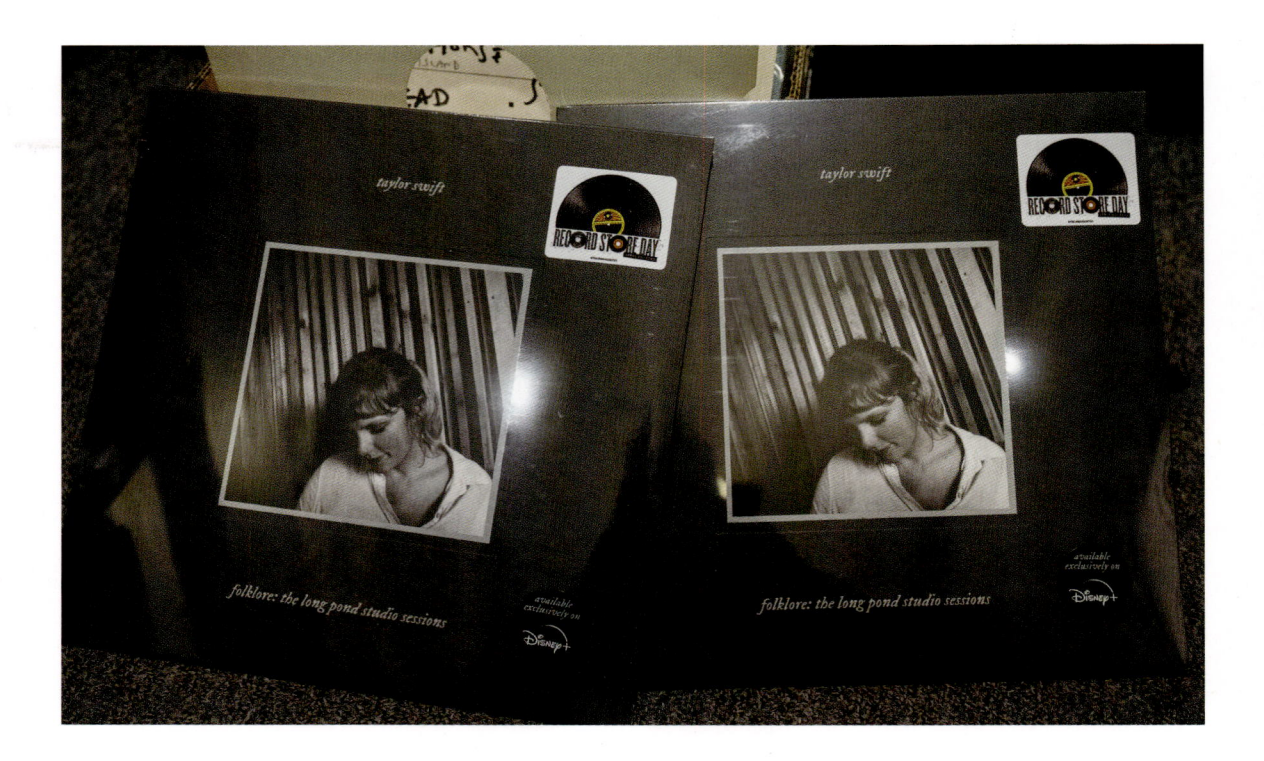

And if listeners were surprised to find out about *folklore* on that July day, well, they weren't so far behind Swift's record label, Universal Music Group's Republic Records: She revealed they didn't know it existed until, oh, a week-ish before it dropped. It was a hell of a trust fall for her second release with the label, her new recording home after the Big Ouch that was her bitter departure from Big Machine Records, which released all of her albums until *Lover*. Imagine Swift essentially tapping UMG on the shoulder and saying, *hey, got a sec? I have an entire album for you that sounds totally different from anything I've ever recorded before—and by the way, yeah, I've recorded this whole thing and have album art ready, don't worry—and also I talk a little thinly veiled smack about my old label in there, too.* Are you sweating a little, too, or is that just me?

"I thought it was going to be stressful and I thought I was gonna have to kind of stand up with shaking hands being like, 'I promise I know what I'm doing, I know there's not like a big single and I'm not doing like a big pop thing and I'm not'—but my label was like, whatever you wanna make, we're so down," she said of the big reveal to the suits.

The album earned 2.3 million units in 2020, making it the best-selling album of the year. It was streamed 72 million times in the United States within 24 hours of its release.

So, yes, it makes sense that UMG was "so down," despite that hard, sepia-toned swerve away from *Lover*'s whole candy-coated pop vibe.

the long pond sessions explored both the loneliness of collaborating on an album in quarantine and the joy of finally reuniting with your collaborators. "In isolation my imagination has run wild and this album is the result," Swift wrote on Instagram in July 2020, "a collection of songs and stories that flowed like a stream of consciousness."

"I miss you terribly," Swift wrote on social media, announcing the cancellation of Lover Fest after repeated postponements. One of her planned appearances was as a headliner at the Glastonbury Festival's 50th year.

Right after the listener hit play, Swift signals that this album is something different: On the aptly-titled first track, "the 1," after a few measures of piano, quickly joined by acoustic guitar, she offers a status update complete with—gasp!—a curse word, informing us she's "doing good" and "on some new shit." The inclusion of a curse word wasn't a first for Swift—that would be on *reputation*'s "I Did Something Bad"— but paired with that sound, that guarded "good" you might dole out to an ex you haven't seen in a while, waiting to see how their version of "good" compares with yours without showing your underbelly, this is a Swift who's signaling something of a reintroduction, waving at us from home through her little section of the Zoom window. It's also her first album to be slapped with an explicit content label—she drops her first on-record F-bomb later in the album, in "mad woman."

Among *folklore*'s new shit (apart from, oh, basically everything) is her collaboration with Dessner, whose face would certainly grace a would-be Indie Rock Mount Rushmore and who co-wrote and/or co-produced 11 of the album's 16 tracks and would become a familiar face in the Swiftiverse moving forward.

Swift had long admired The National, attending concerts and throwing their songs onto curated playlists, and met the band members in 2014 at *Saturday Night Live*. In 2019, her pal Antoni Porowski even posted a photo to Instagram of the two on the set of the music video for "You Need To Calm Down," looking at each other with open delight. It was captioned, "You love The National?! I love The National!!"

FOLKLORE

Swift's massive hilltop estate in Watch Hill, Rhode Island, formerly owned by Rebekah Harkness. "And then it was bought by me," Swift sings in "The Last Great American Dynasty," inspired by Harkness.

"Aaron is one of the most effortlessly prolific creators I've ever worked with," Swift, the woman who would have enough material for a three-plus hour retrospective concert with time enough on her hands to re-release four of those albums before she turned 35, told *Entertainment Weekly* in 2020. "There was something about everything he created that is an immediate image in my head or melody that I came up with. So much so that I'd start writing as soon as I heard a new one. And oftentimes what I would send back would inspire him to make more instrumentals and then send me that one. And then I wrote the song and it started to shape the project, form fitted and customized to what we wanted to do."

The pandemic forced a different recording environment than she'd ever faced, with Dessner at Long Pond Studios, which he owns, in upstate New York, Antonoff in Brooklyn, and Swift at her newly built in-home studio in Los Angeles, dubbed the Kitty Committee Studio in the liner notes for *folklore*, thanks to Swift's three pets. Despite the distance between herself and her collaborators, and the fact that the album marked the first time she strayed greatly from writing about and from her own life experiences, *folklore* communicates the greatest intimacy of all of Swift's albums. You can literally hear her breath on the tracks, can almost feel the flannel of her shirt brushing against your bare arm next to you on the couch. In the past, Swift had shared her teenaged anxieties over short skirts and T-shirts, and she'd made a snowmobile accident danceable. With this album, she relayed the legend of Rebekah Harkness, the previous owner of Holiday House in Rhode Island and fashioned a love triangle among three teenagers from thin air with the trio of "cardigan," "betty," and "august." She imagined herself as a ghost pissed off that she was being improperly mourned, and astrally projected to relay the experiences of frontline pandemic workers. In real life, Swift was reading and watching movies in the early part of lockdown, but mentally she was imagining herself drifting through a misty field in an old-fashioned nightgown, an avenging—if stylishly clad—angel.

In Swift's previous work, she invited listeners inside the pages of her diary. On *folklore* she cracked the door and beckoned us into her home and her innermost daydreams. For once, her day-to-day life wasn't that interesting, but her inner landscape was in full bloom.

"I survived mostly on wine and watching seven hundred hours of TV every day, but I also made *folklore*," she told Rob Sheffield.

She threw out the entire rulebook for *folklore*, realizing that, wait, since she'd *made* the rules, she could change them, too.

"Songwriting on this album is exactly the way that I would write if I considered nothing else other than, 'What words do I want to write? What stories do I want to tell? What melodies do I want to sing? What production is essential to tell those stories?'" she told *Entertainment Weekly*. "It was a very do-it-yourself experience."

Even with all that sweat equity poured in, the daydream quality of *folklore* stayed with Swift. As she prepares to play the songs with Dessner and Antonoff for the first time in person, she says, "I think it will take that for me to realize that it's a real album."

folklore met fans where they were: alone at home, and pretty bummed out about it. It may have been high summer, late July, when Swift dropped her melancholy masterpiece of a surprise on our digital doorsteps, but the leaves changed color when this album came out, the fall vibes were so strong.

It's as if by being forced to slow down, Swift was able to process her experiences and her reactions to the experiences of others, stepping outside the time loop and her usual obligations and worries in service of one great big worry, and suddenly finding time to understand what was going on in her own head. She found herself being triggered by stories about divorce, she said, like the movie *Marriage Story*, even though she'd never been divorced, never even been married, and realized that, *oh*, she was feeling pangs from the messy fallout of her necessary breakup with Big Machine Records and Scott Borchetta, the label's founder and CEO.

The very first song she wrote for the album is the devastating "my tears ricochet," an ode to her unresolved angst over the Big Machine situation. It landed in the storied track 5 slot on *folklore*, the space Swifties know is traditionally reserved for an emotional dagger. In *Long Pond*, Swift doesn't say it's about Borchetta, but does say, "it's about karma, greed, how somebody could be your best friend and your companion and your most trusted person in your life and then they could go and become your worst enemy who knows how to hurt you because they were once your most trusted person." It's her only solo songwriting credit on the entire album and its lyrics imagine a ghost narrator haunting her own funeral, pissed as hell to see a former lover graveside. Swift is unable to move on, but so is the mourner, playing her "stolen lullabies" on repeat. You can feel those layered vocals and shrieking harmonies with herself in your chest.

Later in the album, "mad woman," too, is an ode to copyright law and long-dry contract ink that manages to be emotional and legible even to tweens who don't have a checking account to their name. Swift plays with the dual meaning of "mad" in the song's lyrics, masterfully flipping between anger and what others tell her is lunacy for being angry. When she first heard Dessner's instrumentation, she said, "I thought, oh, this is female rage." It would be a few years before Swift's *The Tortured Poets Department* epic, which she has since classified as "Female Rage: The Musical!" The seeds were certainly planted with *folklore*, where she began cloaking her own very real inner emotions in created characters to make them walk and sing.

The album has moody ruminations on fame ("mirrorball," "peace," and "the last great american dynasty," to name a few, the last being a total bop about the HOA nightmare rich lady whose house Swift bought decades later, picking up the mantle of being the main course in a feast of gossip), love ("the 1," "hoax," the rainbow of "invisible string," the teenage love triangle trilogy of "cardigan," "august," and "betty," the last featuring that Springsteen-y harmonica intro), and more. "This album was a real flotation device for both of us," she remarked to Dessner.

For an album that started in isolation, Swift by and large emerged from the misty veil of her own mind, delighting fans with a newfound sense of identity and purpose in a world ravaged by the pandemic. It wouldn't be the last time she'd surprise the Swifties... or herself.

Not only did Swift get to show off her songwriting muscles in a different way than ever before, but the indie rock sensibility and credibility that Dessner brought to the album, both in practice and reputation, had Swift welcoming a bevy of new fans, welcoming to the stage the legion of Sad Dads of The National. She even collaborated with Justin Vernon of Bon Iver on the standout track "exile," the piano melody and first verse of which were written by Alwyn. By linking arms with Dessner, Swift was able to not only embrace a sound she'd been afraid to approach but also shore up her confidence as a musician. She speaks of being nervous about suggesting Vernon as the male vocal for "exile" in *Long Pond*, while Dessner looks on with an expression of bafflement that she doesn't seem to understand that she's a super-desirable collaborator in herself. She's Taylor Swift.

After an increasingly pop-flavored trajectory throughout her career, dropping that adopted twang of her debut, dipping a toe into mainstream radio with *Red*, being the first person to ever go out dancing with her girls in the city in *1989*, and sinking into the warm bubble bath of long-term love on *Lover*, it seemed that Swift might have stayed that course. Instead, with *folklore*, she revitalized her career and recruited an entirely new segment of fans, gaining critical and commercial acclaim for the risky move to boot. With *folklore*, she became the first female artist to win the Album of the Year Grammy three times. The album topped many best-of-the-year lists and became a defining soundtrack of the COVID-19 era. In 2023, *Rolling Stone* revamped its 500 Greatest Albums of All Time. *folklore* was number 170.

For the first time in her career, Swift threw out her own rulebook. The world had changed, why couldn't her approach to music? This secretive project cast Swift in the lead role in her own story, rather than one (very important) cog in the machine that previously chugged away to make Taylor Swift™. Once she grabbed that spotlight, she didn't let it go, as evidenced by her re-recording project, launching a career retrospective tour before she was old enough to run for president, and on and on and on. She learned that evolving doesn't necessarily mean destroying what came before, but building on it and writing your own, yes, folklore.

"I have this weird thing where, in order to create the next thing, I attack the previous thing," she told *Entertainment Weekly* at the time. "I don't love that I do that, but it is the thing that has kept me pivoting to another world every time I make an album. But with this one, I still love it."

It was with *folklore* that she began seeing herself not just as a person, not just as a singer, but as a full body of work, a cultural force. She didn't just have a discography or a fan base or a shelf creaking with awards—she had a *legacy*.

In the final moment of *Long Pond*, as the camera zooms out and away from the roof of that Hudson Valley abode, Swift can be heard saying, "that oughta do it," then, with Dessner and Antonoff, agreeing that it's time for some whiskey. As the lore goes, they decided that that didn't *quite* do it, and after they found the whiskey, that same night, they began recording *evermore*. 🦋

9

By Moira McAvoy

evermore

Track Listing:

1. willow [3:34]
2. champagne problems [4:04]
3. gold rush [3:05]
4. 'tis the damn season [3:49]
5. tolerate it [4:05]
6. no body, no crime (ft. HAIM) [3:35]
7. happiness [5:15]
8. dorothea [3:45]
9. coney island (ft. The National) [4:35]
10. ivy [4:20]
11. cowboy like me [4:35]
12. long story short [3:35]
13. marjorie [4:17]
14. closure [3:00]
15. evermore (ft. Bon Iver) [5:04]

Deluxe Edition Bonus Tracks:

16. right where you left me [4:05]
17. it's time to go [4:15]

Recorded at Kitty Committee (Los Angeles), Long Pond (Hudson Valley), Scarlet Pimpernel (Exeter), and Ariel Rechtshaid's house (Los Angeles)

Released December 11, 2020

Produced by Aaron Dessner, Taylor Swift, Jack Antonoff, and Bryce Dessner

Label: Republic Records

Notable personnel:

Aaron Dessner: songwriting, drum machine programming, percussion, keyboards, synthesizers, piano, electric guitar, bass guitar, acoustic guitar, synth bass, mandolin, field recording, tambourin, high string guitar, drum kit, rubber bridge guitar, drone, banjo, recording

Justin Vernon: backing vocals, triangle, drum kit, banjo, electric guitar, Prophet X, Messina, synthesizers, field recording, vocals, bass guitar, acoustic guitar, vocal recording

Jack Antonoff: songwriting, drums, percussion, bass, electric guitar, acoustic guitar slide guitar, piano, Mellotron, backing vocals

Marjorie Finlay: backing vocals

William Bowery: songwriting, piano

Marcus Mumford: backing vocals

Bryce Dessner: songwriting, orchestration, piano, pulse, electric guitar

James McAlister: synthesizers, drum machine programming, percussion, keyboards, Vermona pulse, drum kit, additional production

Matt Berninger: vocals

Scott Devendorf: bass guitar, pocket piano

Bryan Devendorf: percussion, drum machine programming, drum kit

Danielle Haim: vocals

Este Haim: vocals

Laura Sisk: recording, vocal recording

Beth Garrabrant: photography

Deluxe edition released December 18, 2020

Total units sold: 10,000,000 (as of November 2024)

Selected awards:

American Music Awards: Favorite Pop/Rock Album 2021

ARIA: Best International Artist 2021

Notable honors:

4 weeks at number one on the Billboard 200

World record broken: shortest gap between two chart-topping albums by a woman on the Billboard 200 for the 140 days between *folklore* and *evermore*'s number-one debuts

Tour: NA (all albums post-*reputation* were bundled into The Eras Tour).

Swift's collaborations with Jack Antonoff and Aaron Dessner continued to pay dividends as the world reeled from the effects of the pandemic.

It's September 2020 and Taylor Swift is out with lanterns looking for herself. The world is not moving on from the COVID-19 pandemic as promised. The era of isolation and introspection continues inching along and the borders between existing in public and existing in private have bent, blurred. She's been spending a lot of time with her past work and past selves as she revisits her pre-*Lover* catalog and its vaults in an effort to own her masters, and artistically, Taylor is on fire in her collaborations with longtime partner Jack Antonoff and newfound comrade Aaron Dessner on the heels of July's seismically successful *folklore*.

Endless reinventions and half a lifetime into her career, Swift has, once again, found herself in uncharted territory. Recorded in total secrecy and seclusion, released without any forewarning, and hereunto her only work explicitly conceived through a lens of fiction, *folklore*'s warm reception seemed to give Taylor a key to the gilded cage in which she's long believed herself trapped. Maybe every single detail of her personal life didn't need to be autopsied and reanimated like a cultural Frankenstein for her art to be understood. Maybe her artistic lineage had branched from the likes of her alleged distant cousin, poet Emily Dickinson, instead of the ever-multiplying parade of ingenues volleying with her along sales charts and magazine covers. Maybe the stories she'd been telling us—and herself—had been wrong.

On her next two original albums and throughout her subsequent public engagements, Taylor Swift will position herself—sometimes satirically, sometimes with excruciating earnestness—as the Machiavellian mastermind she believes the general population believes her to be, leaning in to the trope at times to the detriment of her art and, seemingly, her well-being. But on Swift's second surprise 2020 album, *evermore*, we walk deeper into the woods, the fog of calculation and myth lifts, and Taylor appears as Taylor Swift the human, not Taylor Swift the legend, Taylor Swift the brand, or Taylor Swift the monoculture, one last time.

The pandemic rearranged time, and Swift fans were hit especially hard— and were especially delighted—when more music kept pouring out of their favorite musician.

Taylor's emotional live performances—always legendary career highlights—set the stage of the raw honesty on *evermore*.

Legend has it that Taylor, drunk off the emotional and artistic rush of recording the *Long Pond Studio Sessions* documentary—and also a very conspicuous glass of wine—wrote "'tis the damn season" in one fevered, tipsy swoop, and the rest of *evermore*'s recording process followed in frenetic suit. This lore is not only factually relevant but scene setting: The album's intimacy feels like a whispered secret fluttered between friends when one too many bottles have been drained, the fire is dying, and the night begs for one more honorific secret to be sacrificed.

OPENING THE CLOSET OF BACKLOGGED DREAMS

TRACK 13 IS, at times throughout Swift's discography, a meditation on fame. In the *folkmor* universe, Swift inverts this conceit, with each track acting as an homage to the loss of her grandparents—*folklore*'s "epiphany" dedicated to her paternal grandfather, *evermore*'s "marjorie" in memory of her maternal grandmother—and a deeply personal exploration of grief and regret on a global scale. "marjorie" seems an unlikely song to make it onto The Eras Tour setlist, somber, mournful, intimate, tender, yet Swift sang it night after night, gradually awash in a sea of phone flashlights.

A relatively successful opera singer—particularly in Puerto Rico and Cuba—the titular Marjorie Finlay's influence on Taylor as person and Taylor as artist is indelible. Despite all of her unprecedented fame and success, on "marjorie," it sounds as if Taylor's regret is not only borne of not appreciating the time she had with her grandmother, but for continuing to not live up to the aspirations she'd set for herself in honor of her. To rectify this, Swift brings Finlay to the forefront, her voice interpolated into the studio version of the song. She knows better: She will never be back, but maybe she can be summoned in the studio or onstage in front of thousands of fans.

This is the thesis of Taylor's grief throughout the album: You can move around it, you can barter against its existence, and you can even push through it, but, as you stare out the windows to an end point, closure in which you believe but know you will never, ever have, nearly careening to your own demise, you know this grief will never leave you alone, not really. You can mastermind the release schedule of the entire music industry; you can orchestrate a fan frenzy to murals in Nashville and Targets and record stores the world over; you can craft an explanation for every single possible interpretation of yourself and your art, but you cannot outmaneuver grief, and you certainly cannot outrun yourself.

Taylor is not the first musician in the family! Her grandmother, Marjorie Finlay, won praise, awards, and fans throughout her stage career in the 1950s.

evermore feels as if it's the only album Taylor Swift has ever written for herself. Comparably out of the panopticon of stardom, it seems that Swift, like many of us, connected with, excavated, and re-evaluated every aspect of herself, her life, and her choices during the early days of the pandemic, and, like for many of us, those discoveries seem to have wrought profound grief, the five stages of which Swift traverses throughout the record. As she moves through this cycle, Taylor is not only reckoning with the stories she'd been telling herself in order to live, but explicitly rewriting them. So what if your life isn't what you believed it to be, that you are not who you've needed to be? Maybe, if your sense of self has been built around stories, you can create a new one simply by saying something else.

One thing Taylor has always wanted is to be taken seriously as an artist, or to say, treated the way any man would be. She got her wish with *folklore*, acclaimed by indieheads and pop acolytes alike, receiving rave reviews from the same publications that devoted hundreds of words to Ryan Adams's *1989* cover album while ignoring hers entirely. The momentum keeps going on *evermore*, digging into the lush folk composition and narrative lyricism perfected on *folklore*. There's a great irony to this, as Taylor's early career success was buoyed by personal and specific songwriting and full orchestras of studio musicians.

Taylor has seen all of the tweets about how she has inspired Swifties to open a dictionary for the first time in their lives. She has also, apparently, seen the tweets comparing her with your favorite high school English teacher and, on *evermore*, seeks to both pay homage to and entrench herself in the American literature tradition. "ivy" radiates Emily Dickinson's influence—in some roundabout ways confirmed by the song's feature in an episode of Apple TV's *Dickinson*—"happiness" brings the grandiose desperate longing of Fitzgerald's most impossible imagery from *The Great Gatsby* close to the chest, and "tolerate it," the often extremely and explicitly personal track 5, is canonically inspired by the spectral gothic novel *Rebecca*. Throughout the record, Taylor is saying she is not only the Great American Songwriter, but one of the Great American Writers, period, while also asserting that the most gut-wrenching grief at the core of the album is being haunted.

evermore begins, of course, with denial. "willow" thrums a sultry invitation for someone—maybe a lover, maybe herself, or maybe her fans listening for guidance at every turn—to wreck her plans, cautioning with a gleeful wink that every bait-and-switch throughout her career has been an art piece, begging the question whether ALL of the mythmaking in conversation with her work has been fiction. It is clear from the get-go that, deep in the woods of *evermore*, all bets are off and nothing has been what it seemed.

The following track, fan-favorite anger-laden "champagne problems" is speculated to be about anything from the stolen masters to an exercise in pure narrative fiction to a failed engagement with long-time boyfriend Joe Alwyn, but the song rings most true not as an elegy for a relationship but for a life left unlived. Swift's career was largely built upon love songs; her breakout single was literally titled "Love Story" and ends with a picture-perfect proposal, and the prototypical Swiftian speaker is frequently seeking, cherishing, or lamenting a beloved. On "champagne problems," dripping with desperate regret, Swift seems certain that very narrative is impossible for her: If that love can never come to fruition for her, either as songwriter or person, as she is—ahem—fucked in the head, what else in the arc of her work, and thereby her life, is untrue?

evermore's third track, "gold rush" traffics specifically in the realm of revisionist reverie, a sort of bargaining between past and present. Harkening back to *reputation*'s bubbly "gorgeous," the speaker in "gold rush" finds her flirtation is replaced by bitter incredulousness, admitting she'd crafted the lore of her beloved and their life in her head. The details were there—dinner parties with friends, an Eagles shirt in a shared home, a town on the coast where the couple's romance bloomed—and yet none of it was as Swift wanted to believe it had been. The dinner parties were not warm celebrations but moments on eggshells awaiting contrarian commentary, the shirt a forgotten garment instead of a domestic shrine, the coast an unpinned locale on a map. The incandescently perfect person and the impossibly perfect tale were nothing more than fool's gold taunting her from below the waves of her desire.

The majority of *evermore*, like the majority of Swift's canon, operates as a direct address to a "you," often an object of affection or scorn. As much of the album interrogates interpersonal grief, it would seem, on the surface, that the addressee is a separate entity. However, as the album progresses and the desperate bargaining cycles in and out, you can't help but wonder if the "you" is Taylor herself, with the trope of an intimate relationship a symbolic vehicle for her journey through grief over lives she did not or will not get to lead, of people she has not gotten to be.

1989, which was, in a way, Taylor's last album before becoming Taylor Swift™, opens with a track explicitly about all the potential selves she could conjure for herself, declaring that she could embrace that philosophy forevermore. The word "forevermore" only appears four times across Taylor's discography: in "Welcome To New York," "New Year's Day," "long story short," and "evermore." While Taylor's reputation as an omniscient puppet master is exaggerated to say the least, and all artists repeat motifs throughout their canon, her word choice is precise. As an album, *evermore* is an elegy of the selves that could have existed through the self-determination of *1989*, through the embrace of the beloved on *reputation*. It is clear in the album that neither of those things ever existed to Taylor, not really. Who are we to say that when Taylor sings about turning a life into folklore and banishing any fantasy therein she is not talking about herself?

A fictionalized tale of a lesbian affair, "ivy," deftly pings this pang of preemptive grief. The speaker knows that if she does not have the impossible love of her dreams, one which enlivens and breaks down her stony emotional fortress, she will be doomed to a mundane life of restriction and predictability. Why not think that instead of a literal lover, the song is Taylor addressing a version of herself she only recently discovered and desperately longs to be, yet feels she cannot attain, one which is lethally flawed and magnificently cursed? This curse could be her belief that her

Swifties love a pilgrimage, and "dorothea"'s Tupelo is no exception.

EVERMORE 115

Taylor soaks up the adoration during the post-"champagne problems" applause at Arrowhead Stadium.

work only matters if it is discernibly tied to a man (as symbolized by the concept of marriage), that she must fit a specific vision of herself as an artist as a person to be successful.

It is a gift to learn more about yourself. It is a curse to learn it is not possible to live out those realities. Despite the certain dismissal in "gold rush," it's clear that *evermore*'s protagonist cannot let go of her desire, no matter how much harm it could cause. The allure of a curse never loses the faint glow of a savior. This tension plays out beautifully on the album-closing, Bon Iver–featuring title track "evermore," a transfixing, swelling take on regret, desperation, and hope. Taylor muses over how her life could be different if not for her choices as perceived by the public, how she could retell the story to herself via letters she could never send, longing out the window to a horizon she can only dream of meeting.

Swift is no stranger to a male duet, but in the "folkmore" (a fan-created phrase referring to both *folklore* and *evermore*) universe, these collaborations operate somewhat differently. Instead of a literal other, the male vocalist acts as a megaphone for Taylor's wants, wishes, and outside perspective; an "other" of potential, a potent symbol in the metaphor of heterosexual marriage as career and personal success.

The voice of that very specific allegory is one Taylor lyrically chased throughout the folkmore composition process: The National's Matt Berninger. Standout track "coney island" operates as call and response, Berninger entering almost as an intrusive thought to counter or amplify Taylor's self-deprecating lamentation.

The *evermore* bridge features, in my opinion, the most successful use of a male duet in Swift's catalog, a masterful dialogue between Taylor and Bon Iver with references to "seven," "happiness," and "gold rush." Throughout, Swift recognizes that the situation may not be as hopeless as she once believed, thanks to the belief in the version of herself of which she dreamed, and that maybe that self could still exist somewhere, somehow. After all, in a relatively explicit letter to self, "long story short," Swift sings that her waves will meet her own shore forever and evermore.

Throughout the album, romantic love is almost never attainable. Nostalgic tracks like "'tis the damn season" and "dorothea" touch on tenderness and hope, but for love long past, and songs like "cowboy like me" and "ivy" evoke a sense of doom and fatalism. Track 5 of *evermore*, "tolerate it," deals with an emotionally restrained and dismissive relationship, which, narratively, has a satisfying dovetail into the middling but fun "Goodbye Earl" inspired HAIM-helmed country romp "no body, no crime." Track 6 often operates as a metaphorical energy cleanse from the heaviness of track 5, but on *evermore*, it is a literal murder.

Grief is not linear. Taylor may have said that *Red*'s scattershot structure was meant to mirror the reality of heartbreak, but that concept crystalizes masterfully on *evermore*. The album begins with the first three stages, in order, before ricocheting through the cycle across the tracklist, the stages often swirling among each other within the same song. Denial crops up in "marjorie," "gold rush," and, perhaps most crucially, bonus track "right where you left me;" anger simmers in "tolerate it" and "closure;" bargaining wheels and deals itself through nostalgic relationships on "dorothea," "'tis the damn season," and "coney island;" depression permeates "champagne problems," "coney island" and "happiness."

Acceptance, as in reality, ebbs and flows on *evermore*. The song "happiness" swaps the trademark excess of its inspiration for a sparse air of resignation, reenacting the tired sort of argument you have with yourself that you tell yourself has ended, but only because you're too exhausted to keep having it. Then, the pendulum swings back—it's fine, you're fine, maybe it wasn't that bad, and actually, you will ALWAYS be fine! Playing expertly with this desperate grasp at flattening the narrative, "long story short" makes the nuance and regret of follow-up track "marjorie" ache all the stronger. More anger, denial, bargaining, and depression cycle through, finally pushing Swift toward her window's ledge in the closing eponymous track.

On "evermore," acceptance steps in tentatively, quietly. Taylor rewinds the tape and tells herself the story she's been frantically revising and revisioning. She's still left with herself as she is, and the self she's dreamed up, realizing that, perhaps, the sheer possibility of the dream itself was enough salvation on its own.

The album, in some ways, is a renegotiation of *reputation* and *Lover*, of the people Taylor and her lovers were positioned to be on them, of the story she was telling not only us, but herself. Taylor said she escaped into a world of fiction on these albums as a way to express and process—maybe that world is one where there actually is a sense of closure, even if it's one in possibility in lieu of a definitive answer. Now that The Story—of a career, of a love, of a life—has been definitively declared false, we can move out of the woods into the dawn-drenched clearing of what's to come.

Swifties like to joke that *evermore* is the forgotten folkmore sister, abandoned by her mother. They aren't exactly wrong. The album was lavished in critical acclaim but garnered significantly less commercial success than *folklore*, and Taylor has largely avoided talking in depth about *evermore* at all, once vaguely referring to it onstage during The Eras Tour as "that thing."

For all of Taylor's relative disregard, *evermore*'s set organically grew to be a fan-favorite, community-centered highlight of The Eras Tour, the only era to inspire not only one new show tradition, but three. This is, at first, somewhat surprising, given that beyond album opener "willow," the setlist eschews any of the album's more stadium-screaming-friendly tracks in favor of slower, mournful songs like "marjorie" and "champagne problems." But, we must remember this album is *intimate*. Released at midnight in the middle of an eight-month run between *folklore* and *Fearless (Taylor's Version)*, listening to *evermore* felt like typing your most intimate secrets onto a message board, alone in the thrumming static quiet of your room, then logging off before you could possibly perceive anyone else perceiving you.

Taylor positions herself as a literary heir of Emily Dickinson on *evermore*, and some Twitter sleuths think she may be a very, very, very distant cousin.

118   TAYLOR SWIFT ALBUM BY ALBUM

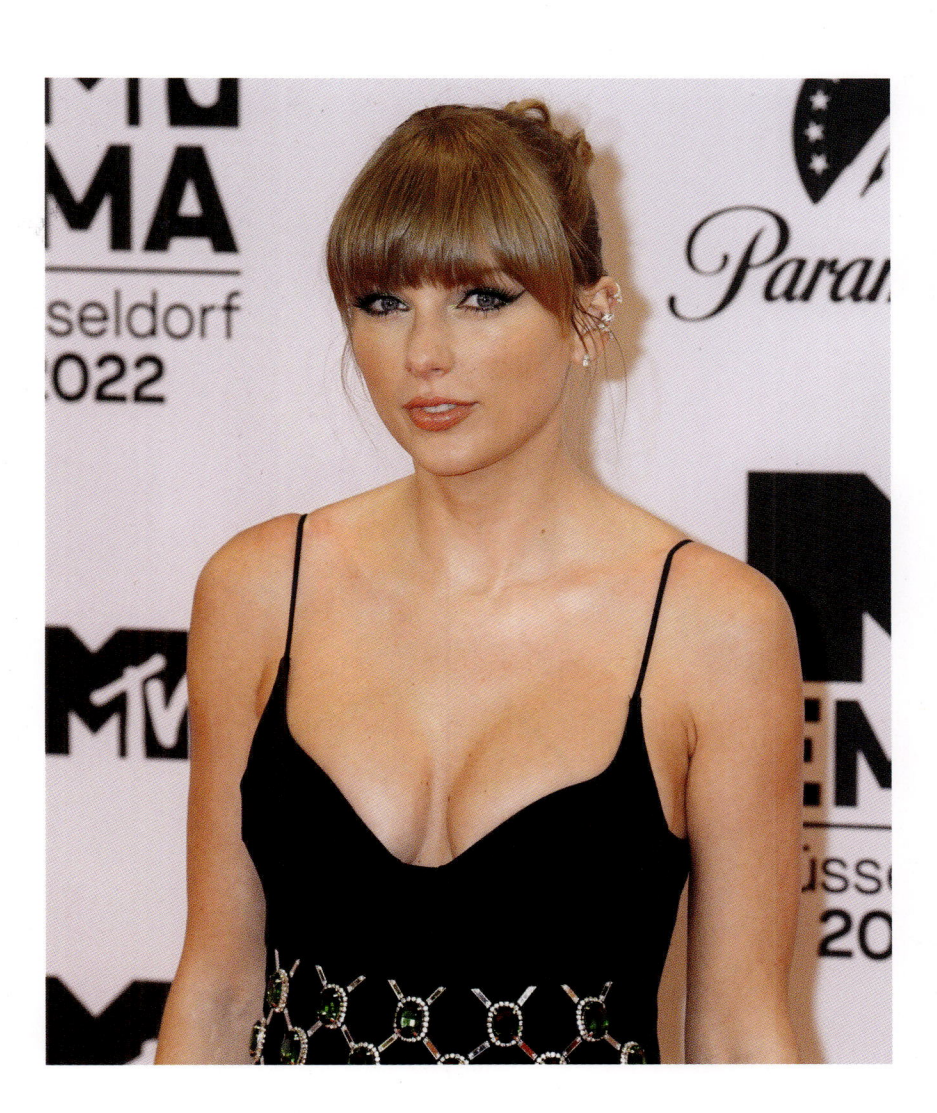

evermore was named the UK's biggest Americana album of 2022.

These ballads of grief and love are some of the most overtly personal tracks Swift has ever released. Of course, the legions of fans who feel innately, personally connected to Taylor would coalesce around their hushed intimacy and novelty to ritualistically enshrine their connection with the other 60,000-plus fans in attendance night after night.

While the phone lights twinkled as Taylor performed "marjorie," handcrafted yellow orbs bobbed throughout the crowd as talismans during the bewitching live rendition of "willow," and throughout the sometimes upwards of ten-minute standing ovation after "champagne problems," the crowd was not simply having fun with each other. They were affirming that they, too, were seated alongside Taylor in that forest, glinting in the dying light of the fire, listening to each secret and regret uttered into the night, and gently letting them go.

EVERMORE

B R I D G E

COPYRIGHTS.
CONTRACTS.
COUNTER OFFENSIVES.

THE SAGA OF Taylor Swift's masters—which resulted in a set of albums known as Taylor's Versions—is a twisting tale of secret negotiations, deep grudges, and shadow internet warfare. It has also, in its way, been educational. The masters battle introduced Swift's fans to the complex financial side of the music industry. It showed them ways a signed legal agreement can determine an artist's future, decades down the line. And it offered a lesson in how, and how not, to shape a public narrative.

Here's a primer for Swift's master class, so to speak, in music industry publishing and payback.

The Taylor Swift Masters Explained

What Is a Master Recording?

A master is the original sound recording of a song—the version released to the public, the source of all subsequent copies. The owner of a master earns royalties when that recording is purchased or streamed. And the owner controls where that recording is played—in TV shows and movies, commercials, and samples from other artists.

What About the Songwriter?

Songwriters own what are known as "publishing rights" over a song's composition, melody, and lyrics. Think of it this way: When Taylor Swift released "Love Story" in 2008, she owned the rights to the song itself. But her label, Big Machine Records, owned the recording, in all its glory—the vocals, the instrumentation, the production.

How Did Taylor's Record Label Come to Own Her Masters?

It's not an uncommon scenario. In many record deals, the label fronts the cost of recording, distribution, and promotion in exchange for ownership of the masters. That can be an attractive deal for an artist upfront because recording and promotion are expensive. But, ultimately, royalties that come from master recordings can make up the bulk of future income.

For decades, artists have pushed back on this arrangement, saying it keeps them from profiting from their own creative work. In 1996, Prince told *Rolling Stone*: "If you don't own your masters, your master owns you."

But Re-Recording All of Your Masters Is a Big Commitment, Isn't It?

We'll refer you to Taylor Swift at the Tribeca Film Festival in 2022: "People often greatly underestimate how much I will inconvenience myself to make a point."

What Happened to Get Her There?

It's complicated. Let's start from the beginning.

THE PLAYERS

Taylor Swift: Prolific songwriter, energetic performer, social media savant, cat lover

Scott Borchetta: Race car driver turned record executive and founder of Big Machine Records, Swift's label from 2005 to 2018

Scooter Braun: Manager of musical talent, including Justin Bieber, Ariana Grande, and, from time to time, Kanye West

Kanye West: Erstwhile rapper and Taylor Swift antagonist, also known as Ye

Justin Bieber: Pop star, Scooter Braun loyalist; opened for Taylor Swift on parts of her Fearless Tour in 2009 and 2010; uses the internet

Kelly Clarkson: Pop star, talk show host, everyone's best friend

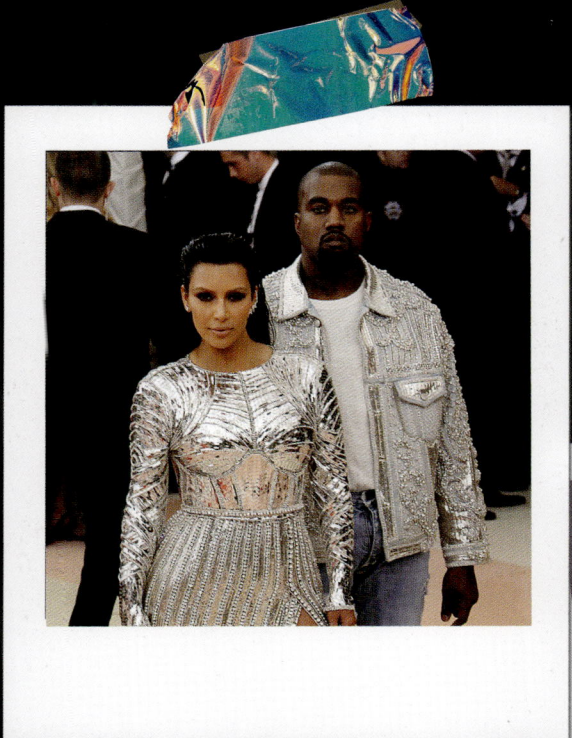

Kanye West and Kim Kardashian at the Met Gala in 2016. Their public dispute with Swift would fuel her anger over Scooter Braun's business deal.

Scooter Braun circa 2019. Swift wrote on Tumblr that she was "grossed out" Braun and Scott Borchetta now controlled her music catalog.

BRIDGE: THE TAYLOR SWIFT MASTERS EXPLAINED

"I honestly owe everything, everything in my life to you," Swift told her fans when she accepted her "Tour of the Year" prize at the 2019 iHeartRadio Music Awards. "And I just wanted to let you know when there's new music, you will be the first to know."

2005: Up-and-coming record executive Scott Borchetta leaves Universal Music Nashville to found his own label, Big Machine Records. The first artist he signs is a 15-year-old country singer-songwriter named Taylor Swift. Their contract calls for six studio albums.

2005–2017: Swift releases *Taylor Swift*, followed by *Fearless*, and subsequently takes over the universe. Borchetta reaps the benefits. They embrace at multiple award ceremonies and profess their mutual love and respect.

2009: Kanye West interrupts Taylor Swift at the MTV Video Music Awards as she's receiving the Best Female Video Award for "You Belong With Me." A feud is born.

June 2016: West releases the song "Famous," featuring a line that makes Taylor Swift incensed: "I feel like me and Taylor might still have sex. Why? I made that bitch famous." West's video features a wax sculpture of a naked Swift lying in bed with him. (It's a large bed that also contains naked figures of, among others, Donald Trump and George W. Bush.)

July 17, 2016: Kim Kardashian, West's then-wife, releases an edited recording of a phone call between Swift and West, suggesting that Swift had pre-approved the "famous" line. (A full recording, leaked later, will show she did not.) #TaylorSwiftIsOver trends on the internet.

August 2, 2016: As Swift continues to be bombarded with online hate, Justin Bieber posts a photo of himself facetiming with West and Scooter Braun. The caption: "Taylor Swift what up." Taylor will not forget this.

November 10, 2017: Swift releases *reputation*, her sixth studio album— and the last one she's contractually obligated to make with Big Machine Records.

2018: Taylor enters negotiations with Big Machine for a future contract. They cannot come to terms. She will later say she tried to buy back her masters but would not agree to Borchetta's offer, which would have required her to "earn back" each previous album by recording a new one.

November 2018: Swift walks away from Big Machine Records and signs with Republic Records, a division of Universal Music Group, under a contract that gives her control of her new masters from the get-go.

June 30, 2019: Big Machine Records is sold for $300 million to Ithaca Holdings, owned by Kanye West's sometime-manager Scooter Braun. Borchetta stays on as CEO after the sale. As an investor in Big Machine, Swift's father makes $15 million from the deal.

June 30, 2019 (a few hours later): Taylor goes on Tumblr to express how "sad and grossed out" she is that, of all people to now control her masters, it's Braun. She accuses him of bullying her during the Kanye feud, and shares the Justin Bieber Instagram post as evidence.

June 30, 2019 (a few hours later): Borchetta posts a countermanifesto on his website, including a screenshot of what he calls his final "extraordinary" offer to Swift. "Taylor had every chance in the world to own not just her master recordings, but every video, photograph, everything associated to her career," he writes. "She chose to leave."

June 30, 2019 (a few hours later): On Instagram, Bieber posts a photo of his younger self and a teen-aged Taylor Swift, apologizes for his 2016 post, and asks Swift to call off fans who are now attacking Braun online: "I usually don't rebuttal (sic) things like this but when you try and deface someone i loves (sic) character that's crossing a line."

July 13, 2019: Kelly Clarkson tweets a suggestion to Taylor: "U should go in & re-record all the songs that U don't own the masters on exactly how U did them but put brand new art & some kind of incentive so fans will no longer buy the old versions." She adds: "I'd buy all of the new versions just to prove a point."

Some commenters are skeptical: Wouldn't that infringe on Big Machine's copyright? It turns out, no: As primary songwriter, Swift owns her music and lyrics. She would essentially be creating covers of her own songs. And by putting a "(Taylor's Version)" tag at the end of each new song, she can signal that it's a new recording and avoid trademark issues over the title.

November 14-18, 2019: Taylor, Braun, and Borchetta engage in a public feud over whether she has permission to play her old songs at the 2019 American Music Awards, where she's accepting an award for Artist of the Decade. Swift activates her fans, who crowdfund the cost of two #ISTANDWITHTAYLOR billboards in Nashville. The fans also go on the offensive online. Twitter removes posts that share Borchetta's and Braun's phone numbers. Braun complains he and his family are getting death threats.

November 2020: Taylor clears the last legal hurdle to re-recording her albums: the expiration of the "re-record clause" in her Big Machine Records contract, which prevented her from re-recording her songs for two years after the original contract ended.

November 16, 2020: Braun sells Swift's masters to Shamrock Holdings, an investment firm owned by the Disney family, for $300 million. (Swift had entered negotiations to buy back her masters from Braun, but negotiations apparently broke down over disputes about nondisclosure agreements.)

November 16, 2020 (later that day): Taylor notes on Twitter that she has started to re-record her older music and "it has already proven to be both exciting and creatively fulfilling." A few days later, *Variety* writes: "Will Swift's pledge to re-record her back catalog deeply devalue Shamrock's investment, or will fans favor the versions they already know and love?"

April 9, 2021: Taylor releases *Fearless (Taylor's Version)*, which includes six previously unreleased songs "From The Vault." It earns more equivalent album units—a measure of sales and streaming—in its first week than the original version earned in its first year.

November 12, 2021: Taylor releases *Red (Taylor's Version)*, a supersized album with 30 songs, including a 10-minute version of "All Too Well." It debuts at number one on the Billboard 200 albums chart. *Billboard* reports that by mid-2023, "for every person who has purchased the original version of *Red*, about 21 people have picked up *Red (Taylor's Version)*."

July 7, 2023: Taylor releases *Speak Now (Taylor's Version)*, which includes six songs "From The Vault." It also debuts at number one on the Billboard 200, putting Swift ahead of Barbra Streisand for the most number-one albums by a female artist.

October 27, 2023: Taylor releases *1989 (Taylor's Version)*, nine years to the day after the original came out. It sells two million copies in just over two months, making it the best-selling album of 2023.

Ongoing: Every time a new Taylor's Version album is released, Swift sends Kelly Clarkson a bouquet of flowers. 🦋

OPPOSITE: **Red has long been a color asssociated with Taylor Swift, and the gown she wore in the video for "I Bet You Think About Me," a vault track on the *Red (Taylor's Version)*, is on display in 2021 at the Taylor Swift Songbook Trail at the Victoria & Albert Museum in London.**

BRIDGE: THE TAYLOR SWIFT MASTERS EXPLAINED   **127**

10 FEARLESS

TAYLOR'S VERSION

Track Listing:

1. Fearless [4:01]
2. Fifteen [4:54]
3. Love Story [3:55]
4. Hey Stephen [4:14]
5. White Horse [3:54]
6. You Belong With Me [3:51]
7. Breathe (feat. Colbie Caillat) (4:23)
8. Tell Me Why (3:20)
9. You're Not Sorry (4:21)
10. The Way I Loved You (4:03)
11. Forever & Always (3:45)
12. The Best Day (4:05)
13. Change (4:39)
14. Jump Then Fall (3:57)
15. Untouchable (5:12)
16. Forever and Always (Piano Version) (4:27)
17. Come In with the Rain (3:57)
18. Superstar (4:23)
19. The Other Side of the Door (3?58)
20. Today Was a Fairytale (4:01)
21. You All Over Me (featuring Maren Morris) (3:40)
22. Mr. Perfectly Fine (4:37)
23. We Were Happy (4:04)
24. That's When (featuring Keith Urban) (3:09)
25. Don't You (3:28)
26. Bye Bye Baby (4:02)

Physical Edition Bonus Track:

27. Love Story (Elvira remix) (3:31)

Recorded at Blackbird (Nashville), Conway Recording (Los Angeles), Electric Lady (New York), Kitty Committee East (London), Long Pond (New York), Prime Recording (Nashville), Rough Customer (Brooklyn)

Released April 9, 2021

Produced by Taylor Swift, Christopher Rowe, Jack Antonoff, Aaron Dessner

Label: Republic

Notable personnel:

Liz Rose: songwriting, 8 tracks

Cobie Caillait: vocals, songwriting on "Breathe"

Maren Morris: vocals on "You All Over Me"

Keith Urban: background vocals, electric guitar on "We Were Happy," 12-string acoustic guitar, vocals on "That's When"

Elvira Anderfjard: production, remixing, background vocals, bass, drums, keyboards, programming

Notable honors:

(Note: Swift didn't submit this album to the Grammy Awards or Country Music Association Awards because she wanted the awards committee to focus on *Evermore*.)

50 million global first-day streams on Spotify

Debuted at number one on the Billboard 200 (Swift's ninth consecutive album to do so)

Spent 11 total weeks in the top 40 of the Billboard 200 in its first year, including two nonconsecutive weeks at number one

Taylor Swift arrives at the 2009 Grammy Awards. She and producer Nathan Chapman (not pictured) picked the original *Fearless* tracks from some 50 possibilities.

Joanna Weiss: Why do you think Taylor chose *Fearless* for her first Taylor's Version album?

Moira McAvoy: Every time I went to The Eras Tour, the loudest era, every single time, was *Fearless*. That was the one where everybody was on their feet. It just feels like the "Taylor Swift™" album to me, for lack of a better word. *Fearless* was her breakthrough. "Love Story" was that moment where Taylor became a force.

Kase Wickman: It's an early album, so she can update some takes on it, but show people, "This is what these [Taylor's Versions] are going to be like. It's not a one-for-one copy, but I'm not reinventing the wheel here. You're getting more, you're getting different, but you're still getting the essence of the album."

JW: Lore has it that Taylor and producer Nathan Chapman recorded more than 50 songs for the original *Fearless*, but only 13 made the cut. In *Taylor's Version*, she added back six of them. Did she make the right choices? Are there any Vault Tracks that shouldn't have been there?

MA: I think one of the reasons the *Fearless* vault was so successful is that every song is a banger. And yet, with the exception of "Mr. Perfectly Fine," it's also understandable how they didn't make it onto the album. But "Mr. Perfectly Fine"—that could have been a single, right after "The Way I Loved You."

JW: "Mr. Perfectly Fine" is a quintessential Taylor Swift song to me. My first reaction is, "What's the point of this? It's so surface, so obvious." And then I realize, a day later, that the song has been playing in my head nonstop, and that it's hooked me with those barb hooks that attach to your brain.

KW: "Mr. Perfectly Fine" has taken on a lot of new meaning in recent years. And it's a bop.

JW: How about the original tracks? If you toggle back and forth between the original recipe of each song and Taylor's Version, what differences do you notice?

KW: They're all director's cuts and remasters. So I could imagine there are spots where she's like, "I'm gonna fix some of the things I did, because that's what I should be doing."

MA: Her vocals are so much better. More mature and just technically better, because Taylor's greatest improvement as an artist has been her vocals. I listened to 75 percent of *Fearless (Taylor's Version)* this morning, just because it's so long—

KW: God, so long. I can't believe how long it is.

MA: But it's almost all killer, no filler. We can get rid of "Change." That's fine. But otherwise, good stuff. And listening to her sing "Fifteen (Taylor's Version)," I think she used that sense of maturity and passage of time in a way that felt very nostalgic for her. That carries through the majority of the album, to the point of making sure she included the laugh in the bridge in "Hey Stephen."

KW: That was another proof point I like in *Taylor's Version*: that Tay laugh. Including that is like saying, "Okay, I'm not going to self-edit. I'm not face-tuning this." It's so goofy, it's very silly. But if you're familiar with the original, then you're like, "It has to be there."

JW: It's fan service.

MA: It's fan service in an earnest sense, where it's going back to what Taylor used to do: see fans as community, as friends. We are all in this together, and this is something we are creating together. The mythos of *Fearless* exists because of the fan reaction to it. That laugh wouldn't be significant if people didn't give it significance over the years, which Taylor knows.

JW: Taylor's fans loved her, from the start, for her authenticity. Do you think *Fearless* OG was about Taylor Swift? That it was authentically her?

Visions of Swift loomed large as The Eras Tour swept the world.

When Taylor wore the Romeo shirt from the original *Fearless* on the cover of *Taylor's Version*, the message went well beyond a fashion statement.

FEARLESS (TAYLOR'S VERSION)   131

In 2009, Taylor's relationship with her fans was mutually supportive and could feel like unmitigated joy. Still, there were signs, even then, that the price of adulation was high. And by the time *Fearless* (*Taylor's Version*) came out, Swift had experienced the highs and lows of celebrity.

MA: Yes. I also think that's part of why Taylor started with it, and why Taylor seemed to actually enjoy it. That was the last era before she became, like, *Taylor Swift*—before that fame. It seems like it was a project that was healing for her: This is what [music] used to be for me before. This is how I can reconnect with that feeling.

JW: But it's different, too. Take the *Taylor's Version* cover, where she's wearing a shirt that looks like the one Romeo wore in the "Love Story" video. The pop psychology take on that shirt is: "I don't need Romeo. Romeo could screw me at any time. I'm gonna do this myself."

KW: It's interesting, looking at the album covers side by side. She's facing different directions. And while neither of these photos is candid, one looks very manufactured: "We're gonna make it so your hair is just so on this album, Baby Taylor." And there's a subtle change in angle: The original version is head on, level with her. *Taylor's Version* is taken from slightly below. So it's Big Taylor in charge. Taylor, self-possessed. Taylor doing it, versus "someone is telling me what to do."

JW: That makes me wonder: Do you think when the original *Fearless* came out, Taylor had an inkling of what was going to happen—what that album was going to do to her career, her life?

OPPOSITE: **A happier era for *Fearless* OG: Taylor Swift, Scott Borchetta, and Nathan Chapman accepted the award for Album of the Year at the 2009 Academy of Country Music Awards.**

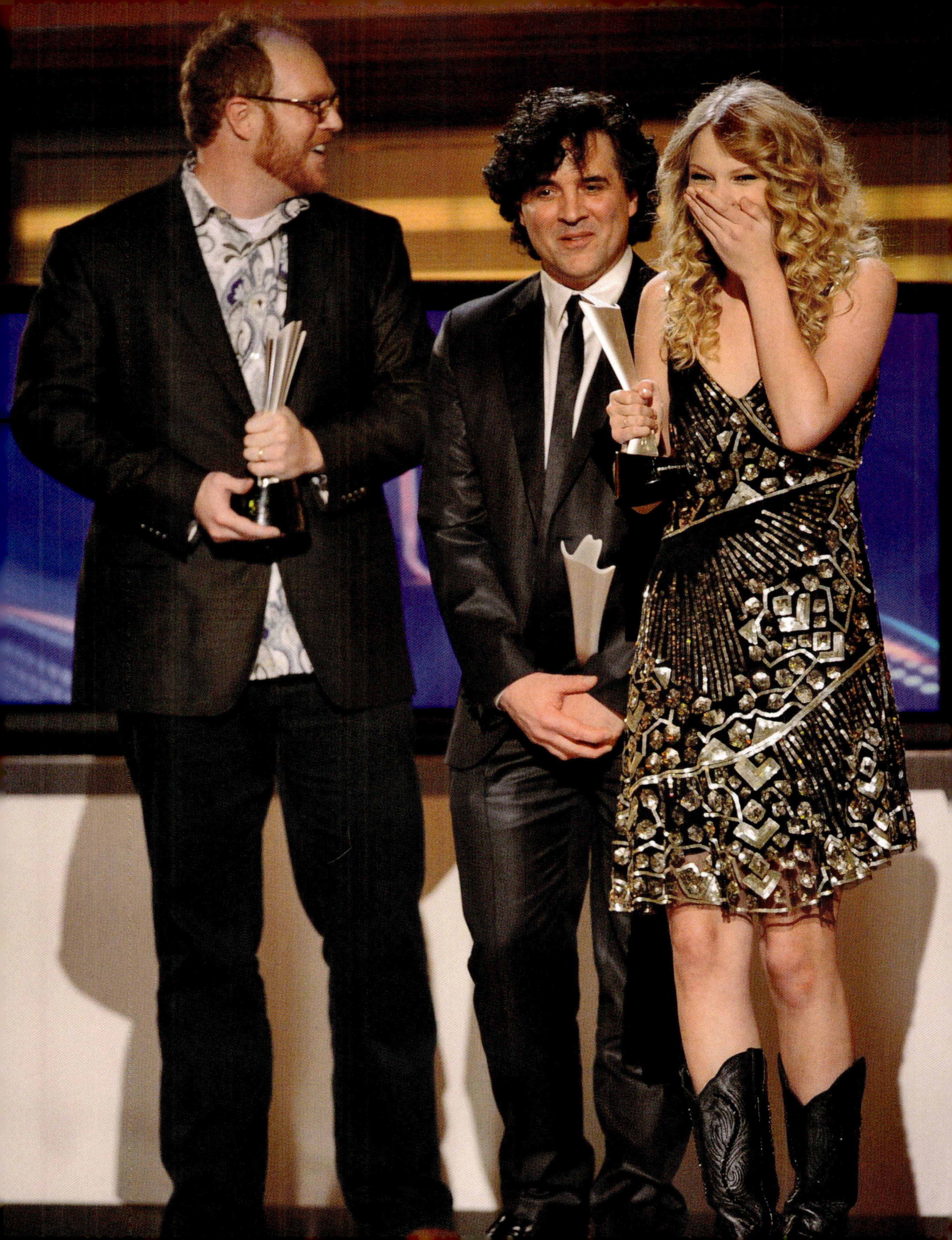

KW: No. You can't.

MA: Up until very recently, Taylor Swift has seemed very aware of the improbability of the success she's had. Up until at least 2022, she seemed surprised by the heights that continue happening.

JW: But the Taylor's Versions come out of the loss of innocence. At this point, her wide-eyed wonder at what has happened to her has turned into, "I'm a business. I'm a commodity."

MA: I think there's something to be said for the fact that she was able to tap back into that sense of innocence, even if just for the 20-odd songs on this album.

KW: With still-genuine gratitude, but also awareness of the downside—how terrible people can be, in a business sense. Has anyone taught the general population as much about copyright law as this woman? It's very impressive that she can say, "I'm re-recording these. Here's why. Let me tell you a little something about masters."

JW: In a metaphoric sense, it gets you back to "Fifteen," right? This is what I thought I wanted. This is what I know now.

MA: I think it's a test case for the Taylor's Versions, and also for the stage of her career she was in. Contemporary Taylor thinks fame is a prison. But at that point, in 2021, I think she had this platonic-ideal level of fame she'd always wanted: I'm in the cultural zeitgeist. I have the general public on my side.

JW: When you think about the differences between Original Recipe and Taylor's Version, is there anything lost, or is it all gain?

MA: It feels like all gain. And that's because she seems really invested in the underlying narratives: Here's growth, here's reclaiming my history, here's going back to my youth, here's how we've grown as a fandom.

ABOVE: **A rack of *Fearless* bracelets at a pop-up boutique in Los Angeles on the opening night of *The Eras Tour* movie. Of all of the eras, *Fearless* might have gotten the biggest crowd reaction.**

OPPOSITE: **Taylor in OG time, performing "Love Story" on the Fearless Tour. That song was a key reason *Fearless* launched her into the stratosphere.**

KW: I think this project has been successful because she managed to use her pull to say, "When you play this song, you will play *this* version of the song, right?" You have to look for the original recordings. The *Taylor's Version* tracks have become *the* version, because the other ones are so thoroughly buried. And so, you know, talking about the differences is tough because—

JW: These are now the canon.

KW: Exactly. She's managed to, literally, rewrite history, which is what she wanted to do. It's stunning to think about how successful she was. 🦋

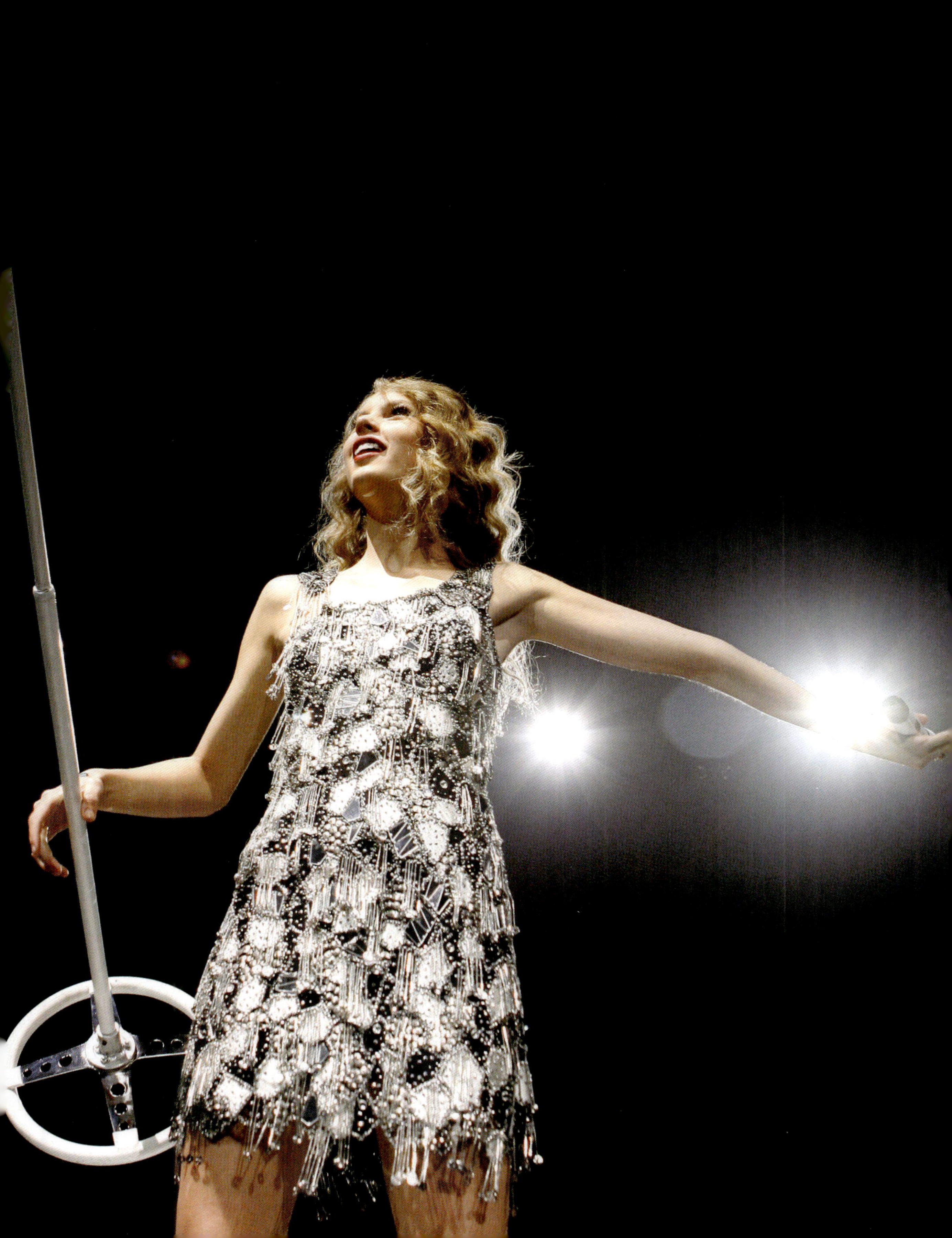

11 RED

Taylor's Version

Track Listing:

1. State Of Grace (Taylor's Version) [4:55]
2. Red (Taylor's Version) [3:43]
3. Treacherous (Taylor's Version) [4:02]
4. I Knew You Were Trouble (Taylor's Version) [3:39]
5. All Too Well (Taylor's Version) [5:29]
6. 22 (Taylor's Version) [3:50]
7. I Almost Do (Taylor's Version) [4:04]
8. We Are Never Ever Getting Back Together (Taylor's Version) [3:13]
9. Stay Stay Stay (Taylor's Version) [3:25]
10. The Last Time (ft. Gary Lightbody) (Taylor's Version) [4:59]
11. Holy Ground (Taylor's Version) [3:22]
12. Sad Beautiful Tragic (Taylor's Version) [4:44]
13. The Lucky One (Taylor's Version) [4:00]
14. Everything Has Changed (ft. Ed Sheeran) (Taylor's Version) [4:05]
15. Starlight (Taylor's Version) [3:40]
16. Begin Again (Taylor's Version) [3:58]
17. The Moment I Knew (Taylor's Version) [4:45]
18. Come Back...Be Here (Taylor's Version) [3:43]
19. Girl At Home (Taylor's Version) [3:40]
20. State Of Grace (Acoustic Version) (Taylor's Version) [5:21]
21. Ronan (Taylor's Version) [4:24]
22. Better Man (Taylor's Version) (From The Vault) [4:57]
23. Nothing New (ft. Phoebe Bridgers) (Taylor's Version) (From The Vault) [4:18]
24. Babe (Taylor's Version) (From The Vault) [3:44]
25. Message In A Bottle (Taylor's Version) (From The Vault) [3:45]
26. I Bet You Think About Me (ft. Chris Stapleton) (Taylor's Version) (From The Vault) [4:45]
27. Forever Winter (Taylor's Version) (From The Vault) [4:23]
28. Run (ft. Ed Sheeran) (Taylor's Version) (From The Vault) [4:00]
29. The Very First Night (Taylor's Version) (From The Vault) [3:20]
30. All Too Well (10 Minute Version) (Taylor's Version) (From The Vault) [10:13]

Recorded at Ballroom West (Los Angeles), Blackbird (Nashville), Capitol B (Los Angeles), Conway Recording (Los Angeles), Electric Lady (New York City), The Garage (Topanga), House Mouse (Stockholm), Instrument Landing (Minneapolis), Kallbacken (Stockholm), Kitty Committee (Belfast), Long Pond (Hudson Valley), Prime Recording (Nashville), Sterloid Sounds (Los Angeles)

Released November 12, 2021

Produced by Taylor Swift, Christopher Rowe, Shellback, Aaron Dessner, Jack Antonoff, Elvira Anderfjärd, Dan Wilson, Jeff Bhasker, Jacknife Lee, Butch Walker, Espionage

Label: Republic Records

Notable personnel:

Chris Stapleton: vocals

Phoebe Bridgers: vocals

Ed Sheeran: vocals, background vocals, acoustic guitar

Jacknife Lee: bass, guitar, keyboards, piano

Owen Pallett: string arrangement

Butch Walker: background vocals, bass, drums, guitar, keyboards, percussion

Aaron Dessner: songwriter, producer, various instruments

Jack Antonoff: songwriter, producer, various instruments

London Symphony Orchestra

Selected awards:

MTV Video Music Awards: Best Director (*All Too Well: The Short Film*)

MTV Video Music Awards: Best Long-Form Video (*All Too Well: The Short Film*)

MTV Video Music Awards: Video of the Year (*All Too Well: The Short Film*)

Billboard Music Awards: Top Country Album; Top Country Artist; Top Country Female Artist; and Top Billboard 200 Artist 2022

American Music Awards: Artist of the Year; Favorite Pop Female Artist; Favorite Country Female Artist; Favorite Country Album; Favorite Pop Album; Favorite Music Video 2022

Grammy Awards: Best Music Video (*All Too Well: The Short Film*)

NME Awards: Best Reissue

Notable honors:

Debuted at number one on Billboard 200

Swift's fourth number one on the Billboard 200 in less than 16 months, setting a new record for achieving the milestone

New record for most single-week new entries (26 tracks) on Billboard Hot 100

"All Too Well (10 Minute Version) (Taylor's Version) (From The Vault)" becomes longest song ever to top Billboard Hot 100

Guinness Book of World Records: Most day-one streams of an album on Spotify (Female)

First female artist with over 100 million Spotify streams in a day

Groundwork that Swift laid with *Red* and its tour, including the iconic hat she wore while performing "22," became unforgettable concert traditions in Swiftian lore.

Kase Wickman: *Red* (*Taylor's Version*) is, of course, most notable for unleashing "All Too Well (10 Minute Version) (Taylor's Version) (From The Vault)" on the world. Did we need it?

Joanna Weiss: When I originally heard that there was a 10-minute version, I thought, "How could that possibly be a good idea?" Then, I listened to it and I wasn't bored. She builds on things in a smart way from a craftsperson's point of view and manages to make it less repetitive than you could imagine it would be. My biggest surprise was when I learned that her relationship with Jake Gyllenhaal lasted three months. You got 10 minutes of serious feels out of this!

KW: And that's the edited-down version! Liz Rose, her co-writer, has said she came to her with about 24 minutes of material, and they edited it down. It feels like a lot of the actual lyrics and base ingredients were there from the original *Red* era.

Moira McAvoy: I don't think we needed the 10-minute version, though. I think "All Too Well" original recipe is a perfect song, and one of Taylor's most well-executed songs, and trying to add to it in the name of fan service and lore building kind of misses what made the original what it was. I think the 10-minute version leans in to a lot of Taylor's less successful creative impulses. Especially the fact that it's 10 minutes and 13 seconds *exactly*—I have mixed feelings on it.

JW: *Red* was always a confusing album, because it's the bridge album. You hit a regular radio listener in 2012 with "We Are Never Ever Getting Back Together" and it was like, what the hell is happening? What is she doing? But I've been proven wrong by so many of Taylor Swift's mic drops. You start with skepticism and come around to, "she somehow made it work."

OPPOSITE: *Red (Taylor's Version)* was, in Jack Antonoff's words, "a wild rollercoaster and a goddamn honor."

138   TAYLOR SWIFT ALBUM BY ALBUM

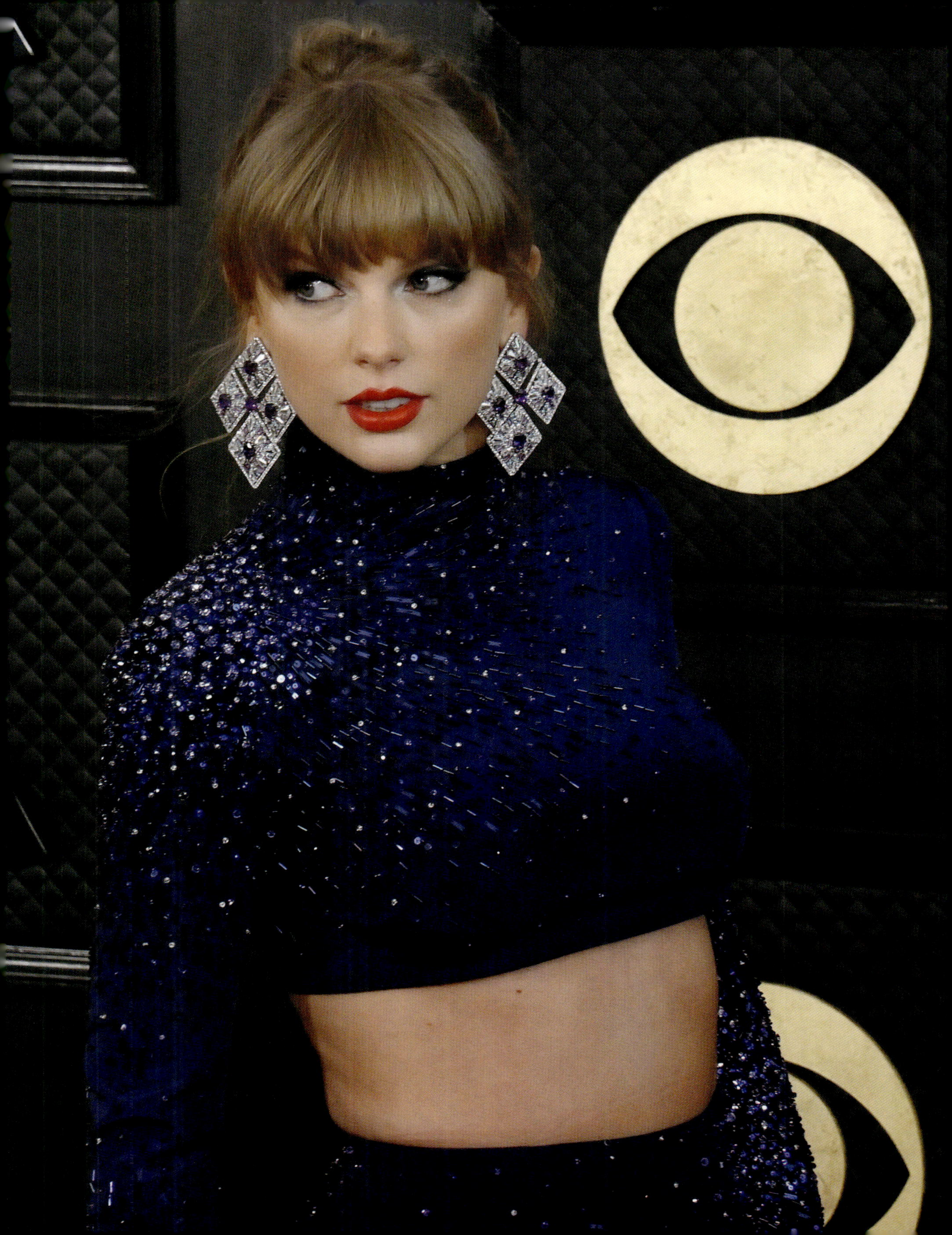

LEFT: **On *Red (Taylor's Version)*, a more mature Swift brought new dimension to performing songs exploring some of her earliest heartbreaks.**

OPPOSITE: **Think 10 minutes is too long? Think again. "You guys sent a 10-minute song to number one for the first time in history honestly WTH," Swift wrote on social media. She also scooped up an MTV Video Music Award, pictured, for best longform video.**

KW: Yes! The number of times I've gone from "I don't know…" to "yes, please" after hearing new Taylor tracks. *Red* was a big turning point for her. What's it like revisiting that evolution on *Taylor's Version* now?

JW: One of the things that struck me about *Red (Taylor's Version)* is that she sounds so much older. You can really hear the 22 to 32 age jump in every song. And she sounds like she's having some fun.

MM: I think she specifically had a lot of fun trying to reclaim the *Red* era for herself. She was going through a lot when she made *Red*. The original album's last track, before the bonus tracks, is "Begin Again." I think there was a lot of joy and healing for her in taking all of that back and having this era on her terms. It seemed like she got a lot of closure, or maybe closure with the idea that she *won't* get closure. Because if you listen to some of it, it's like, "Oh, you're still *very* upset."

KW: We know she wrote something like 25 songs in the year after *Speak Now*, and Big Machine was like, great job, let's effing rock. And she said, "Meh, it feels a little samey to me," scrapped those songs and brought in Shellback and Max Martin to try something new. She was interested in evolving, but not doing something new just to do something new. She wanted it to make sense. This was legitimately her crossover album, and songs from this period were the last time she was nominated for Grammys in a country category. That's such an interesting contradiction, that she is so compelled to move on but is also holding on to all these past things, and still acknowledges and lives with them through the Taylor's Version project and The Eras Tour.

140   TAYLOR SWIFT ALBUM BY ALBUM

RED (TAYLOR'S VERSION)   141

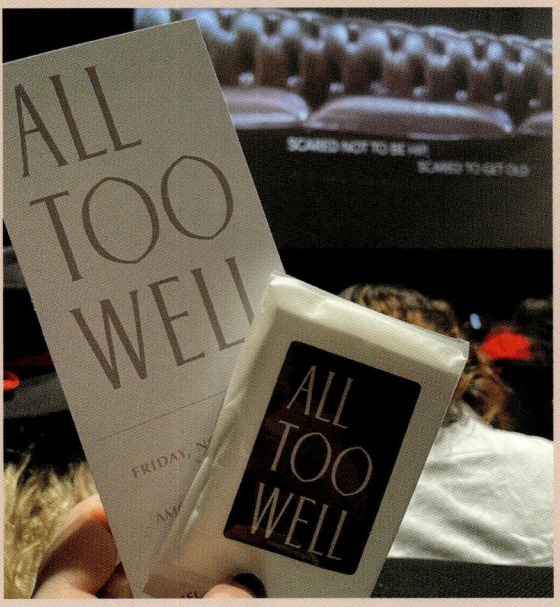

LEFT: **At the Tribeca Film Festival premiere of** *All Too Well: The Short Film*, **audience members were given branded tissues at the door, always a sign something serious is about to go down.**

ABOVE: **Swift played director for** *All Too Well: The Short Film*, **which she presented at the 2022 Tribeca Film Festival.**

JW: Isn't that the whole Taylor Swift thing, though? It's like you're going through a museum and her songs are under glass canisters, and you can visit them. With only that slight tweak of hindsight. Although there's more change on this album. She's injecting it with some modernity via whom she chooses to guest. I don't know whether she was getting bored of doing the Taylor's Versions, or whether she was dissatisfied with *Red* in particular, that made her want to make those tweaks.

142 TAYLOR SWIFT ALBUM BY ALBUM

MM: I hadn't thought about that, with the guests on the Vault Tracks being artists like Phoebe Bridgers, who was not recording music in 2012. Phoebe Bridgers was a child in 2012. It feels like this peek behind the curtain—Taylor tweaking things to fit the modern iteration of her approach to her art. To me, that goes along with having a renewed sense of agency over that era: "I am the artist who can make all of this happen, and here are the people who are exciting me now. If I'm putting this out into the world now, what do I actually want that to mean?"

KW: How do we feel about the Joni Mitchell of it all, especially thinking about the cover art changes? The original *Red* album art was an obvious homage to Mitchell's *Blue*. There are some lines in the song "Blue" that I could see Taylor relating to, where she's saying, "my songs are a tattoo. There's an empty space for you." And Taylor's songwriting, like Mitchell's, centers around the universal living in the specific: "I'm going to talk about this scarf. I'll tell you what color it is. I'll tell you where I was. This is how it smells." She's evoking this very specific image and item that's clearly a tangible thing that exists in the world. I don't have that specific scarf, but it's universal in that I, too, have things that I've held on to that I don't need, and the memory is like picking a scab. The *Taylor's Version* album cover is still an homage to Joni, but tweaked: She's still shadowed, but her eyes are out and visible, unlike the original art.

JW: It's more about Taylor than the title, with this composition.

MM: What's striking me about the new cover is that she is in the car, very prominently, facing the same direction—but she's looking back. It feels very intentional, like "I am moving on from this." Not to sound too literal and cheesy—though Taylor is sometimes literal and cheesy—this time is literally in her rearview mirror. The album title being on a piece of jewelry is also interesting to me, because outside of *folklore* and *evermore*, that's the least obtrusive title she's ever had.

"I just couldn't stop writing," Swift said of the supersized album *Red*, which she made even longer for the *(Taylor's Version)* release.

RED (TAYLOR'S VERSION)

KW: And her name isn't even on this cover.

JW: This art invites sleuthing, right? You have to look really, really closely at everything; you have to pay such meticulous attention to detail. And she knows people are going to do it. She's giving them both challenge and the opportunity.

KW: The other three Taylor's Version albums all have a prologue attached, and *Red (Taylor's Version)* doesn't. It's just the lyrics, plus an image of the handwritten "All Too Well" extended lyrics. Compared to the other Taylor's Versions, the only contextualization or artist's statement she wants to offer in the liner notes is, "Here's the handwritten lyrics for 'All Too Well.' Bye."

MM: By not having a prologue, she's letting the art speak for itself. Like, "I've talked about it. We've said all we need to say. I'm releasing a short movie to say what I need to say. And then the album is just the album, and the album is just for me."

KW: At the Tribeca Film Festival, talking about *Red*, she said, "I write about girlhood a lot, and this was about the moment of girlhood calcifying into bruised adulthood." Being an adult is a never-ending project of iterating on yourself in this way, and she's done it in the public eye.

MM: You have this album where "22" is the breakout single: "Oh my god, I'm an adult, but I'm still so young, everything's great, blah, blah, blah. And then you have, in "All Too Well (10 Minute Version)," the line, "it's supposed to be fun turning twenty-one." It's a very nostalgic look back at what this period of her life *actually* was, despite what she wanted it to be, and then, in the original track ordering, goes directly into "22."

KW: And this album is *long*. Thirty tracks!

MM: On *Red*, you have this exercise in maximalism that she was told is too much at the time. But when you're reclaiming this era of your life, maybe that's where you're like, "Yeah, I am a lot, this is me, have some more."

JW: It feels like she's saying, "I was overindulgent with my feelings at the time, and you are now going to overindulge with me, in a ten-minute song."

KW: "It's about a brief relationship when I was in my early twenties."

MM: Taylor has implied she feels stuck at the age where she became famous—a teenager, on the cusp of adulthood and maturity. *Red* is the album that, in her mind, was about that leap, and then a decade later, she's still feeling trapped there, for lack of a better word, partly because of her level of fame. If you look at songs like "Clara Bow" or "mirrorball," there's this idea she has to keep projecting what she thinks people want of her, and that that's the key to maintaining her success.

JW: She also occasionally, in song, reflects on the life she might have had. That comes up in *Midnights*, too, right? That she might have had an option for normalcy but she really had her eye on the ball. What she wanted, and the way she wanted it, was incompatible with that life.

KW: But the way she talks about feeling stuck is, again, a universal nostalgia, and something she shares and enables and welcomes with her fans. Going to Eras and hearing her sing "22" with the people I was 22 with, I'm just like, *oh*. It feels intentional that she's resurfacing all these songs about the people she's been, and they remind the listeners about all the people they have been and still are within the container that they are now. And that's the bruised adulthood: just pasting layers on layers on layers. When we say she's stuck, I don't necessarily think it's harmful stuck. Maybe it's healthy to be able to acknowledge all the people you have been that make you who you are.

Swift took home an armful of American Music Awards for her work on *Red* (*Taylor's Version*).

RED (TAYLOR'S VERSION) 145

12

By Joanna Weiss

Midnights

Track Listing:

1. Lavender Haze [3:22]
2. Maroon [3:38]
3. Anti-Hero [3:20]
4. Snow On The Beach (ft. Lana Del Rey) [4:16]
5. You're On Your Own, Kid [3:14]
6. Midnight Rain [2:54]
7. Question...? [3:30]
8. Vigilante Shit [2:44]
9. Bejeweled [3:14]
10. Labyrinth [4:07]
11. Karma [3:24]
12. Sweet Nothing [3:08]
13. Mastermind [3:11]

3 a.m. Edition Bonus Tracks:

14. The Great War [4:00]
15. Bigger Than The Whole Sky [3:38]
16. Paris [3:16]
17. High Infidelity [3:51]
18. Glitch [2:28]
19. Would've, Could've, Should've [4:20]
20. Dear Reader [3:45]

The Til Dawn Edition Bonus Tracks:

21. Hits Different [3:54]
22. Snow On The Beach (ft. more Lana Del Rey) [3:49]
23. Karma (ft. Ice Spice) [3:21]

146

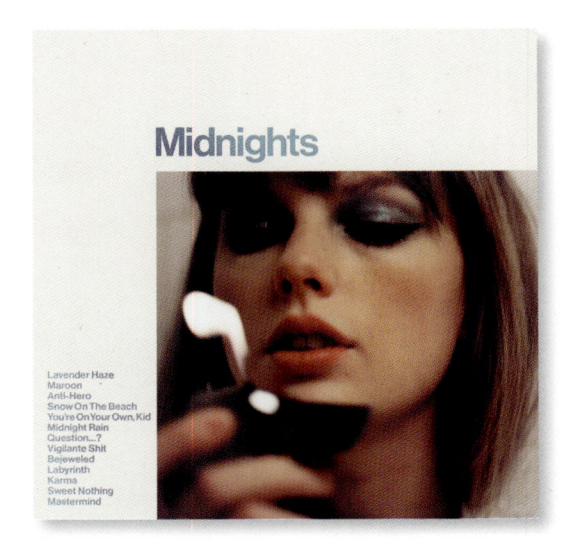

Recorded at Electric Lady (New York City), Henson Recording (Los Angeles), Rough Customer (Brooklyn)

Released October 21, 2022

Produced by Taylor Swift, Jack Antonoff, Sounwave, Jahaan Sweet, Keanu Beats, Aaron Dessner

Label: Republic Records

Standard, Lavender/Deluxe, and 3 a.m. editions released October 21, 2022

Late Night and The Til Dawn editions released May 26, 2023

Selected awards:

Grammy Awards: Album of the Year 2024

Grammy Awards: Best Pop Vocal Album 2024

MTV Video Music Awards: Album of the Year 2023

iHeartRadio Music Awards: Pop Album of the Year 2023

iHeartRadio Music Awards: Song of the Year, "Anti-Hero"

People's Choice Awards: The Album of 2022

Nickelodeon Kids' Choice Awards: Favorite Album 2023 (*Midnights*, 3 a.m. edition)

Notable honors:

12 (nonconsecutive) weeks at number one on the Billboard 200

OPPOSITE: **A larger-than-life ad for *Midnights* looms over the hmv Vault record shop in Birmingham, England—featuring the sultry Taylor photo from the album cover.**

Taylor Swift
Midnights

own it on vinyl & CD

Notable personnel:

Jack Antonoff: percussion, programming, synthesizer, background vocals, drums, Mellotron, Wurlitzer organ, bass, electric guitar, piano, acoustic guitar, crowd noises, slide guitar

Aaron Dessner: percussion, keyboards, synth bass, piano, electric guitar, synthesizer, acoustic guitar, bass, harmonica

Sam Dew: background vocals

Zoë Kravitz: background vocals

Jahaan Sweet: synth pads, bass, flute, synthesizer, keyboards

Sounwave: programming

Dominc Rivinius: snare drum, drums

Evan Smith: saxophone, clarinet, flute, organ, synthesizer, percussion

Bobby Hawk: violin

Dylan O'Brien: drums, crowd noises

Lana Del Rey: vocals

Rachel Antonoff: crowd noises

Austin Swift: crowd noises

Sean Hutchinson: drums, percussion

Mikey Freedom Hart: keyboards, programming, synthesizer, theremin, organ

Keanu Beats: synthesizer

Michael Riddleberger: drums

Zem Audu: saxophone

Kyle Resnick: trumpet

Yuki Numata Resnick: violin

Benjamin Lanz: drums, trombone

James Krivchenia: drums

Bryce Dessner: electric guitar

Bryan Devendorf: drums

James McAllister: drums, synthesizer

Thomas Bartlett: keyboards, synthesizer

Of course, Taylor Swift would be lying awake in the middle of the night. This is an artist who catalogs her thoughts like an archivist, who sifts through the debris of her relationships like an archeologist, who manages her image as meticulously as she crafts her songs, who obsesses over her discourse with fans and her place in the music industry. And who also, by the way, is a typically anxious millennial, navigating the pressures of modern femininity.

There's a lot to think about when the lights go out, and it was surely just a matter of time before Swift would turn those thoughts into songs. This was the concept behind *Midnights*, her 10th studio album, which she teased as "the stories of 13 sleepless nights scattered through my life" and released when the clock struck 12 a.m. Eastern on October 21, 2022. Hours later, she unveiled the 3 a.m. Edition with seven more tracks. When you start to share your secret ruminations—and you happen to be Taylor Swift—it turns out you have a lot to say.

Midnights was a departure for Swift, and also a return. Some assumed that after getting critical raves for the acoustic-driven *folklore* and *evermore*, she would drift back toward her Americana roots. Some thought that after spinning out stories about fictional teenagers, true-crime cases, and real-life heiresses, she would choose to stray farther from her hashed-over autobiography.

Instead, the old Taylor was back—back from the woods, back with the synthesizers cranked to high gear, back to sharing her interior monologue. Except that the Taylor we meet on *Midnights* is different from the ones we've seen before. Yes, she's been troubled, vengeful, even vindictive in songs, but this time the atmosphere is there to match. The music swirls in moody electronic set pieces. The melodies can be so close to monotone that they feel like incantations. On the cover, she stares seductively at the flame from a cigarette lighter, the prom queen donning black, swearing under her breath, and dreaming of setting the school on fire. She might be more relatable than ever.

Everyone has a dark side, after all. And even those of us who don't have a rapt international audience feel the need to shape the image we present to the world. For years, as she stumbled through emotional setbacks and public feuds, challenges in work and challenges in love, Swift worked hard to assert a certain public narrative. She was a heroine. She was a striver. She was a victim of bad actors and manipulators. She was cornered, with no choice but to fight back with the sonic tools at her disposal. In *Midnights*, she suddenly suggests that, in her late-night thoughts and sometimes in real life, she was always a little complicit in the madness.

It takes a certain amount of bravery to share that idea out loud, or maybe just a confidence that you won't be punished for it. When *Midnights* came out, Swift had hit a cultural high. She was a critical darling, solidly back in her fandom's good graces. Her Taylor's Version gambit was a smashing commercial success. She was ensconced in a long-term relationship, with a place to retreat from the noise. There had never been a safer time to share some brutal truths—about the life she had willed into existence and the consequences for her own psyche.

"Anti-Hero," the tongue-in-cheek excavation of Swift's anxieties, won her the Song of the Year award at the iHeartRadio Music Awards.

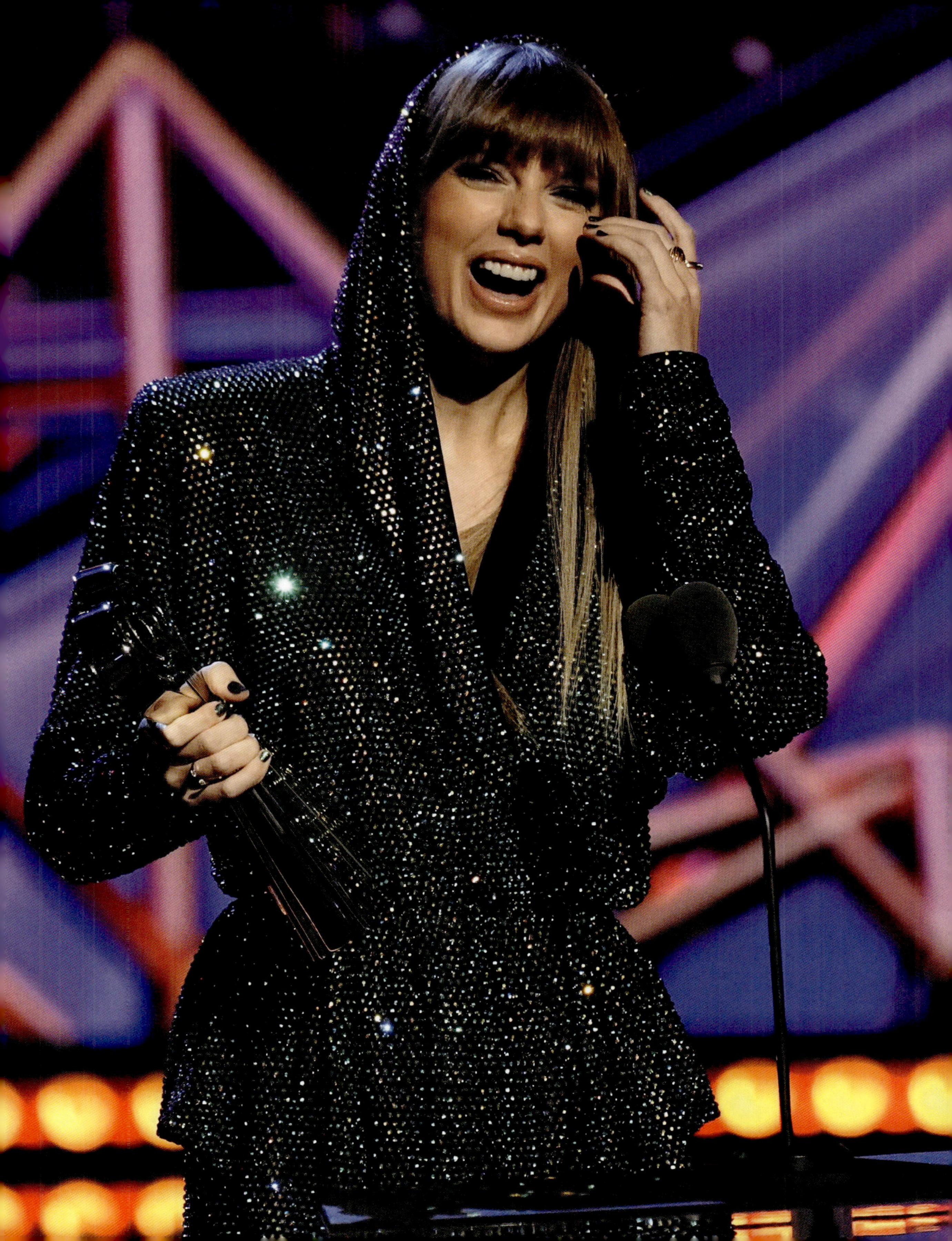

And it turned out, everyone wanted to listen. Within 24 hours of its release, *Midnights* was Spotify's most-streamed album in a single day. It would go on to win Album of the Year and Best Pop Vocal Album at the Grammys and take the top album prize at the MTV Video Music Awards, the People's Choice Awards, and the Nickelodeon Kids' Choice Awards (presumably for the PG version). More significant than the trophies, though, was the way the album would alter the language of Swift World. *Midnights* created a new standard greeting ("It's me, hi…"). It sparked an explosion of friendship bracelets. It gave Swift permission to embrace the complicated, imperfect, sometimes-self-defeating person she is, and still kiss off the haters with a signature Taylor Swift laugh.

Swift must have been laughing about the power she held over pop culture as she orchestrated the *Midnights* rollout. It was a mix of peeling back the curtain—sharing her week-one publicity plan, for instance, in an Instagram post—and toying with her fandom, like a cat playing with its prey. She first announced the album at the 2022 VMAs, promising more information at midnight that night, setting a countdown clock on her website. Later, she launched a TikTok series dubbed "Midnights Mayhem With Me" where she revealed a new song title every day, using an old-fashioned Bingo cage and an oversized red phone receiver as props.

The vibe was playful, quirky, and the tiniest bit sinister, part *Austin Powers* and part *Twin Peaks*, and a perfect match for the album as a whole. Mostly co-written and co-produced by Jack Antonoff, with a sprinkling of Aaron Dessner in the 3 a.m. installments, the *Midnights* tracks are layered with sound and loaded with effects that feel like characters themselves. Swift's voice is breathy and low, sometimes altered electronically to the point that it's unrecognizable. The songs are a swirl of dark dreams, deep doubts, and full-on revenge fantasies, with a sly sense of humor running through nearly all of them.

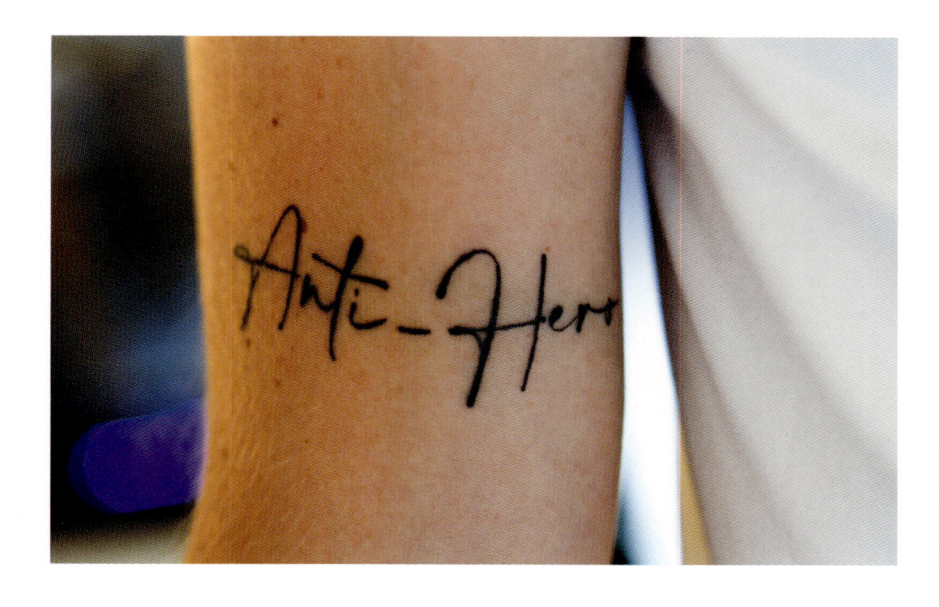

How relatable was Taylor Swift's dark persona? A fan in Germany got a tattoo of her song title.

Taylor Swift and Joe Alwyn in a rare public sighting in 2019. Their relationship was, for a time, a refuge from the madness—and he co-wrote the song "Sweet Nothings" under a pseudonym, William Bowery.

That vision is most realized in "Anti-Hero," the debut single and opening statement, a mix of brutal honesty about her insecurities and self-awareness about how absurd her problems must look to the outside world. In the tongue-in-cheek video, a wide-eyed Taylor stumbles through horror movie tropes and Alice-in-Wonderland dreamscapes and exchanges drink after drink with a dark-id version of herself. She enacts a nightmare involving fictional grown-up children who murder her for her money, and conjures a way to get revenge from the grave. And she pokes fun of her own tics, from her performative generosity to her overuse of social media. (An online backlash followed a brief scene where she stepped on a scale that read "FAT," and the offending shot was retrospectively edited out. The internet monster isn't just a phantom in Swift's mind.)

For much of *Midnights*, Swift returns to her old habit of excavating past romances and examining her emotional states. It's tempting to play detective and pinpoint a moment in time for each song, but she keeps things metaphoric enough to blur the record. "Lavender Haze," the thrummy opener, explores the start of a relationship, when she tries to block out the skeptics and the inner doubts and just luxuriate in the present. "Snow On The Beach" is a treatise on the rules of attraction, with Lana Del Rey's vocals shimmering in the background and her hazy aesthetic hovering in the foreground.

MIDNIGHTS

In "Labyrinth"—a stated favorite of *Rolling Stone* Swiftologist Rob Sheffield— synth lines swirl like eddies as she contemplates the risk of starting something new. In "Sweet Nothings," co-written by then-boyfriend Joe Alwyn, she allows herself to hope as she describes a relationship that's a refuge from the pressures of the world, her chord progression subtly shifting from minor key to major.

Swift's catchy bonus songs tend to be the most earnest, from the wailing "Would've, Could've, Should've" to the plaintive "Hits Different" and the sorrowful "Bigger Than The Whole Sky," which some fans took as the heartbreakingly perfect description of emotions after a miscarriage. But *Midnights* also leads us, again and again, to self-criticism. ("Isn't it fascinating how quickly we vacillate between self-love and self-loathing at this hour?" she wrote in the liner notes.) In "Maroon," with its throbbing bass, Swift dwells on the memories that linger at the end of an affair; she'd assigned colors to the stages of a relationship in "Red," but she never got as grim as this. In "Question...?" and "High Infidelity," she ponders forbidden trysts and the act of dragging someone else down with her. In "Vigilante Shit," where the hi-hat ticks like a time bomb, she takes on the persona of a mistress who exacts punishment on the cheater. If it's a little on the nose—like a femme fatale costume she found at Party City—you can't fault her for enjoying the bash.

If not all of those songs would make it to the top of the Taylor Swift canon, maybe it's because they tread common ground, picking apart her human-level relationships. The most resonant singles on *Midnights* play with the public Taylor, a larger-than-life creation of her own unrelenting will.

"Midnight Rain," where the altered-voice effect looms heavily, finds Swift wrestling with the trade-offs she's made for her career—fleeting moments of regret, offset by the admission that this extraordinarily public existence was the path she truly wanted. Track 5, "You're On Your Own, Kid," tracks her progression from dreamy ingenue to battle-scarred player and muses on the loneliness of success and the value of self-love. "Bejeweled" is a cheerier variation on that theme, a personal pump-up anthem and a statement of survival, with a video that luxuriates in over-the-top glamour and feeds her fandom's appetite for Easter eggs.

But she seems to be enjoying herself the most in "Karma." Built off a dreamy, distorted sample from Australian producer Keanu Beats, it spins a triumphant story of someone who took her knocks, again and again, and came out on top. In the video, Swift is variously dressed as Nemesis, the Greek goddess of retribution; Dorothy from *The Wizard of Oz*; and, most tellingly, the filament in a light bulb, slaying her demons with ideas. Lyrically, "Karma" is an Easter egg hunt of its own: Which past tormenter is getting a comeuppance with which sly line? Gone is the indifference she feigned in *Lover*. She's relishing the sweetness of revenge.

Except that small-k karma doesn't come close to explaining everything that has happened to Taylor Swift, Inc. It's not some benevolent force or deep cosmic vibration that propelled Swift to the top of the musical universe. It's a superhuman drive, a refusal to lose, a willingness to make bold plans and see them through.

OPPOSITE: **Swift closed out The Eras Tour with her** *Midnights* **era, culminating with "Karma."**

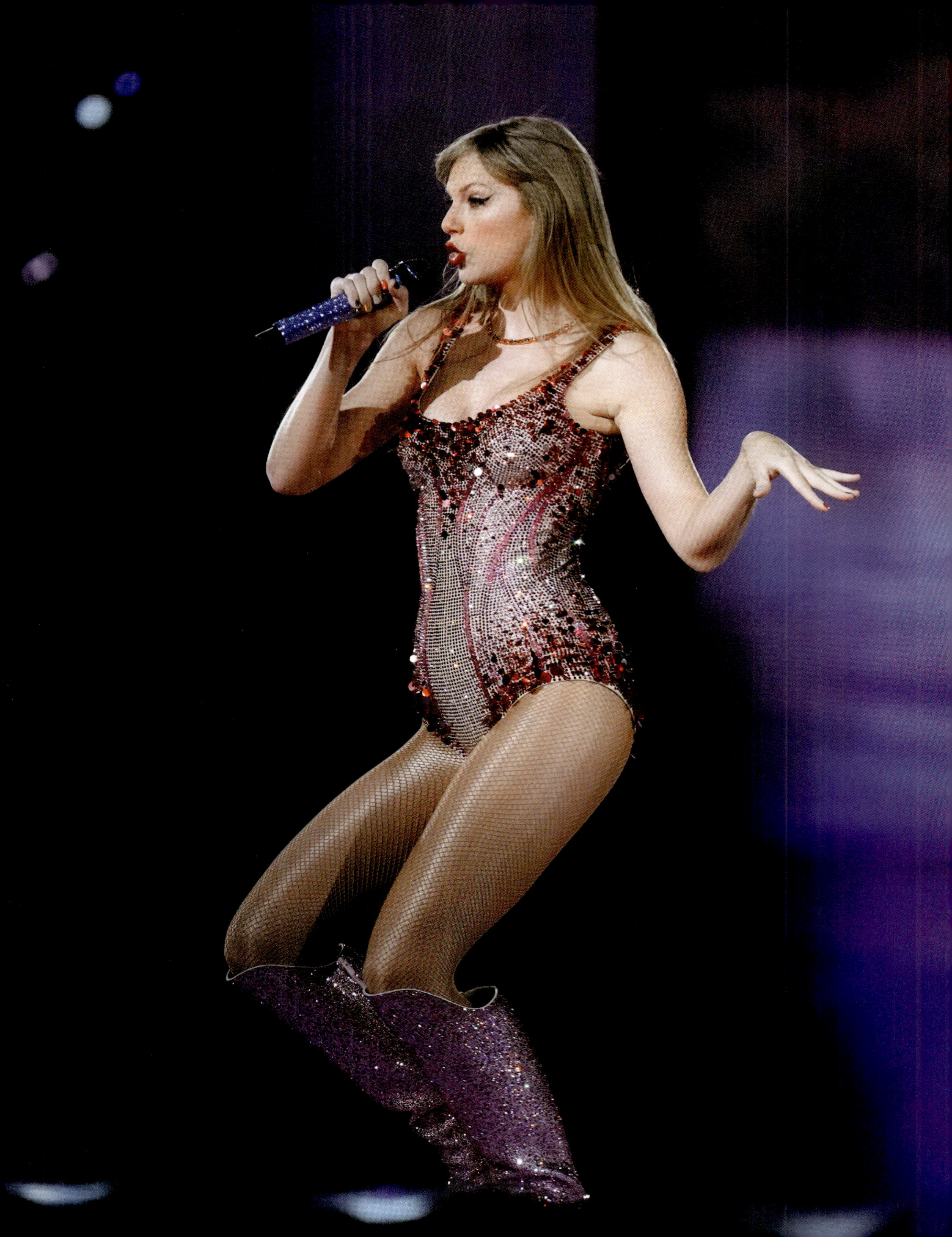

NO SONG, FOR SO LONG

IT'S ONE OF the most popular, replayable, sing-along-worthy songs on *Midnights*. And it didn't make it onto Spotify for six months.

That would be "Hits Different," Swift's upbeat-yet-downcast song about breakup and regret, co-written by Jack Antonoff and Aaron Dessner, and guaranteed to burrow into the recesses of your brain. It's visceral and profane, with a bridge that Swift has described as one of her favorites and a haunting final verse that suggests that its protagonist—whether it's a fictional character or Taylor herself—is going off the deep end. In other words, it has everything.

But it wasn't on the original edition of *Midnights*. Or the 3 a.m. Edition. Or four of the physical editions (Jade Green, Moonstone Blue, Mahogany, and Blood Moon, whose back covers combined to make a clock). For six months, you could play "Hits Different" only if you went to Target and purchased the retailer's exclusive deluxe Lavender Edition, which included the song as a bonus track. Swift finally unleashed the streaming version on May 26, 2023, in a *Midnights: The Til Dawn Edition* release that also included a "Snow On The Beach" re-take with more Lana Del Rey vocals and a "Karma" remix featuring Ice Spice.

This is what happens in the modern music industry—at least, when it comes to a certain entrepreneurial artist whose financial dealings hinge on retail partnerships, overlapping products, complex contractual timing arrangements, and efforts to drum up buzz and sales with tantalizing record drops. There will be waiting. And there will be payoff: Within three months, "Hits Different" had surpassed 200 million streams on Spotify. And whenever Swift played it on The Eras Tour as a surprise song—even a week after its streaming release—the stadium sang along, word for word.

Another album, another Target exclusive.

TAYLOR SWIFT ALBUM BY ALBUM

Weeks after *Midnights* came out, Swift lifted a detail from one of her lyrics and wore cat-eye makeup to the MTV Europe Music Awards.

That's the message of "Mastermind," the final track of the original 13. A proud confession of her scheming that manages to squeeze in the word "Machiavellian," it ends with a twist: The object of her machinations knew what she was doing all along, and wanted it this way.

This was, by now, the story of Swift's post–Taylor's Versions public life. She embraced her fans as pseudo friends, but held them at arms' length. She set them off on scavenger hunts and sometimes led them astray. She held the cards, she played the tease, and they kept coming back for more.

Which all suggests that *Midnights* was another puzzle piece in her master plan. If those late-night ideas had been simmering for years, there had to be a reason she was unleashing them now. Perhaps she was thinking about her next earthquake of a career move, something bigger and louder than anything she'd done before. Perhaps it would help, as she plotted it all out, to be in possession of a buzzy new album that re-established her pop credentials. On *The Tonight Show* the week that *Midnights* came out, she sat on Jimmy Fallon's couch in a loud checkered pantsuit and dropped a tantalizing hint.

Fallon: You haven't toured in, like, four years. We want you to.
Swift (with a knowing smile): I think I should do it.
Fallon: Are we talking sooner than later?
Swift: You know, I should do it.

A week later, she announced The Eras Tour. If anything was going to cement Taylor Swift's victory over the doubters, liars, and cheats—to meet her sky-high expectations or surpass her wildest dreams—this tour would be it. And it's surely no accident that "Karma" closed it out.

While promoting *Midnights*, Taylor announced her next big move: The Eras tour.

156 TAYLOR SWIFT ALBUM BY ALBUM

THE TAYLOR SWIFT GRAMMY AWARDS

THE 66TH GRAMMY Awards came a mere three days before the Asian leg of The Eras Tour, but Taylor Swift was present at the party—managing, with every moment on camera, to upstage a major awards show and make the night about her.

There was her grand entrance at the Crypto.com Arena, stalking through the ballroom fashionably late, in the middle of host Trevor Noah's monologue. (Noah joked she was boosting the economy of every table she passed.) There was the moment when she hijacked her own acceptance speech for Best Pop Vocal Album to announce her surprise new album, *The Tortured Poets Department*. (She had announced *Midnights* two years earlier at the MTV Video Music Awards, to a more rapturous response than she got inside the Grammys arena.)

There was the moment she seemed to avoid eye contact with Celine Dion, who handed her the trophy for Album of the Year. (Swift executed a quick PR recovery response, posting a photo of herself embracing Dion backstage.) There was the way she grabbed the hand of fellow Album of the Year nominee Lana Del Rey and pulled her onstage for the victory speech. (Some observers thought it was awkward. Del Rey later posted online she was fine.)

In an earlier time, the online backlash to any one of these controversies would have stung. But by this point, Taylor was inoculated. As she jetted off to Japan to play more sold-out stadiums, she must have known she had given her audience exactly what it wanted: another reason to talk about Taylor Swift.

At the Grammy Awards, Swift's 13th award (for Pop Vocal Album) seemed secondary to her big announcement: another new album was coming.

MIDNIGHTS 157

Swift had announced the existence of *Midnights* when she accepted the Video of the Year award at the MTV Video Music Awards.

ABOVE: **To sing "Lavender Haze" on The Eras Tour, Taylor embraced light purple, faux fur, and a sly attitude.**

RIGHT: **Swift and Lana Del Rey—whose vocals infuse the song "Snow On The Beach"—sat together at the 66th Grammy Awards. When Swift beat out Del Rey for Album of the Year, she pulled her friend up onstage.**

13

Speak Now

TAYLOR'S VERSION

Track Listing:

1. Mine (Taylor's Version) [3:51]
2. Sparks Fly (Taylor's Version) [4:21]
3. Back To December (Taylor's Version) [4:54]
4. Speak Now (Taylor's Version) [4:02]
5. Dear John (Taylor's Version) [6:45]
6. Mean (Taylor's Version) [3:58]
7. The Story Of Us (Taylor's Version) [4:27]
8. Never Grow Up (Taylor's Version) [4:52]
9. Enchanted (Taylor's Version) [5:53]
10. Better Than Revenge (Taylor's Version) [3:40]
11. Innocent (Taylor's Version) [5:01]
12. Haunted (Taylor's Version) [4:05]
13. Last Kiss (Taylor's Version) [6:09]
14. Long Live (Taylor's Version) [5:17]
15. Ours (Taylor's Version) [3:55]
16. Superman (Taylor's Version) [4:34]
17. Electric Touch (ft. Fall Out Boy) (Taylor's Version) (From The Vault) [4:26]
18. When Emma Falls in Love (Taylor's Version) (From The Vault) [4:12]
19. I Can See You (Taylor's Version) (From the Vault) [4:33]
20. Castles Crumbling (ft. Hayley Williams) (Taylor's Version) (From The Vault) [5:06]
21. Foolish One (Taylor's Version) (From The Vault) [5:11]
22. Timeless (Taylor's Version) (From The Vault) [5:21]

Recorded at Big Mercy (Brooklyn), Blackbird (Nashville), The Clubhouse (Rhinebeck), The Dwelling (New York City), EBC (London), Electric Lady (New York City), Hutchinson Sound (Brooklyn), Kitty Committee (Belfast), Long Pond (Hudson Valley), Pleasure Hill (Portland), Prime Recording (Nashville), Rough Customer (Brooklyn), Sound House (Lakeland)

Released July 7, 2023

Produced by Taylor Swift, Christopher Rowe, Aaron Dessner, Jack Antonoff

Label: Republic Records

Notable personnel:

Patrick Stump (Fall Out Boy): electric guitar and vocals "Electric Touch (Taylor's Version)"

Hayley Williams (Paramore): vocals "Castles Crumbling (Taylor's Version)"

London Contemporary Orchestra: strings "Back To December (Taylor's Version)," "Enchanted (Taylor's Version)," "Haunted (Taylor's Version)"

Selected awards:

Billboard Music Awards: Nominated but lost Top Country Album 2023

Notable honors:

2 weeks at number one on Billboard 200

Swift's 12th album to top the Billboard 200 chart, a new all-time record for the most number-one albums by a female artist; most consecutive years (5) with a new number-one album

All 22 tracks charted on the Billboard Hot 100

Record broken: The most single-day streams for a country album on Spotify

First woman to chart four albums in *Billboard*'s Top 10 in the same week; first woman and living soloist to chart 11 albums simultaneously; first to have nine albums each sell at least 500,000 copies in a week

Kase Wickman: *Speak Now* was originally released October 25, 2010, and *Taylor's Version* was released July 7, 2023. She went from being on the edge of 21 to 33-and-a-half when this came out. That's quite a jump. In its various forms, how do you feel about *Speak Now*?

Moira McAvoy: *Speak Now* was, for many years, until *evermore* came out, my favorite Taylor Swift album. "Long Live" dropping my senior year of high school alone is enough. It is, beginning to end, her only self-written album. I don't know if *Taylor's Version* actually sticks the landing like the original album. I love that the album overall really leaned in to country and pop-punk and rock as genres and how a lot of the songs dive in and out of genres. Something about her being 17 to 19 years old brings a lot of important excitement and passion to the original album. That's hard to capture in the same way more than a decade later.

Joanna Weiss: She really is advancing as a lyricist, even though a lot of it feels self-indulgent, emotionally. Which is, again, where she was—and which I think I can forgive and indulge more when she's 20 than when she's 33, which is the core of my issue with songs like "Dear John." *Lover* feels to me like an album that someone in their 30s would write. It's an "I'm an adult now and it's sort of weird!" album. *Speak Now* is, "I'm almost 20, holy shit, I'm not going to be a teenager for long anymore, but I'm feeling the feels, and what am I going to do?" It really feels like a snapshot of that moment.

MM: There was something about seeing Taylor in that stage of her career where everything seems possible if she has ownership of it and she's still excited about it, while also processing a lot of seemingly big and traumatic feelings. It's a sad album at the core. Her parents are getting divorced during the Speak Now World Tour. She's writing "All Too Well," apparently, on the tour. I think *Taylor's Version* left something to be desired, because I think a lot of that passion and excitement are gone, which I think is the result of being 33 years old instead of 19, and not actively going through that moment. Back when people didn't know when the Taylor's Versions were going to be released, it looked possible that *Speak Now* (*Taylor's Version*) would come out when Taylor was 32. People wondered, what is she going to do with that line in "Innocent": "32 and still growing up now"?

KW: Although it's funny—with that song, she has the line, "who you are is not who you've been." Taylor's whole thesis is that who you are *is* who you've been. It may not be who you are anymore, but who you *have been* is so important to who you are.

JW: We talked, with *Fearless* (*Taylor's Version*), about how she established that she was truly recreating the tracks, as opposed to reinventing the tracks. Would you have wanted her to reinvent these *Speak Now* tracks a little more, do more than just note for note and laugh for laugh, really take the songs apart?

MM: I think there's something compelling about seeing what her thought process was going into each album through listening for differences on the Taylor's Versions. With *Speak Now* (*Taylor's Version*), we didn't get that peek behind the curtain. That was not, seemingly, a great time in her personal life, so it would make sense for her to not really want to dig into that process or those emotions again in the same way she did with the other albums.

JW: As a teenager, a lot of excuses are made for you: It's okay, because everyone knows how horrible and hormonal teenagers are. At 19, you're an adult. You're not necessarily equipped to be an adult by our society, but you are expected to be an adult. And again, you're expected to have these very mature reactions and emotions, make decisions. When I was 19, I was a total moron. I was feeling a lot of things, and I was literally trying to figure out who I was.

KW: When I die, burn my journals! I think about that a lot listening to this album. There are so many things in my life I wish I could do differently, and I feel like it's ballsy for her to go back and be like, "Okay, I'm not reinventing this. I'm not rewriting." There are a few notable changes, but to have your 19-year-old-self's words come out of your adult mouth and be like, "Yeah, that's me"—that's bold. In the prologue to this Taylor's Version, she talks about

Vault track "When Emma Falls In Love" was reportedly inspired by longtime pal Emma Stone. Here, Swift supports Stone on the red carpet of Stone's 2010 comedy *Easy A*.

SPEAK NOW (TAYLOR'S VERSION)   163

"It's here. It's yours, it's mine, it's ours," Swift wrote on the release day of *Speak Now (Taylor's Version)*, calling it "an album I wrote alone about the whims, fantasies, heartaches, dramas, and tragedies I lived out as a young woman between 18 and 20."

self-criticism and internalizing others' criticism and wishing she'd spoken up for herself over and over in her career. What do you think of her commentary here around ownership, both of her own work and of her actions?

JW: I've watched and re-watched the VMAs Kanye moment, and that was the thing that really struck me: She was, in that moment, mute. She did not know how to react, which is not a criticism. I don't know how anyone could viably react to an unexpected moment like that. Beyoncé called her back onto the stage to complete her speech, and she didn't say anything about the Kanye moment, even to the press.

She waited and waited and waited to respond to that until she was able, basically, to respond to it in music. It's interesting to hear her articulate that regret and that motivation.

MM: Something that started with *Speak Now* is the tightrope she's been walking with her fame and what she does or doesn't say publicly, and what she does or doesn't say in her songs. The more stratospherically famous she's gotten, the less she comments outside of song. That sense of restraint does actually make sense for what did or didn't change on *Speak Now (Taylor's Version)*, and she's obviously very aware of it.

TAYLOR SWIFT ALBUM BY ALBUM

KW: Yes, she's become more conscious of the megaphone she holds, and that this level of fame is a lose-lose situation. In the prologue to the original release, she also talks about regretting staying quiet in the moment, but suggests things like writing a letter you'll never send, or publishing a book and saying what you need to say. It's less direct than her updated version. What do we think of this shift?

JW: Writing a letter you'll never send is really good adult advice. I do it all the time: Get it out, say it to yourself, but don't hit "send" until you've taken a walk around the block, and then you rewrite it.

MM: But then you have "Dear John" as the track 5 on this album: the letter she didn't send, but thankfully *did* sing.

KW: How about the album art? The original album cover is her last princessy ballgown, and the *Taylor's Version* is more mature, and reads to me as still posed but more organic. It's a similar idea to the original, but evolved.

JW: It's like those projects where you take a picture once every year. You really can see how she has grown up: She's a girl in one and a woman in another, literally. It's just striking to see how young she looks. It underscores the idea we talked about: Here's this 30-year-old, reliving 19.

MM: There is no text on the cover whatsoever, and the whole conceit of the album is what you do or don't say. "How do I say it through music? What stories am I telling?" Just letting the album speak for itself when she had so much regret around overcommunicating or undercommunicating before is a really powerful message, especially with that direct gaze into the camera that she's replicated between the two covers.

KW: And maybe, on an album that's all about regret and forgiveness—of herself and others—she's finding peace through accepting that the past is past, and that she can re-record and re-examine, but fundamentally, it's not going to change. Like she's saying, yes, I acknowledge and now, literally, own all these past versions of who I've been, and I recognize how they make me who I am. 🦋

Taylor Lautner, the inspiration for "Back To December," has since married another woman named Taylor, who is also a Swiftie.

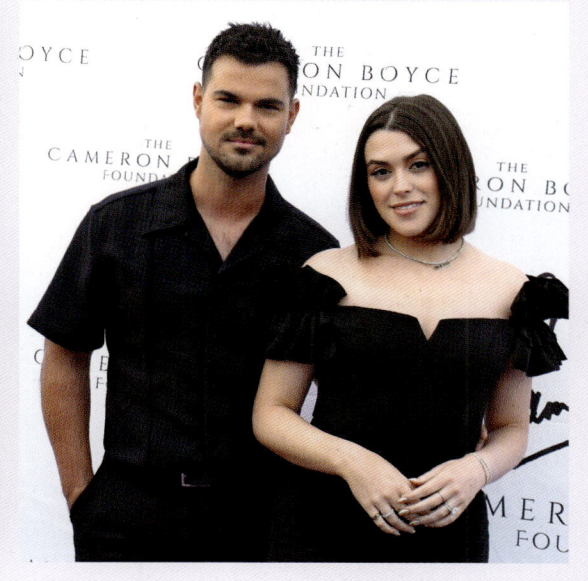

Taylor Lautner and his wife, known widely as "Girl Taylor," shared videos on TikTok ahead of the album's release set to "Dear John," showing Lautner in a hotel robe with his head bowed in prayer. The hashtag? #prayforjohn.

SPEAK NOW (TAYLOR'S VERSION)

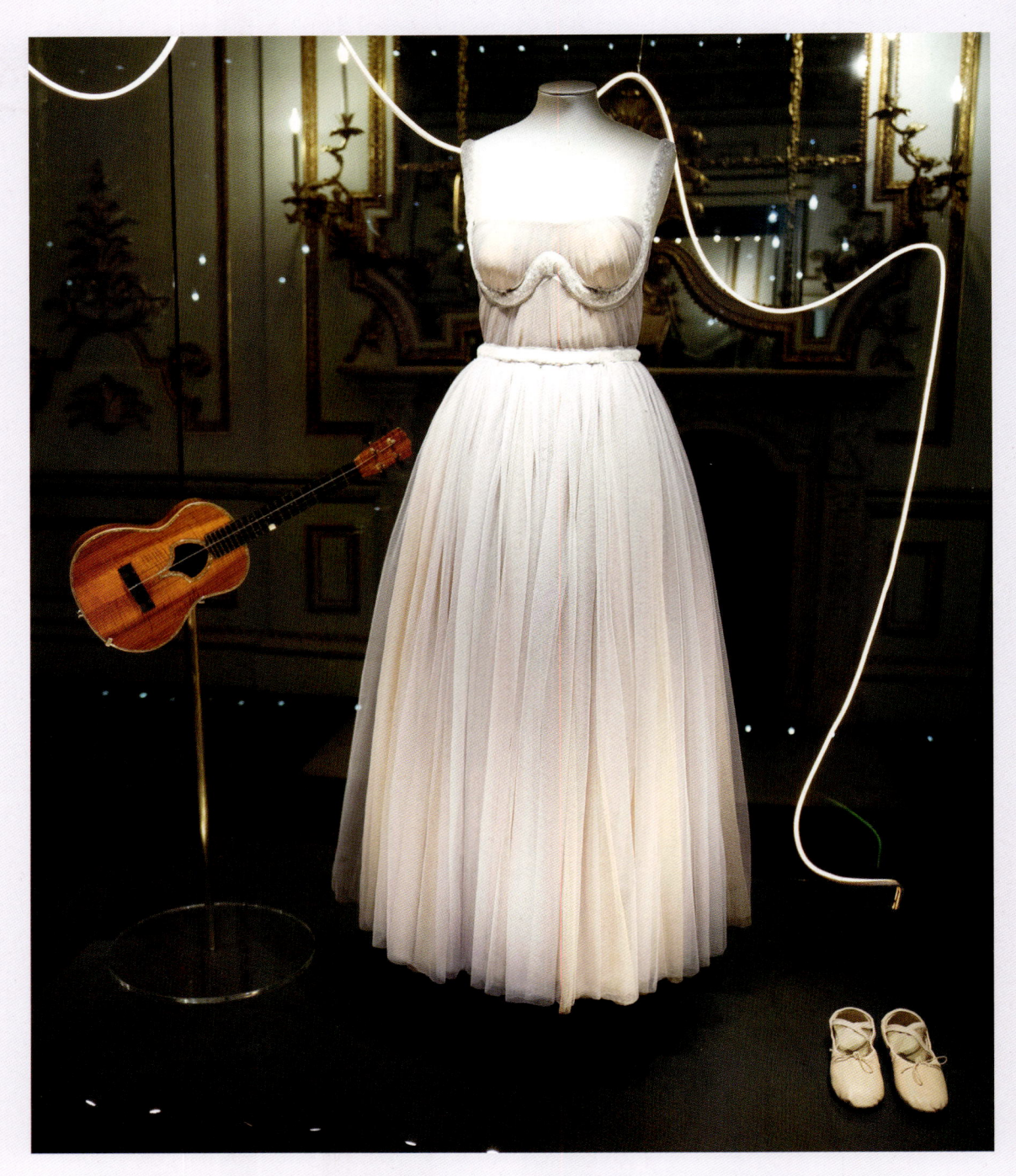

ABOVE: **It belongs in a museum! The dreamy Reem Acra-designed dress Swift wore on the re-released album's back cover was part of a traveling exhibit.**

OPPOSITE: **Another dynamic album, another unforgettable outfit. The *Taylor's Version* songs, recaptured and reclaimed, were as dynamic and impactful to herself and her fans as her Eras Tour outfits. This shimmering bodysuit became one of (if not *the*) look that defined her record-breaking tour.**

TAYLOR SWIFT ALBUM BY ALBUM

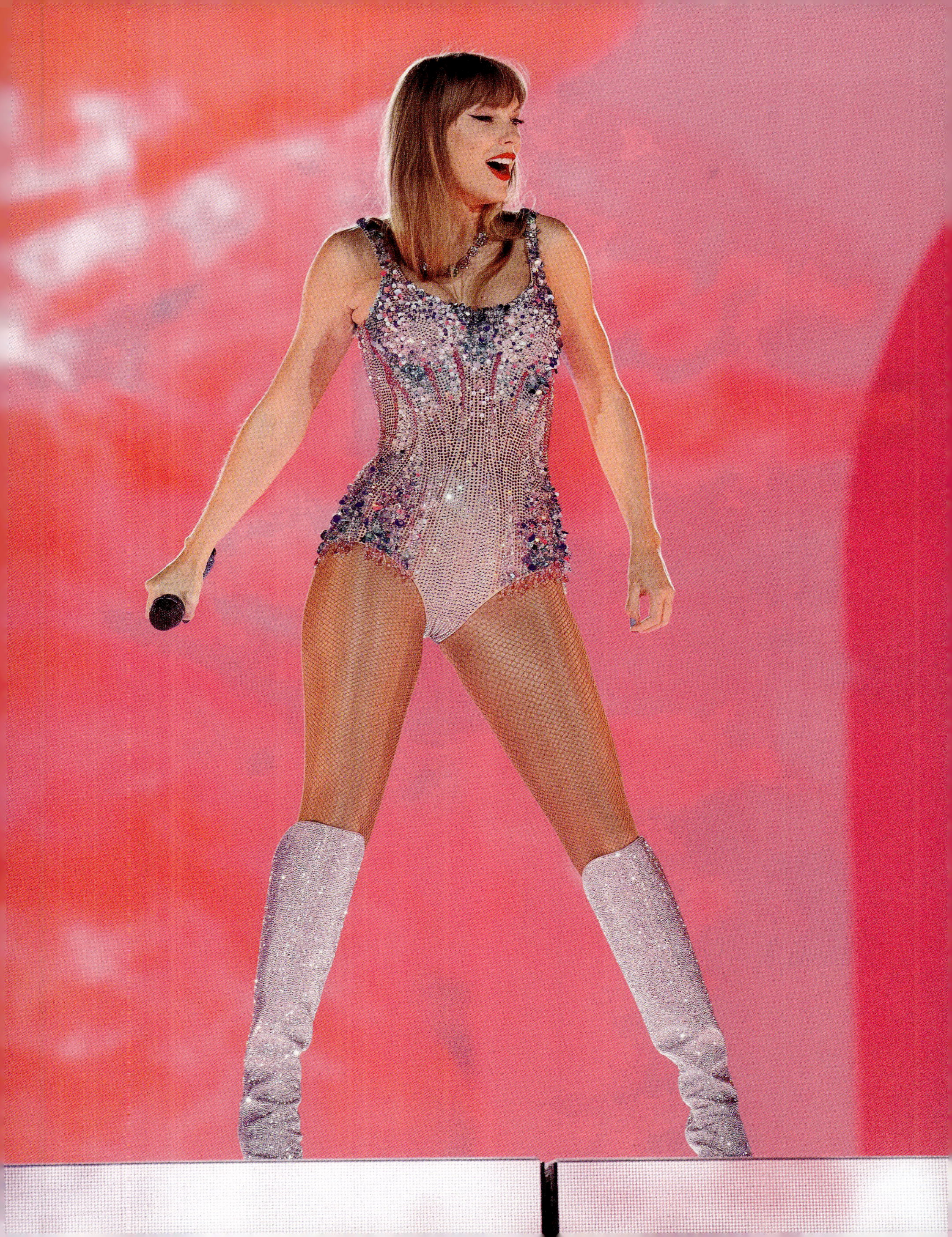

14

1989

TAYLOR'S VERSION

Track Listing:

1. Welcome To New York (Taylor's Version) [3:32]
2. Blank Space (Taylor's Version) [3:51]
3. Style (Taylor's Version) [3:51]
4. Out Of The Woods (Taylor's Version) [3:55]
5. All You Had To Do Was Stay (Taylor's Version) [3:13]
6. Shake It Off (Taylor's Version) [3:39]
7. I Wish You Would (Taylor's Version) [3:27]
8. Bad Blood (Taylor's Version) [3:31]
9. Wildest Dreams (Taylor's Version) [3:40]
10. How You Get The Girl (Taylor's Version) [4:07]
11. This Love (Taylor's Version) [4:10]
12. I Know Places (Taylor's Version) [3:15]
13. Clean (Taylor's Version) [4:31]
14. Wonderland (Taylor's Version) [4:05]
15. You Are In Love (Taylor's Version) [4:27]
16. New Romantics (Taylor's Version) [3:50]

From The Vault:

17. "Slut!" (Taylor's Version) (From The Vault) [3:00]
18. Say Don't Go (Taylor's Version) (From The Vault) [4:39]
19. Now That We Don't Talk (Taylor's Version) (From The Vault) [2:26]
20. Suburban Legends (Taylor's Version) (From The Vault) [2:51]
21. Is It Over Now? (Taylor's Version) (From The Vault) [3:49]

Tangerine Edition Bonus Track:

22. Sweet Than Fiction (Taylor's Version) (Tangerine Edition) [3:54]

Deluxe Edition Bonus Track:

23. Bad Blood (ft. Kendrick Lamar) (Taylor's Version) [3:20]

Recorded at Audu (Brooklyn), Big Mercy (Brooklyn), Conway Recording (Los Angeles), Electric Lady (New York City), The Hideaway (London), Hutchinson Sound (Brooklyn), Kitty Committee (New York, London, Belfast), Mandarin Oriental (Milan), Pleasure Hill (Portland), Prime Recording (Nashville), Rough Costumer (Brooklyn), Sharp Sonics (Los Angeles), Studio 112 (Jonstorp)

Released October 27, 2023

Produced by Taylor Swift, Christopher Rowe, Jack Antonoff, Ryan Tedder, Noel Zancanella, Imogen Heap, Shellback, Patrik Berger

Label: Republic Records

Notable personnel:

Imogen Heap: background vocals, drums, kalimba, keyboards, percussion, programming, vibraphone

Kendrick Lamar: vocals

Jack Antonoff: programming, synthesizer, electric guitar, bass guitar, drums, acoustic guitar, background vocals, Mellotron, percussion

Ryan Tedder: background vocals, piano, synthesizer, acoustic guitar, drum programming, electric guitar, programming

Noel Zancanella: drum programming, synthesizer, bass guitar, programming

Mike Meadows: synthesizer, acoustic guitar, electric guitar, background vocals, synthesizer programming

Amos Heller: bass guitar, synth bass

Christopher Rowe: background vocals, trumpet

Paul Sidoti: electric guitar, background vocals

Patrik Berger: bass guitar, electric guitar, programming, synthesizer

Tangerine edition released October 27, 2023

Deluxe edition released October 27, 2023

Total units sold: 2,000,000 (as of January 2024)

Selected awards:

Nominated for a Juno award

Notable honors:

6 weeks at number one on the Billboard 200

Taylor's 13th number-one album

Records broken: Most weeks at number one as a solo artist (per Billboard); first-ever album to sell more than 1,000,000 vinyl copies in a calendar year

Moira McAvoy: Let's chat about album art.

Kase Wickman: This is the first Taylor's Version where she offered different versions of the art. You can choose your own adventure: Which reinvented Taylor would you like? Is your flavor here? She's talked about the album art for Original Recipe, where she was saying, "Interpret this how you want. I don't want to show what emotion I want you to feel. I'm just giving you this snapshot of this moment in my life, a literal snapshot." But in these, she was revealing more of herself. Here, she's free and open. She's on the beach. She's alone on the beach. But these photos are candid enough that you feel someone there. Her friends could have taken this photo.

Joanna Weiss: It's New York as—I'm gonna say it—a blank slate, a place where you rewrite yourself and your story. That exuberance in the re-record is the feeling she can rewrite her story again and again in this setting. She had to walk through fire to get this opportunity. She chose to walk through the fire. Now she's reentering, and as she says in the prologue, she's reinventing.

MM: The prologue even starts with a story about cutting off her youthful Cinderella locks. New city, new haircut, new person.

KW: Culturally, cutting your hair is a sign of grief. She's not necessarily cutting bangs here, but it's like breakup grief.

JW: Very explicitly, you're saying good-bye to a part of yourself. You have made this choice to excise a part of yourself.

MM: I think it's a personal choice she made, but artistically, it's also really cogent. The last real formal track on original-recipe *Red* is "Begin Again." It's this idea of moving out from that narrative—and also, here, moving into that entirely different version of herself, that takes place in New York. This album is the vehicle for that. The idea of having long hair as you get older is seen as more childish, so the cut brings a sense of moving on from adolescence. She's saying, "This is my adulthood, this is my agency."

On the re-record, I think there's a sense of confidence that you can also hear as more evident with 10 years of distance in her voice. I was listening to "Welcome To New York," and she sounds triumphant in the re-recording of that song.

JW: The original version has that wide-eyed feeling: "I'm 23, I just moved to a new city and I'm making it my whole personality." This exercise of re-recording and revisiting your own work with a decade of distance is a really interesting project because your whole perspective changes, and I don't think you can help but put that into the music.

MM: I agree—especially for artists whose work is so personal and autobiographical. To me, *1989* feels like the bridge in her discography where it goes from lowercase "taylor swift" to uppercase "TAYLOR SWIFT," and I think Taylor also recognizes that.

JW: She's not trying or striving anymore. She has arrived and she knows she's arrived: "As it turns out, I am very good at this, and do not need to throw 30 tracks out to prove it and can have a succinct 13-song tracklist."

KW: So the original flavor and the re-record are interesting because she said, "Okay, everyone's picking on me for writing about boys. I write about boys too much. Fine, fuck you, meet my friends. I'm not gonna write about boys." And it didn't work.

MM: Taylor becomes so angry later in her career, right? Except for OG *1989*, which is an album that feels hopeful in a way the majority of her discography doesn't.

JW: The frame of mind she was describing back then is so optimistic. She's moving to New York, she's hired the right people. She's reaching for this point in her career where it's like, "I've arrived and now I can live my life the way I need to live it." But it didn't work. She could never keep up with the needs of her public because our culture cannot stand to see somebody in the same place for very long. They have to bring that person up or bring that person down. Stasis is not possible.

OPPOSITE: **Swift announced *1989 (Taylor's Version)* on The Eras Tour, a record given 5/5 stars from *The Guardian*, *NME*, and *Rolling Stone*, among others.**

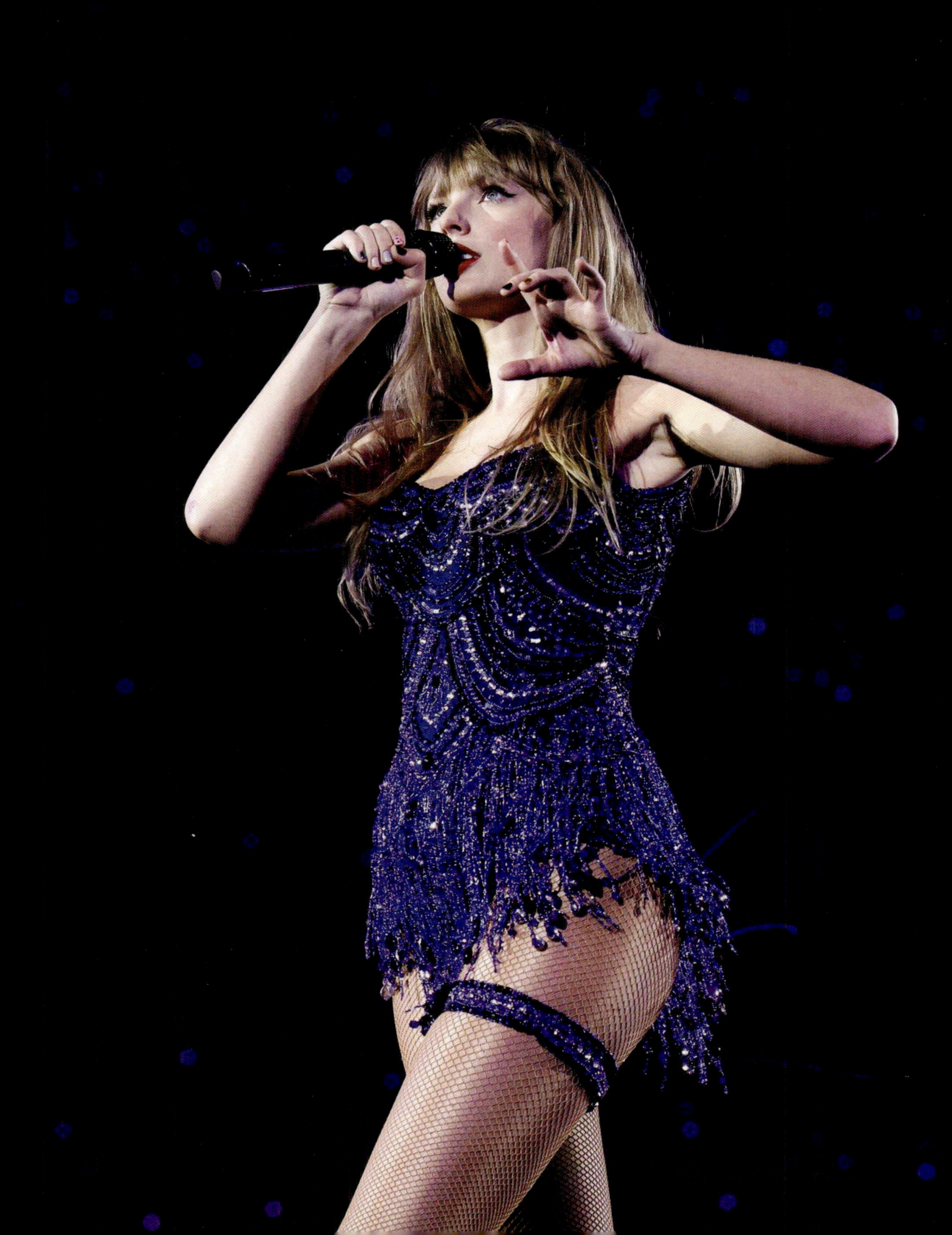

Taylor attends the 2015 MTV Music Awards with a handful of the "Bad Blood" Girl Squad.

MM: And the fact that that didn't happen is so hurtful to her. The tension for me in the re-record is that there was a sense of agency and power and control—not even optimism, but confidence—in the original that has been shattered going into this. And I think you can sense that insecurity, especially with the inclusion of a song like "Slut!" where it's like, "I need you to know how I felt about this because, even though it's evident in the art, I don't know if that's understood."

JW: Let me spell it out for you in four letters….

MM: I am filling in the blank space—see, I did it, too—because you guys seemingly didn't get it. It seems like Taylor was hoping this would be the turning point where the art was its own thing and Taylor, the individual, was her own thing, and they could exist separately in the public sphere. That very clearly didn't happen, and that is the grief of a lot of the rest of her music. I'm wondering how we think that informed the re-record of *1989*—specifically, with some of the Vault Tracks she chose to include, like "Slut!," in terms of Taylor really pointedly trying to communicate with her fans.

JW: "Slut!" is so on the nose in a way that's disappointing to me. I can see why she would feel it, but also why she would hold it back if she's thinking, "I don't want to give them the satisfaction. I'm not writing about boys. I will not."

MM: To then include "Slut!" as the first Vault Track and position it like it was going to be the next single, trying make sure it was the first thing everyone heard—is really interesting. Taylor uses her art to speak for her contemporary feelings, even for music that was recorded months, if not years, before the album comes out, right? And I feel like part of what makes *1989* so successful is that otherwise it is so clear and cohesive without having to be so on the nose. I feel like after the prologue communicated the message of "the general public are vulturous snakes and I can never live in peace" in and of itself, I don't know if we needed another track to do it.

Even though the aesthetic moves us toward the coast, 1989 (*Taylor's Version*) is a New York City album. Here, she stuns in The Big Apple with aplomb.

KW: My favorite Vault Track ever—"Is It Over Now?"—was one of those "I'm gonna self-edit" attempts. But I think it's a very honest song that could have been on the original album for sure.

MM: On so much of the OG album, Taylor really leans in to the pattern of the happy songs being upbeat classic pop songs and the more emotionally complicated songs being the slower ballads. That's not how Taylor's songwriting works overall, and it's certainly not how Taylor's songwriting is operating on The Vault.

KW: I wonder if she was thinking, "I'm going to apply some classic conceits and strictures of pop music. This will be a short album. I've got my secret track. This is what you want from me, and I will give you what you want."

JW: "I'm checking off these boxes."

KW: But so successfully. It does not stand to me as inauthentic. There are some unusual choices for her, but it's not like, "Oh she's just doing her best whoever impression."

JW: Is this the moment where I bring up Ryan Adams? His song-by-song cover album got more critical mention than the original 1989 did, which is crazy. And that's the thing about pop, right? She does the best version of it there can be because she's really talented and she's Taylor Swift. She still has to face all of the biases against pop. It still isn't appreciated for the craftsmanship that it is until Ryan Adams comes around, then, all of a sudden, it's like, "Oh, these are some pretty good songs." But that's another one of the risks in this treacherous thing she did by becoming a pop star. She put herself in a box where the establishment, the arbiters of culture, were going to accept her only in a certain way.

1989 (TAYLOR'S VERSION)

ABOVE: **Taylor kicks back (kind of!) on The Eras Tour. In her reintroduction for the new version of** *1989*, **she left little to the imagination. Perhaps that explains her ease on stage, here.**
OPPOSITE: **No matter the record, tour, or audience, Taylor ensures her fans know she loves them.**

MM: Especially as she went in wanting to create this perfect thing—and I think *1989* is a perfect pop album. Going back to the prologue, her take on this era seems to be one of failure, even though she created this album that had, at the time, her highest charting singles, was so well received by fans, went on this sold-out international tour with all of these celebrities coming as her surprise guests. She has all of this, and still is looking back at it saying, "I failed." But with 10 years of hindsight, it becomes evident that was not an era of failure. I do think the misogyny against pop music had a lot to do with the critical dismissal, and I think that really crystallized the industry for Taylor in a way I think she's still navigating.

JW: It's totally wrong, and pre–Scooter Braun, it feeds her growing realization that in the industry, she's the talent. She's the thing.

MM: They would be nothing without her.

TAYLOR SWIFT ALBUM BY ALBUM

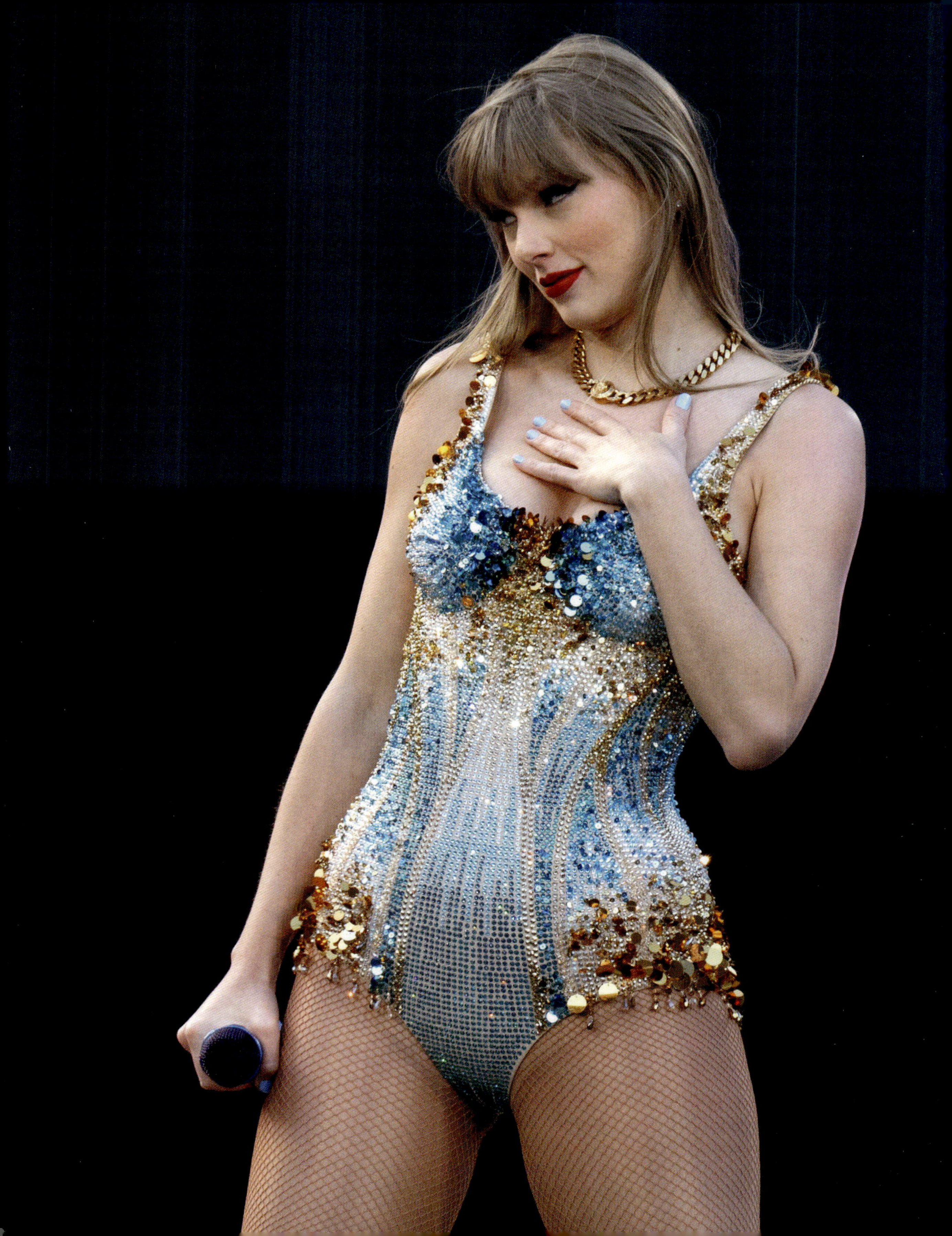

15

By Kase Wickman

THE TORTURED POETS DEPARTMENT

Recorded at Audu (Brooklyn), Big Mercy (Brooklyn), Conway Recording (Los Angeles), The Dwelling (New York City), Electric Lady (New York City), Electric Feel (Los Angeles), Esplanade (New Orleans), Hutchinson Sound (Brooklyn), Long Pond (Hudson Valley), Miloco (London), Narwhal (Chicago), Pleasure Hill (Portland), Prime Recording (Nashville), Rue Boyer (Paris), Smilo Sound (Orcas Island), Tiny Telephone (Oakland), Unknown locations (Biarritz, Los Angeles, Paris)

Released April 19, 2024

Produced by Taylor Swift, Jack Antonoff, Aaron Dessner, Patrik Berger

Label: Republic Records

Notable personnel:

Post Malone: vocals, cowriter

Emily Jean Stone aka Emma Stone: oddities

Florence Welch of Florence + The Machine: vocals, drums, percussion, piano, cowriter

Glenn Kotche of Wilco: drums and percussion

Bryce Dessner: synthesizer, piano

Jack Antonoff: various instruments and percussion, background vocals

Aaron Dessner: various instruments and percussion

The Anthology **released** April 19, 2024, two hours after original release

Selected awards:

Billboard Music Awards: Top Billboard 200 Album 2024

Notable honors:

17 weeks at number one on Billboard 200

Personal record broken: highest single-day and single-week streams for an album on Spotify

Swift's seventh album to open with more than a million units

Six-time Platinum certified by RIAA

Only artist to hold top 14 spots on Billboard Hot 100 simultaneously: All 31 songs from *The Anthology* debuted on the Hot 100, and Swift set the record for most simultaneous entries (31) on the list by a female artist and first woman to have more than 50 top-10 songs in her career

Third-ever album and first by a female artist to spend its first 12 weeks atop *Billboard*

Tour: The Eras Tour, March 2023–December 2024, 149 shows, 21 countries

On May 9, 2024, after releasing *The Tortured Poets Department* while on a six-week hiatus from The Eras Tour, Swift took the stage in Paris. She'd reworked the show to include several songs from the new album, complete with new sets, costumes, and even her very own UFO. This dress is covered in lyrics from "Fortnight."

Track Listing:

1. Fortnight (ft. Post Malone) [3:48]
2. The Tortured Poets Department [4:53]
3. My Boy Only Breaks His Favorite Toys [3:23]
4. Down Bad [4:21]
5. So Long, London [4:22]
6. But Daddy I Love Him [5:40]
7. Fresh Out The Slammer [3:30]
8. Florida!!! (ft. Florence + The Machine) [3:35]
9. Guilty as Sin? [4:14]
10. Who's Afraid of Little Old Me? [5:34]
11. I Can Fix Him (No Really I Can) [2:36]
12. loml [4:37]
13. I Can Do It With a Broken Heart [3:38]
14. The Smallest Man Who Ever Lived [4:05]
15. The Alchemy [3:16]
16. Clara Bow [3:36]

The Anthology Extended Tracks:

17. The Black Dog [3:58]
18. imgonnagetyouback [3:42]
19. The Albatross [3:03]
20. Chloe or Sam or Sophia or Marcus [3:33]
21. How Did It End? [3:58]
22. So High School [3:48]
23. I Hate It Here [4:03]
24. thanK you aIMee [4:23]
25. I Look In People's Windows [2:11]
26. The Prophecy [4:09]
27. Cassandra [4:00]
28. Peter [4:43]
29. The Bolter [3:58]
30. Robin [4:00]
31. The Manuscript [3:44]

Fool me once: Taylor Swift takes the stage at Los Angeles's Crypto.com Arena on February 4, 2024, to accept the Grammy for Best Pop Vocal Album for *Midnights*. It's her 13th Grammy, and close watchers are convinced, *convinced* that Swift, draped in a white custom Schiaparelli gown paired with black opera-length gloves and chunky chain jewelry, perhaps a more mature take on her *reputation* aesthetic, will announce a release date for *reputation* (*Taylor's Version*) sometime that night. Hell, maybe she'll just say it's out, boom, no preamble. After all, "there will be no further explanation, there will just be reputation" and all that.

Instead: "I want to say thank you to the fans by telling you a secret that I have been keeping from you for the last two years, which is that my brand-new album comes out April 19th. It's called *The Tortured Poets Department*. I'm going to go and post the cover right now backstage."

And so she did. It's a sepia-toned photo of Swift prostrate on a hotel bed in a slinky camisole and tap pants, the upper part of her face out of frame, her hands clenched across her torso. Shot by Beth Garrabrant, who photographed Swift for the album art of all her releases from *folklore* onward, it's moody as all hell. "All is fair in love and poetry," Swift captioned the cover.

Awestruck fans flocked to Wembley Stadium in June 2024 for the first eight nights of Swift's record-breaking Eras Tour. It was here where she'd even surprise them with a special guest on stage—Super Bowl winner and boyfriend Travis Kelce.

178 TAYLOR SWIFT ALBUM BY ALBUM

It's important to keep in mind the year that Swift had had prior to the announcement of *The Tortured Poets Department*. A few high-level bullet points:

- In March 2023, she embarked on The Eras Tour, which would last until December 2024, with 149 shows total, becoming the highest-earning tour in history by raking in nearly $2 billion.

- In April 2023, the world learned that Swift and actor Joe Alwyn, who had been dating since 2017 and who kept their relationship largely out of the public eye, had recently broken up.

- Soon after, Matty Healy, the frontman of rock group The 1975 who had crossed paths with Swift many times over the years, was spotted at several Eras Tour shows, even playing guitar onstage with opener Phoebe Bridgers at dates in Nashville and Philly. He and Swift are spotted holding hands and being datey-datey. The relationship, situationship, whatever you want to call it, is controversial among Swift's fans, and doesn't last long, though, as we'll see, it leaves a lasting mark via Swift's work.

- Still later that summer, NFL player Travis Kelce sees Swift play in Kansas City and makes a play to get the singer's attention. As the world finds out in September, when Swift appears in a VIP box at Arrowhead Stadium (yes, Virginia, at the same venue where he saw her) to watch Kelce play and then drives off into the sunset with him after, it worked.

- She released two more Taylor's Version albums, plus the theatrical and home releases of a concert documentary of The Eras Tour, also record breaking.

- Oh, and the same evening she announced *Tortured Poets*, she returned to the stage to accept her fourth Album of the Year Grammy, pulling her tally ahead of Paul Simon, Frank Sinatra, and Stevie Wonder's three each, making her the winningest artist of the honor ever.

She had had, to put it mildly, a *lot* going on at the moment.

Come April 19, Swift releases *The Tortured Poets Department*. In her midnight release tweet, she calls it "an anthology of new works that reflect events, opinions and sentiments from a fleeting and fatalistic moment in time—one that was both sensational and sorrowful in equal measure. This period of the author's life is now over, the chapter closed and boarded up."

Fool me twice: Given the moody album imagery, track names, and released lyrical snippets like "I love you, it's ruining my life" and "even statues crumble if they're made to wait," fans interpreted some very English tea leaves ahead of release, predicting the album would center on the demise of her relationship with Alwyn. But on first listen, the bulk of the songs—sad, angry, absolutely biting—seem to be inspired by a different Englishman: Healy. Well, *well*.

THE TORTURED POETS DEPARTMENT

Fool me—you know what, let's stop counting, because it starts to get a little embarrassing how many fast ones Swift was able to pull on even the most sharp-eyed of Easter egg hunters. At 2 a.m., she tweets again: It's a double album. The expanded version, with 15 more songs, brings the grand total of tracks up to 31 songs. "I'd written so much tortured poetry in the past 2 years and wanted to share it all with you," she wrote of the expanded album, dubbed *The Tortured Poets Department: The Anthology*. "And now the story isn't mine anymore...it's all yours," she wrote.

Well, at least all those clocks set to 2:00 in images leading up to release day finally made sense.

In "Clara Bow," Swift cycles through It Girls of the ages, herself included. The real-life Bow died at only 60, going from screen star to receiving shock treatments for schizophrenia and becoming a virtual recluse.

180 TAYLOR SWIFT ALBUM BY ALBUM

Channeling her inner witch, Swift pays tribute to Stevie Nicks (right) at the 2010 Grammy Awards.

YOU LOOK LIKE...

WHILE MUCH OF *The Tortured Poets Department* finds Swift grappling with the blurry (nonexistent?) line between Taylor Swift: Performer and Taylor Swift: Real Human Person, listeners also catch a glimpse of her rifling through the filing cabinets of who has come before her and who will come after, hunting for her rightful spot in the taxonomy. She's no longer the ingenue of "Tim McGraw," who would go on to open for Tim McGraw. Now she's a star-maker herself, looking on with pride as former tour openers, like Sabrina Carpenter, find massive success of their own. She once called performing with Stevie Nicks at the Grammys "a fairy tale;" over a decade later Nicks wrote a poem for the liner notes of *The Tortured Poets Department*, with the dedication "For T—and me."

Nicks gets a lyrical shout-out on the album, too, in the track "Clara Bow." Named in honor of a woman dubbed "the original It Girl," the song reflects on how the world likes its female idols: beautiful and silent. Swift acknowledges being compared with stars before her, and how someone else will someday take her place, too. "Did you always know you'd be picked like a rose," she wonders, mirroring awestruck fans and interviewers asking about her fame and fortune. What's left unsaid, but nonetheless hovers at the edges of the song: As soon as a rose is snipped from its bush, destined to be put on display and admired for its beauty, that's the very moment it begins to die.

THE TORTURED POETS DEPARTMENT

If Swift considers *Red* her breakup album, *Tortured Poets* must be her rage album. Read the lyrics, her so-called tortured poetry, then I challenge you to name someone she's not pissed at. Friends, family, fans, ex-lovers: No one is spared on the 31 heart-wrenching tracks, which see Swift exploring different flavors of that anger, tinting them shades of bitter, numb, reflective, grieving, and heartbroken in turn. It's no mistake that in the run-up to the album's release, Swift curated playlists of her past work sorted into the stages of grief. Coming out of arguably the busiest year of a very busy career and life, she found herself changed and reckoning with the loss of all the selves she used to be, from little-kid Taylor to loved-up adult superstar Taylor.

On *Tortured Poets*, Swift grapples with her unique position in the world: Through her music, she spills her guts on demand for millions every day, digging up her deepest pains and greatest joys and setting them to a beat. Swift reveals her truest truths to her listeners, who, in turn, feel like they know her intimately and feel qualified to opine and advise. Feelings, however, are not facts, and the relationship is parasocial. At once overexposed and not truly known, Swift tells the story, most notably on "But Daddy I Love Him," of a woman so besieged by the good intentions of others that she can't experience good things, no matter how hard she tries. She's snared in a net she so painstakingly wove for herself.

There's so much pain and rage and feeling on display in the album that Swift has jokingly referred to it several times as "Female Rage: The Musical." The 2 a.m. double-album surprise proved to be divisive with fans, with complaints that Swift needed an editor to cull the tracklist, that it was just *too much* to process.

Given Swift's eventful year in both the personal and professional spheres, she'd likely agree: Yeah, it is a lot to process! Imagine living through it! Then, layer on a level of fame that means you can't step out for a slice of pizza without your face ending up on the gossip sites and see how chipper you're feeling about the whole thing.

Still, Swift has proven herself to be nothing if not a workaholic with little to no work-life balance: She processes her feelings about work by creating more work, and so the cycle continues. By flooding the zone with so much new material, in addition to the daily headlines generated by her tour and speculation about her personal life, Swift performed her personal bloodletting ritual and vented her big feelings about recent events and knew that with so much to choose from, it would be difficult for fans and the media to fixate on just one thing too closely. It's the multiplatinum pop star equivalent of posting a massive carousel of photos on Instagram, none of which you want to explain specifically, with a vague caption like "life lately."

As if she wasn't busy enough, Swift also released a concert film while still on The Eras Tour.

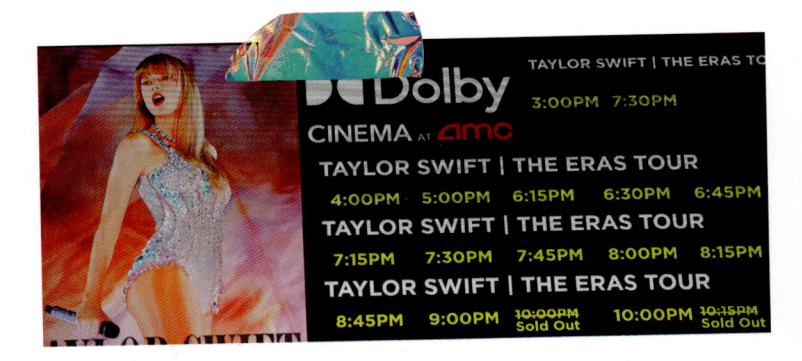

182   TAYLOR SWIFT ALBUM BY ALBUM

PROFANE AND PROFOUND

RESEARCH HAS SHOWN that cursing can trick your brain into perceiving pain less acutely, like dropping an f-bomb when you stub your toe. Sometimes a good profanity really *is* the best medicine.

With that in mind, is it really a surprise that on the somewhat-less-than-shiny-happy *Tortured Poets Department*, Swift curses up a storm?

Swift went from a single meek "damn" on her debut album, in "Cold As You," to dropping 18 f-bombs on a single *Tortured Poets* track, "Down Bad." On Spotify, 11 of the full 31 *Anthology* tracks earn the little "E" for explicit.

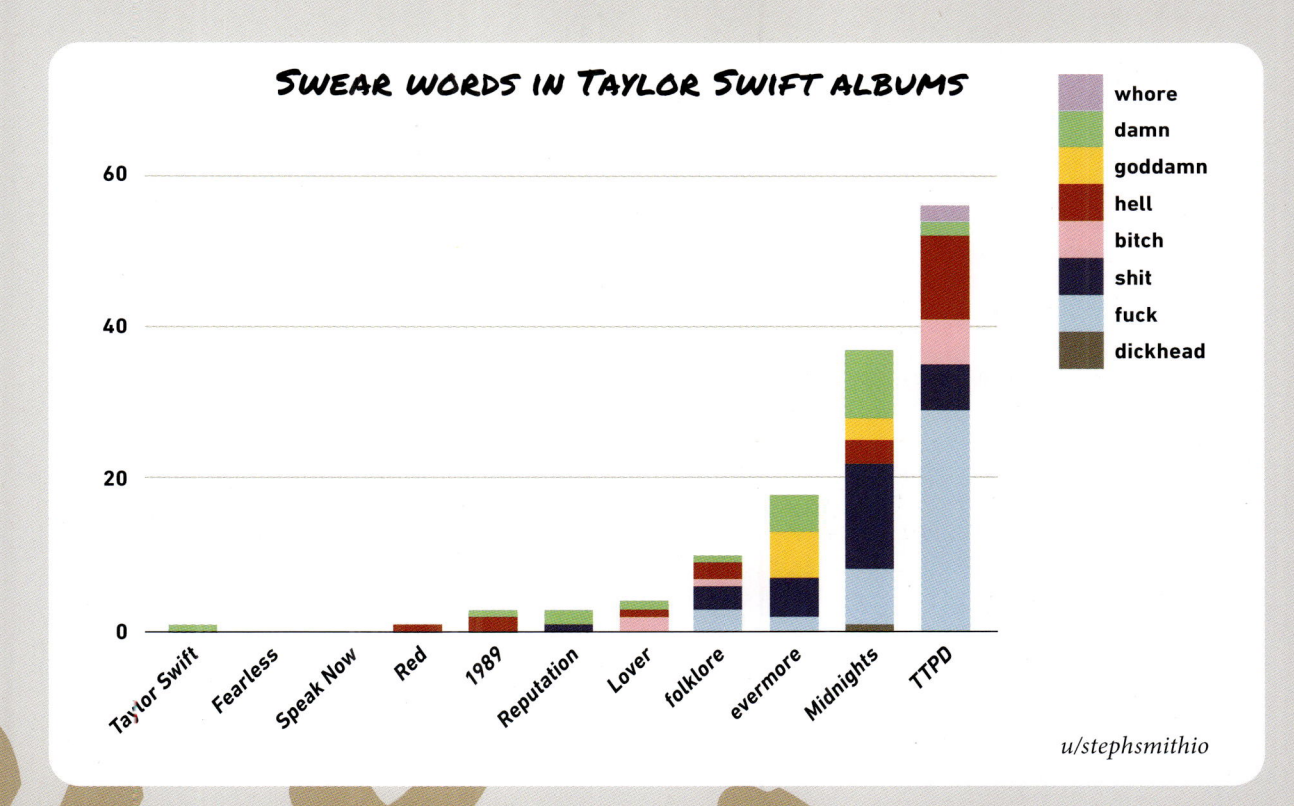

Swear words in Taylor Swift albums

Legend: whore, damn, goddamn, hell, bitch, shit, fuck, dickhead

Albums (left to right): Taylor Swift, Fearless, Speak Now, Red, 1989, Reputation, Lover, folklore, evermore, Midnights, TTPD

u/stephsmithio

Yes, she does kiss her mother with that mouth. *Tortured Poets* had 5,600 percent more profanity than her debut album. "Down Bad" was the most curse-heavy track.

THE TORTURED POETS DEPARTMENT

A dress worn by Taylor Swift in the "Fortnight" music video is displayed behind glass during the "Taylor Swift Songbook Trail Exhibition" at the Victoria & Albert Museum in July 2024 in London. "Pretty much everything in ["Fortnight"] is a metaphor or reference to once corner of the album or another," she later wrote.

Additionally, remember that Swift has said that the morning after she, Antonoff, and Dessner recorded *folklore: the long pond sessions*, they started writing and recording *evermore*. The only difference between that pair of albums and *The Anthology* is that she only waited two hours to release the second half, instead of five months.

Though *Tortured Poets* is Swift's moodiest compilation, favoring electronica-leaning beats to back mournful vocals on which Swift often harmonizes with a backing track of her own voice, perhaps representing the selves she has been and has since lost (appropriate for a woman on a retrospective world tour where she literally dresses up as past versions of herself, donning the costumes of her own youth), it ties back lyrically and melodically to much earlier work in spots. Take "The Smallest Man Who Ever Lived": Swift reveals, for the first time, the flip side of the coin she put on the table in *Speak Now* with the Kanye West pardoning track "Innocent." In the earlier song, more than a decade before, she sings that "who you are is not what you did." On "Smallest Man," older and wiser, with the scar tissue of having forgiven more men who treated her poorly and saw her as a symbol of something instead of as a human woman with a beating heart that is susceptible to bruising and breaking, she swears to "forget but not forgive" the titular diminutive dude, and slams the final nail into the coffin by declaring, over a drumline worthy of My Chemical Romance's *The Black Parade*, that "you are what you did." This Swift is done doling out the get-out-of-jail-free cards of her early career.

In "So Long, London," too, one of the most heart-wrenching of her famed track 5 placements, Swift plays sonically with including a heartbeat-like rhythm in her backing track as she sings about trying to revive both a relationship and her own joy. She gives up on the first, that pulse fading away after pounding with intense effort throughout the song, but the well-wishers gathered around the bedside are still waiting to see how the second patient turns out. That "gray face" she referenced in the gasp-inducing *Midnights* bonus track "You're Losing Me" is "just getting color back" in "So Long," but there's still plenty of healing to be done. When she sings that she's "pissed off [she] gave you all that youth for free," she is likely referring to the end of her six-year relationship, spanning her late twenties to early thirties, but could also be wagging a finger at her fan base, borrowing her feelings to explain their own, for over a decade, with no way for them to return the favor. In "But Daddy I Love Him," the track 6 indictment of public opinion, she points out that "growing up precocious sometimes means not growing up at all," questioning whether she ever even truly experienced that girlhood that so much of her work revolves around. In "The Prophecy" and "Cassandra," she mulls the past and the future, and how much is preordained and forced. Considering she floated herself as a "Mastermind" on *Midnights* and has spoken many times about teasing work years in advance, it would seem that Swift is having some feelings about the house she's built. She did, after all, set the iconic *Lover* dollhouse set on fire onstage every night of The Eras Tour.

In a twist, she also tweaked the list of that tour to make room in the grueling three-hour-plus runtime for a whopping seven tracks from *Tortured Poets* after its release, donning a wedding dress emblazoned with the lyrics "I love you, it's ruining my life" to perform "But Daddy I Love Him," "So High School," "Who's Afraid of Little Old Me?," "Down Bad" (complete with a simulated UFO abduction, no less), "Fortnight," and "The Smallest Man Who Ever Lived," then tearing it off to reveal another two-piece costume for the barnburner high-functioning depression anthem "I Can Do It With a Broken Heart."

That song is an undeniable bop, and it's unsurprising it has been adopted as sort of "the show must go on" theme music for the thirty-something set. The lyrics are uncomfortable, Swift describing fans hankering for "more" even as she admits that "I cry a lot but I am so productive." A voice counts Swift in with a four-count throughout the song, a hint at the actual voice Swift hears in her earpiece, the one telling her to get out there and perform on cue, not the "soliloquies I'll never read" of fan opinion about her personal life that she references in "But Daddy." The staging of the song on tour, too, was a pantomime representing the divide that exists between the heartbroken Swift rolling around on the ground in turmoil wearing a tarnished wedding dress in the front portion of the set, then being picked up off the ground by a posse of tuxedoed gentlemen (at one date, this role was played by real-life boyfriend Travis Kelce in an awwww-inducing cameo), stripped down to a sparkly midriff-baring costume, sexed up, powdered, and then pushed to perform. She goes from pouting and drooping to giving it her all, showing off a dazzling smile as she describes how sad she is. As a fan, you want to dance along with her and apologize for what you've done, all at the same time. Swift returns to a familiar thesis statement for the album—and, honestly, for her continuing career—with "The Manuscript." "The story isn't mine anymore," she sings, her vocals as intimate as whispering a secret into a confidant's ear. It's a distillation of her monologues about "All Too Well," where a painful memory metamorphoses into a shared experience in a singable, hummable container. You hear the Joan Didion quote so often because nobody has ever said this true thing better: "We tell ourselves these stories in order to live."

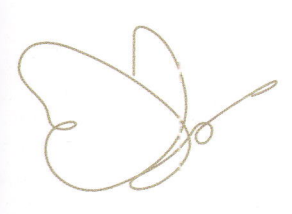

THE TORTURED POETS DEPARTMENT

ABOUT THE AUTHORS

Kase Wickman

Joanna Weiss

Kase Wickman is a culture journalist, editor, and all-around joy to have in class. Her reporting, criticism, and commentary has appeared in the *New York Times*, the *Washington Post*, *Rolling Stone*, and *New York Magazine*, among other publications. She is the Culture and Society reporter at *Vanity Fair*, and her first book, *Bring It On: The Complete Story of the Cheerleading Movie That Changed, Like, Everything (No, Seriously)*, was published in 2022 by Chicago Review Press. Kase lives on the East Coast with her husband, daughter, and 12-foot-tall lawn skeleton, Terror Swift.

Joanna Weiss is the editor of *Harvard Magazine* and a longtime writer and editor in Boston. Her writing has appeared in *Politico Magazine*, *The Atlantic*, *Slate*, *The Boston Globe*, *The Economist*, and others. Her *Boston Magazine* story "For Those Moms About to Rock," about the rock band she formed with four working-mom friends during the pandemic, has been optioned for film by 20th Century Studios. As a late-breaking musician, she looks to Taylor Swift as a model for songwriting, though she will likely never write a 10-minute-version of anything.

Moira McAvoy

Moira McAvoy lives, writes, and markets shows in Washington, DC. A founding editor of *Bad For You*, McAvoy has also served on the editorial staff of *NANO Fiction* and *The Rappahannock Review*, and previous work can be found in *The Rumpus*, *The Financial Diet*, *wig-wag*, and elsewhere. When not attending a next favorite concert—or promoting yours—Moira can be found taking long walks, making memes, and testing theories about Taylor Swift's music. McAvoy is currently within the top 500 all-time global listeners for five different Swift tracks (and counting).

ACKNOWLEDGMENTS

Kase: First, I'd like to thank my very favorite Swiftie. Several people, my daughter included, are wondering if I'm referring to them. My answer is: Yes. Of course I am.

Working on this book wouldn't have been possible without the patience of my family. Chris, who is appropriately mind-blown when I go full yarn-wall explaining lore to him, and Luna, the star of every show (and every phone call I tried to have for this project). She recently asked me to "tell Taylor that I think she'll be very famous when she grows up and that I love her and that I'd like to meet her and I think she'd like me." If someone could relay that message, I'd appreciate it.

Thank you to Jordan and the Quarto team. Look what you made us do.

Thank you to my colleagues who have foolishly enabled me to somehow turn my fascinations into an entire career, and to Maggie, Michelle, Claire, Sarah, Elaine, Spo, Angela, the Snug, and so many more who have scream-sung with me through the years.

Writing can be lonely work, but thanks to my two wonderful co-authors, this project wasn't quite so lonely. Joanna and Moira, thank you for your camaraderie, edits, meandering conversations, patience, tolerance of my need to share every single horrifying piece of weird AI art I come across, and, obviously, for your respect for THE LAW. I'm so sorry that I didn't acknowledge that I was recording before I started writing this note. I hope you can somehow forgive me. In all seriousness: I had the time of my life fighting dragons with you.

Joanna: This project begins with my daughter Ava, who has been my spirit guide to the world of Taylor Swift—from our night in the *1989* tour press seats to our car rides listening to "All Too Well" to our epic Eras Tour tailgate with her besties and their moms. Thanks, too, to her brother Jesse for tolerating *Lover* and *Midnights* on a continuous loop during car rides to school. Thanks to my bandmates in The Lazy Susans and Mini Split for helping me find my inner pop star (because everybody has an inner pop star). And special thanks to Dan DeLeo, my co-collaborator in all things, for teaching me everything I need to know about music.

I wouldn't have found my way to this book if Cloe Axelson, a genius editor at Boston's WBUR, hadn't encouraged me to document my Eras night in the Gillette Stadium nosebleed seats. Thanks to Jordan and the Quarto team for finding that piece and inviting me along for this ride.

The past year of Swift immersion wouldn't have been nearly as enchanting without Kase and Moira, two brilliant writers who have taught me so much about the Taylorverse. You're the best Slack buddies a GenXer could wish for.

Moira: Like so many of my peers, I first fell in love with Taylor Swift's music as an overly-emotional teen, her debut album the iPod-helmed soundtrack to an era where I felt like I was on the precipice of the Big Something of being a person. Her music was personal, relatable, grand in the way only a teenager can be, but the true magic came from the community that would bloom in its wake. Swiftieism dragged me headfirst, fearless, and is now a facet of nearly every relationship in my life.

Thank you to my brother Brian—my original Taylor bestie, concert companion, and sad-banger appreciator. Thank you to my parents, Sharon and Brian, for being steadfast readers of my work, long-suffering listeners to whatever I was playing far too loudly in the car/in the shower/in my headphones, and for supporting me through anything and everything (like pursuit of a Creative Writing degree during a recession). Thank you to the educators (formal or otherwise) who mentored me—Beth and Noreen and Alison and Brian and Elizabeth and Colin—for their enthusiastic encouragement of my work as their student and passion as a person. Thank you to Brad Efford for his support as editor and collaborator. Thank you to Ander Monson for tolerating enough of my Taylor posting to connect me to this project.

Thank you to ALL of my impossibly loving friends for their hours of listening to me rant about the Swiftie cinematic universe and whine about deadlines, especially Caro, Elizabeth, Madee, Sree, Haley, Colleen, Christine, and Claire. I truly am only me when I'm with y'all.

Thank you to Helmi—my copyeditor, fact checker, meme-inspirer, cheerleader, and, so luckily for me, my partner in Taylorism and life. I'm so grateful you showed up at my proverbial party.

Thank you to Joanna and Kase for their unfailing humor, generous wisdom, abundant patience, and overall impeccable vibes. Long live all the mountains we moved!

Thank you to Jordan and the entire team at Quarto for their support throughout this process.

Thank you to everyone who has ever indulged me in a group chat, drunkenly screamed along with me to a song, soberly screamed along with me to a song, sent me a meme, asked me about a theory, shared a memory, or suffered through an unbidden Socratic seminar on all things Swift. You've given me a reality beyond what thirteen year old me (blasting "Mary's Song)" could've ever dreamt, and I've truly had the time of my life with you.

INDEX

A
Adams, Ryan, 113, 173
"All Too Well (10 Minute Version)," 54–55, 138, 144
All Too Well: The Short Film, 55
"All Too Well," 33, 51, 126, 138, 162
Alwyn, Joe, 92, 99, 107, 113, 179
Anderson, Abigail, 19, 24
"Anti-Hero," 151
Antonoff, Jack, 57, 62, 80, 87, 99, 101, 104–105, 107, 150, 154, 184

B
"Back To December," 38–39
Beats, Keanu, 152
"Begin Again," 57, 140, 170
Bell, Lewis, 87
Berninger, Matt, 117
"The Best Day," 24, 94
"Better Than Revenge," 33, 38–39
Beyoncé, 27, 164
Bhasker, Jeff, 57
Bieber, Justin, 122, 125
"Bigger Than The Whole Sky," 152
Big Machine Records, 13, 34, 87, 102, 105–106, 125
"Blank Space," 62–63, 65
Bluebird Cafe (Nashville), 11, 13
Bon Iver, 107, 117
Borchetta, Scott, 13, 34, 105, 122, 125–126
Braun, Scooter, 122, 125–126
Bridgers, Phoebe, 143, 179
"But Daddy I Love Him," 182, 185

C
"cardigan," 98, 105
"champagne problems," 113–114, 117–119
Chapman, Nathan, 52, 62, 130
The Chicks, 10, 15, 92, 94
"Clara Bow," 144, 180, 181
Clark, Annie, 87
Clarkson, Kelly, 122, 126
"Clean," 65–66, 69
"coney island," 117
COVID-19 pandemic, 95, 98–100, 110
"Cruel Summer," 87, 100

D
"Dear John," 38, 162, 165
"Delicate," 76, 79, 83
Del Rey, Lana, 151, 157
Dessner, Aaron, 99, 101, 103–107, 150, 154, 184
diary entries, 52–53, 90–91
Dickinson, Emily, 110, 113
Dion, Celine, 157

E
"Enchanted," 33–34
Eras Tour, 33–34, 54, 130, 154–156, 179, 185
Eras Tour Book, 36
evermore, 100, 107, 108, 110–114, 116–119, 184
"evermore," 114, 116, 118

F
Fearless, 14, 20, 23–24, 29–31, 125
Fearless (Taylor's Version), 118, 126, 128–132, 134
Feeney, Adam King, 87
"Fifteen," 24
"Fifteen (Taylor's Version)," 131
Finlay, Marjorie, 112
folklore, 15, 76, 96, 98–107, 112–113, 184
"Fortnight," 185

G
Garrabrant, Beth, 100, 178
"gold rush," 114, 116–117
"Gorgeous," 80, 114
Grammy Awards (2024), 157, 178–179
Gyllenhaal, Jake, 51, 138

H
Harkness, Rebekah, 105
Healy, Matty, 179
Heap, Imogen, 69
"Hey Stephen," 23, 30, 131
"Hits Different," 152, 154

I
"I Bet You Think About Me," 51
"I Can Do It With a Broken Heart," 185
"I Did Something Bad," 103
"I Forgot That You Existed," 86
"I Knew You Were Trouble," 51, 52
"I Know Places," 63, 65
"Innocent," 42–43, 162, 184
"Is It Over Now?," 173
Ithaca Holdings, 125
"It's Nice To Have a Friend," 93
"ivy," 113–114, 117

J
Jonas, Joe, 29–30

K
Kardashian, Kim, 74, 125
"Karma," 152, 156
Kelce, Travis, 179
King, Joey, 41
Kitty Committee Studio, 104

L
"Labyrinth," 152
Lamar, Kendrick, 69
Lautner, Taylor, 38, 165
Lee, Jacknife, 57
Lefsetz, Bob, 39, 41, 43
Lightbody, Gary, 57
"London Boy," 92
"Long Live," 82, 162
Long Pond Sessions, 101–102, 106–107, 111
Long Pond Studios, 104
"long story short," 114, 117
"Look What You Made Me Do," 74–76, 79
Lover, 63, 84, 86–87, 92–95, 100, 118
"Lover," 93
"Love Story," 24, 29–30, 113, 130, 132

M
McEntire, Reba, 10, 15
McGraw, Tim, 12
"mad woman," 103, 106
"The Man," 92, 95

"marjorie," 112, 117–119
Martin, Max, 52, 62, 80
"Mary's Song," 11, 15
masters
    battle over, 120, 122, 125–126
    defining, 122
    loss of control of, 86–87, 95, 125
    rerecording versions of, 95, 110, 126
    Vault Tracks and, 19, 51, 54, 126, 172–173
Mayer, John, 38, 43
"Mean," 33, 38–39, 41–42, 52
Midnights: The Til Dawn Edition, 154
Midnights, 144, 146–148, 150–152, 154–156, 178
"Mine," 33, 38
"mirrorball," 76, 144
"Miss Americana & The Heartbreak Prince," 87
Miss Americana, 87, 92, 95
Mitchell, Joni, 52–53, 143
"Mr. Perfectly Fine," 130
MTV Video Music Awards (2009), 26–27, 38–39, 42, 164

N
The National, 99, 103, 107
"Never Grow Up," 33
"New Year's Day," 82, 114
Nicks, Stevie, 39, 181
1989, 35, 58, 60–67, 69, 114, 170
1989 (Ryan Adams cover album), 113
1989 (Taylor's Version), 126, 168–170, 172–174
Noah, Trevor, 157

O
Obama, Barack, 27
Obama, Michelle, 42
"the 1," 103
"Our Song," 12–13
"Out Of The Woods," 62
Owl City, 34

P
"Paper Rings," 92, 100
Paramore, 35

perfumes, 34
Perry, Katy, 69, 92
"Picture to Burn," 17, 19
politics, 92
Porowski, Antoni, 103
profanity, 183
"The Prophecy," 185

Q
"Question...?," 152

R
"...Ready For It?," 78
Red, 35, 46–53, 57, 182
Red (Taylor's Version), 51, 54–55, 126, 136–138, 140, 142–144
Republic Records, 102, 125
reputation, 72, 74–76, 78–80, 82–83, 86, 95, 103, 118, 125, 178
Rose, Liz, 13, 16, 23–24, 33, 54, 138
Rosen, Judy, 35

S
Secret Sessions, 63
sexism, 87
"Shake It Off," 62, 66–67
Shamrock Holdings, 126
Sheeran, Ed, 57
Sheffield, Rob, 152
Shellback, 52, 62, 74, 80
"Slut!," 172
"The Smallest Man Who Ever Lived," 184, 185
"Snow On The Beach," 151
"So Long, London," 184–185
"Soon You'll Get Better," 92, 94
Speak Now, 32–43, 48
"Speak Now," 33
Speak Now (Taylor's Version), 126, 160–162, 164–165
Speak Now World Tour, 162
Spotify, 64
Stone, Emma, 163
"Style," 69
Styles, Harry, 51
Swift, Andrea Finlay, 94–95
The Taylor Swift Holiday Collection, 14
Swiftmas, 63

T
Target, 36, 154
Taylor Swift (album), 8, 10–13, 16–17, 19, 125, 132
Taylurking, 54
teenagers, 10–11, 13, 30
"Tell Me Why," 23
"This Love," 62
"Tied Together With a Smile," 13, 17
"Tim McGraw," 11, 16–17, 48
"'tis the damn season," 111, 117
"tolerate it," 113, 117
The Tortured Poets Department: The Anthology, 180, 184
The Tortured Poets Department, 39, 106, 157, 176–185
"22," 52, 57, 144

V
Vernon, Justin, 107

W
Walker, Butch, 57
"The Way I Loved You," 24, 130
"We Are Never Ever Getting Back Together," 51–52, 57, 138
"Welcome To New York," 60–61, 114, 170
West, Kanye, 26–27, 35–36, 42–43, 74–75, 122, 125, 164
"White Horse," 23, 24, 29, 76
"Who's Afraid of Little Old Me?," 185
Williams, Hayley, 35
"willow," 113, 118–119
woodvale, 100
"Would've, Could've, Should've," 152

Y
"You Belong With Me," 23, 29, 76
"You Need To Calm Down," 92, 103
Young, Adam, 34

IMAGE CREDITS

Alamy: 11 (B.A.E. Inc), 13 (EXImages), 16 (ZUMA), 21 (Lee/Everett Collection), 22 (ZUMA), 28 (Lee/Everett Collection), 36 (Jennifer Cohen), 43 (WENN), 48 (WENN), 49 (Media Punch), 51 (Thomas Jackson), 52 (Taylor Swift), 59 (Imaginechina), 66 (Phil McCarten), 71t (Imaginechina), 71b (Tammie Arroyo), 73 (Geisler-Fotopress), 75 (WENN), 82 (ZUMA Press), 93 (dpa), 94 (McClatchy Tribune), 99 (ABACA Press), 102 (Stephen Chung), 103 (Barry Lewis), 110 (APA-PictureDesk), 199 (Ian West), 123r (Jeffrey Meyer), 12r (./.), 127 (EMPPL PA Wire), 131t (Barry King), 131b (John Davies), 132 (John Angelillo), 135 (Sayre Berman), 139 (UPI), 140 (dpa), 141 (Doug Peters), 156 (e. backlund), 159t (Album), 159b (Sipa USA), 165r (Barry King), 167 (imageSPACE), 171 (TCD/Prod. DB), 172 (dpa), 173 (Hoo-Me/SMG), 175 (Jane Barlow), 177 (Thomas Jackson), 178 (Vuk Valcic)

Associated Press: 9, 12, 15 (Charles Sykes/Invision/AP), 18, 25, 26, 27tl, 27tr, 27b, 29l, 30 (Sipa USA via AP), 33, 34, 37, 40, 41, 42, 44, 47 (Owen Sweeney/Invision/AP), 55, 56 (Matt Sayles/Invision/AP), 61 (Frank Micelotta/Invision/AP), 62l (John Shearer/Invision/AP), 64 (Greg Allen/Invision/AP), 65 (John Shearer/Invision/AP), 67 (Dennis Van Tine/Geisler-Fotopres/picture-alliance/dpa/AP Images), 68 (Matt Sayles/Invision/AP), 77, 78 (Evan Agostini/Invision/AP), 83 (Wade Payne/Invision/AP), 85 (Chris Pizzello/Invision/AP), 88 (Chris Pizzello/Invision/AP), 91 (Evan Agostini/Invision/AP), 97 (Jordan Strauss/Invision/AP), 98 (Chris Pizzello/Invision/AP), 101 (Charles Sykes/Invision/AP), 109 (Jordan Strauss/Invision/AP), 111, 123l (zz/XPX/STAR MAX/IPx), 130, 132, 134, 138 (Scott A Garfitt/Invision/AP), 142t, 145 (Jordan Strauss/Invision/AP), 149 (Chris Pizzello/Invision/AP), 153, 157 (Chris Pizzello/Invision/AP), 158 (Charles Sykes/Invision/AP), 164 (Evan Agostini/Invision/AP), 165l (Frank Micelotta/Invision/AP), 166 (Scott A Garfitt/Invision/AP), 174 (Sipa USA via AP), 180, 181, 182, 184 (Scott A Garfitt/Invision/AP)

Authors' Collections: 10r, 14, 80 (courtesy Julia), 115, 116, 142b

Getty Images: 10l (*Star Tribune* via Getty Images), 29r (Raymond Boyd / Michael Ochs Archives), 31 (Tim Mosenfelder/Archive Images), 50 (John Leyba, *Denver Post*), 53 (Henry Diltz, Corbis Premium Historical), 62r (Lester Cohen, WireImage), 70 (James Devaney, GC Images), 86l (Gotham, GC Images), 86r (Patrick McMullan), 92 (MAGALI COHEN, AFP), 95 (Jun Sato, GC Images), 120 (Future Music Magazine/Future), 147 (Mike Kemp/In Pictures), 150 (Picture Alliance), 151 (Jackson Lee/GC Images), 155 (Picture Alliance)

Courtesy Alyssa Lawson: 18r, 19

Courtesy Helmi Henkin: 81

Quarto Publishing Group Collection: 8, 14, 32, 39, 46, 48, 58, 72, 84, 96, 128, 136, 146, 154, 160, 168, 176

Shutterstock: 104, 106, 143, 108, 163